EARLY GREEK PHILOSOPHY

ADVISORY EDITOR: BETTY RADICE

JONATHAN BARNES is Professor of Ancient Philosophy in the University of Geneva. He was educated at the City of London School and at Balliol College, Oxford. For ten years he was a Fellow of Oriel College, Oxford, and for sixteen a Fellow of Balliol. He has held visiting posts in Canada, France, Germany, Italy, Switzerland and the USA. He is a Fellow of the British Academy and an Honorary Fellow of the American Academy of Arts and Sciences. His publications include *The Ontological Argument* (1972), *Aristotle's Posterior Analytics* (1975), *The Presocratic Philosophers* (1979), *Aristotle* (1982), *The Toils of Scepticism* (1990) and *Logic and the Imperial Stoa* (1997). Jonathan Barnes has also written the introduction to Aristotle's *Ethics* in the Penguin Classics.

Early Greek Philosophy

JONATHAN BARNES

PENGUIN BOOKS

PENGUIN BOOKS

Published by the Penguin Group
Penguin Books Ltd, 80 Strand, London WC2R 0RL, England
Penguin Putnam Inc., 375 Hudson Street, New York, New York 10014, USA
Penguin Books Australia Ltd, Ringwood, Victoria, Australia
Penguin Books Canada Ltd, 10 Alcorn Avenue, Toronto, Ontario, Canada M4V 3B2
Penguin Books India (P) Ltd, 11, Community Centre, Panchsheel Park, New Delhi – 110 017, India
Penguin Books (NZ) Ltd, Private Bag 102902, NSMC, Auckland, New Zealand
Penguin Books (South Africa) (Pty) Ltd, 24 Sturdee Avenue, Rosebank 2196, South Africa

Penguin Books Ltd, Registered Offices: 80 Strand, London WC2R 0RL, England

First published in Penguin Classics 1987
Second revised edition 2001

037

Set in 10/12.5 pt PostScript Adobe Minion
Typeset by Rowland Phototypesetting Ltd, Bury St Edmunds, Suffolk
Printed and bound in Great Britain by Clays Ltd, Elcograf S.p.A.

ISBN-13: 978-0-140-44815-3

www.greenpenguin.co.uk

MIX
Paper from
responsible sources
FSC
www.fsc.org FSC® C018179

Penguin Books is committed to a sustainable
future for our business, our readers and our planet.
This book is made from Forest Stewardship
Council™ certified paper.

CONTENTS

v

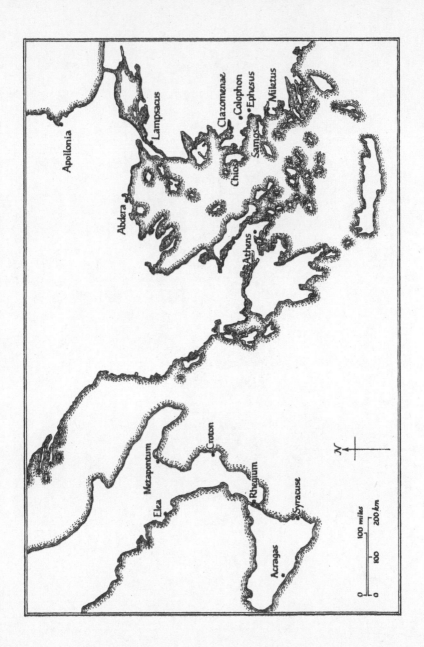

Apollonia

Lampsacus

Clazomenae
Colophon
Chios
Samos·Ephesus
Miletus

Abdera

Athens

Elea

Metapontum

Croton

Rhegium

Syracuse

Acragas

N

0   100 miles
0   100   200 km

PREFACE TO THE
SECOND EDITION

The first edition of this book was prepared some fifteen years ago. Since then, the Presocratic philosophers have been attacked by an overwhelming barrage of scholarly books and articles. In revising *Early Greek Philosophy* I have made no attempt to master all this recent literature; but I hope that I have taken appropriate notice of any pertinent novelties.

One remarkable discovery must be singled out: the reconstitution and publication of the 'Strasbourg Papyrus' of Empedocles has added vastly to our knowledge of that curious thinker. The chapter on him has accordingly been remodelled. So too – but for different reasons – have the chapters on Heraclitus and on Democritus. But otherwise the new edition differs little from its predecessor in structure and in substance: the selection of texts is virtually the same, and so too is their arrangement.

The Introduction, and the linking passages in the chapters, have been lightly retouched. The list of Further Reading has been updated.

As for the translations which make the body of the book, they have all been tested against the Greek (or Latin) originals. Further reflection, or a new critical edition, has occasionally led me to prefer a different wording in the ancient text – and hence in the English translation. In addition, I have found and corrected a depressingly large number of errors in the first edition. Finally, I have made frequent changes of a stylistic nature in order the better to capture certain nuances of the Greek, or to be faithful to repetitions in the original, or to turn a clearer or a happier English phrase. For one reason or another, pretty well all the translations have been altered; and that, I hope, is enough to justify the phrase 'Second Edition'.

In preparing the revised version I have been greatly helped by my assistants, Maddalena Bonelli and Andreas Schmidhauser. And I am particularly indebted to my wife, Jennifer, for aid and advice.

Geneva
December 2000

INTRODUCTION

The First Philosophers

According to tradition, Greek philosophy began in 585 BC (on 28 May) and ended eleven centuries later in AD 529. It began when Thales of Miletus, the first Greek philosopher, predicted an eclipse of the sun (hence the precise date). It ended when an edict of the Christian Emperor Justinian forbade the teaching of pagan philosophy. The tradition is inaccurate at both ends; for Thales observed but did not predict a solar eclipse, and Justinian may have wished to stamp out pagan philosophy but did not have his wish. Nevertheless, the traditional dates may stand as convenient and memorable boundaries to the career of ancient philosophy.

That career can be divided into three periods of unequal duration. First, there were the salad years, from 585 until about 400 BC, when a sequence of green and genial individuals established the scope and determined the problems of philosophy, at the same time forging its conceptual instruments and fixing its general structure. Then came the period of the Schools – the period of Plato and Aristotle, of the Epicureans and the Stoics, and of the Sceptics – in which elaborate systems of thought were worked out and subjected to strenuous criticism. This second period ended in about 100 BC. The long third period was marked in the main by scholarship and syncretism: the later thinkers studied their predecessors' writings with assiduity; they produced commentaries and interpretations; and they attempted to extract a coherent and unified system of thought which would include all that was best in the earlier doctrines of the Schools.

The present book is concerned with the first of the three periods, with early Greek philosophy. This period is commonly called the 'Presocratic' phase of Greek thought. The adjective is ill-chosen; for Socrates was born in 470 and died in 399, so that many of the 'Presocratic' philosophers were contemporaries of Socrates. But the label is familiar and it would be idle to attempt to erase it.

The Presocratic period itself divides into three parts. There was first a century of bold and innovatory thought. Then the early adventures were subjected to stringent logical inspection: the dawn they had heralded seemed a false dawn – their discoveries chimerical and their hopes illusory. Finally, there were years of retrenchment and consolidation, in which thinkers of very different persuasions attempted each in his own way to reconcile the aspirations of the first thinkers with the criticisms of their successors.

These schematisms impose a scholastic fixity on what was in reality fluid and irregular. The Greeks themselves, when they came to write the history of their own thought, were even more schematic. They liked to talk about 'Schools' of philosophy and about 'Successions' of philosophers, in which each thinker had a master and a pupil, and each philosophy a set place. Any such constructions are artificial; but they supply a framework within which the history of thought can be expounded and comprehended. Moreover, it is true, as a rough approximation, that the Presocratics form a unitary group, that they differ in fundamental ways both from their unphilosophical predecessors and from their great successors, and that within the era which their fortunes span three main periods can be distinguished.

Such naked abstractions require a decent historical covering. When we think of Greece we habitually think first of Athens, supposing that the city of Pericles and the Parthenon, of Socrates and Aristophanes, was the centre and focus of the Greek world, artistically, intellectually and politically. In truth, none of the earliest philosophers was Athenian. Philosophy began on the eastern shores of the Aegean, in small independent city-states which had at that time no political ties with Athens. These Greek states of Ionia were torn by internal strife and threatened by external enemies. Yet for a century and a half, from about 650 to 500 BC, they enjoyed a remarkable efflorescence: they burgeoned economically, they bloomed politically, and they flourished in art and in literature, producing majestic architecture, noble sculpture, exquisite poems, elegant vase-paintings.

Miletus was the birthplace of Greek philosophy. The Milesians were an uncommonly vigorous lot. Internally, their politics were turbulent – they knew faction, strife and bloody revolution. Externally, they were neighboured by two powerful empires, first the Lydians, with whom they maintained an uneasy symbiosis, and after 546 the Persians, by whom they were eventually destroyed. Despite these unpropitious circumstances, the Milesians were commercially indefatigable. They traded not only with the Eastern empires but also with Egypt, establishing a trading emporium at Naucratis on the Nile delta. In addition they sent numerous colonies to settle in Thrace and by the Bosphorus and along the coast of the Black Sea; and they had connections with Sybaris in south Italy. It was in this gifted township that Thales, Anaximander and Anaximenes, the first three philosophers, lived and worked.

The intellectual activity which they pioneered soon spread abroad. Xenophanes came from Colophon and Heraclitus from Ephesus, two city-states some fifty miles to the north of Miletus. Pythagoras was born on the island of Samos, which lies close to the mainland halfway between Ephesus and Colophon. Later, Melissus lived on Samos while Anaxagoras came from Clazomenae, north of Colophon. With Democritus, whose country was Abdera, philosophy crossed the Hellespont and entered European Greece. The first Athenian philosopher was Archelaus, a pupil of Anaxagoras.

By then, the west had made its contribution. Pythagoras emigrated from Samos to the Greek colony of Croton in south Italy. Alcmaeon was a native of Croton. Parmenides and Zeno were born in Elea on the west coast of Italy. Empedocles came from Acragas in Sicily.

This geographical diversity did not mean that the Presocratics were isolated workers, writing in ignorance of one another's thoughts. Although communications were slow and frequently dangerous, many of the early philosophers were itinerant. Pythagoras migrated. Xenophanes and Empedocles both tell us that they travelled. Parmenides and Zeno are supposed to have visited Athens, where Anaxagoras spent much of his life before he retired to exile and to Lampsacus on the plain of Troy.

There is little direct evidence of intellectual converse among the early philosophers, and the influences and interactions which scholars commonly assume are largely speculative. But such speculation is plausible; for much in the history of Presocratic thought is most intelligible on the hypothesis of mutual contact. Consider, for example, Melissus. He came from the eastern Aegean, and he was working at most a decade or so after Parmenides, who was a westerner. Melissus does not mention Parmenides, whether for criticism or for praise; yet it is quite certain that he knew his work intimately: either he had met Parmenides, or he had heard his views from the mouth of a third party. There is no reason to think of an Eleatic 'School', nor the slightest reason to imagine that Parmenides and Melissus held joint seminars, or that they met on a regular basis and discussed their thoughts together. None the less, they worked together – or rather, every sentence of Melissus' philosophy was influenced by the philosophy of Parmenides.

I have spoken of the Presocratics as 'philosophers' or as 'thinkers'. The word 'philosophy' comes from the Greek *philosophia*, the etymological meaning of which is 'love of wisdom'. The Greeks used the term in a broad sense, to cover most of what we now think of as the sciences and the liberal arts; and a stock definition explained that the 'wisdom' which a philosopher loves is 'knowledge of things human and of things divine'. The later School philosophers generally divided this ambitious subject into three parts: logic, ethics and physics. Logic included the study of language and meaning as well as the study of thought and argument. Ethics included moral and political theorizing, but it also embraced topics which would now fall under the heading of sociology and ethnography. Physics was defined very generously: it was the study of nature and of all the phenomena of the natural world.

In terms of this later threefold distinction, the Presocratics were regarded primarily as 'physicists'. Ethical and logical matters did indeed exercise some of them; but their chief interest was physics: Aristotle calls them *phusikoi* and their activity *phusiologia* – they were 'students of nature' and their subject was the 'study of nature'. To the modern reader that will sound more like science than philosophy – and indeed the modern discipline of physics derives its content no less than its name from the Greek *phusikoi*. But the modern distinction between empirical science and a priori philosophy had no importance in the earliest phase of Western thought, when wisdom was not yet distributed among departments and thinkers were innocent of specialization.

Thales, then, was the first *phusikos*, the first 'natural philosopher'. The written works of the early thinkers frequently bore the title *On Nature (Peri Phuseôs)*; and even if such titles were bestowed not by the authors but by later scholars, they were largely appropriate. For the general enterprise of the early philosophers was to tell the truth 'about nature': to describe, to organize, and to explain the universe and its contents. The enterprise involved, at one end of the scale, detailed accounts of numerous natural phenomena – of eclipses and the motions of the heavenly bodies, of thunder and rain and hail and wind and in general of 'meteorological' events, of minerals and of plants, of the procreation and growth and nourishment and death of animals, and of mankind and of the biological, psychological, social, political, cultural and intellectual aspects of human life. All this we might justly count as 'science'; and we should regard the Presocratics as the first investigators of matters which became the special objects of astronomy, physics, chemistry, zoology, botany, psychology and so on. At the other end of the scale, the Presocratic enterprise involved larger and more obviously 'philosophical' questions: did the universe have a beginning, and if so, how did it begin? What are its basic constituents? Why does it move and develop as it does? What, in the most general terms, is the nature and the unity of the universe? And what can we hope to learn about it?

Not all the Presocratics asked all these questions, and not all of them wrote in such comprehensive terms 'about nature'. But they all wrote within that general framework, and they all deserve the honorific title of *phusikos*. Whether we should now call them philosophers or scientists or both is a matter of no importance.

The sequence of the *phusikoi* who are the heroes of this book were not the only intellectual adventurers of early Greece – indeed, they were not the only thinkers to engage in *phusiologia*. The didactic poets of the age sometimes indulged in philosophical reflection – or at least in some heavy moralizing. The Athenian playwrights of the fifth century BC had an interest in philosophical matters – the tragedian Euripides shows a keen awareness of Presocratic speculation, and the comic poet Aristophanes parodies philosophical and scientific notions. The histories of Herodotus and of Thucydides are coloured by observations and reflections of a philosophical nature. The so-called 'Sophists' – men such as Protagoras, Gorgias, Hippias – who were contemporaries of Euripides and Thucydides and who professed to teach rhetoric, made enterprising, extensive and controversial forays into philosophical territory. Several of the early medical writings associated with the name of Hippocrates are thoroughly 'Presocratic' in their concerns and in their methods.

Thus a history of Presocratic philosophy is not a history of early Greek thought. None the less, Presocratic philosophy is not an arbitrary entity, a heap of random gleanings from the field of early thought. Nor is it a modern invention. As Aristotle saw, the Presocratics form a coherent group: it was they who began philosophy, they who prepared the way for Plato and for the philosophical Schools of the following generations.

Presocratic philosophy did not spring into existence from nothing. The commercial and political relations between the Ionian Greeks and their eastern neighbours brought cultural connections along with them. Not all observers approved of these connections:

The Colophonians, according to Phylarchus, originally practised an austere mode of life, but when they made ties of friendship and alliance with the Lydians they drifted into luxury, parading with gold trinkets in their hair – as Xenophanes says:

> Learning effete vanities from the Lydians
> while they were free from hateful despotism,
> they paraded in the town square in purple robes,
> no fewer than a thousand of them in all,
> haughty, delighted by their elegant coiffure,
> drenched in the perfume of synthetic ointments. [21 B 3]

(Athenaeus, *Deipnosophists* 526AB)

But effeminacy was not the only Lydian gift. There are clear lines of contact between Ionian pottery and sculpture on the one hand and Lydian art on the other. The Lydian language had some influence on Ionian poetry.

Scholars both modern and ancient have supposed that there were also connections between the earliest Greek thought and the intellectual concerns of the Eastern empires. The advanced astronomy of the Babylonians, for example, must surely have become known on the shores of Asia Minor and have stimulated the Ionians to study astronomy for themselves. Thales' knowledge of the eclipse of the sun of 585 BC must have been derived from Babylonian learning. Other, more speculative, parts of Presocratic thought have parallels, of a sort, in Eastern texts. In addition, there was the Egyptian connection. The Greeks themselves later supposed that their own philosophy owed much to the land of the Pharaohs. But although some Eastern and Egyptian fertilization can scarcely be denied, the most characteristic and significant features of early Greek thought have no known parallels in Egypt or in Babylonia or in Lydia.

The Greek philosophers also had Greek predecessors. Poets had written in their fantastical way about the nature and the origins of the universe: there were stories of the god Heaven and his mate the goddess Earth; there were mythical histories of the human race; et cetera. There are similarities between certain aspects of these tales and certain aspects of the early philosophers' work. But Aristotle made a sharp distinction between what he called the 'mythologists' and the philosophers; and the differences are far more remarkable than the similarities.

Just as the early thinkers sought the origins of the universe, so later scholars have sought the origins of these first thoughts about the universe. It is foolish to claim that the Presocratics began something entirely unprecedented in the history of human intellectual endeavour – no one ever does that sort of thing. But the best researches of scholarship have produced little in the way of true antecedents; and it is reasonable to conclude that Miletus in the early sixth century BC saw the birth of science and philosophy. That conclusion does not ascribe any supernatural talent to Thales and his associates. It merely implies that they were men of genius.

First Philosophy

In what did their genius consist? What characteristics defined the new endeavour? Three things in particular mark off the *phusikoi*.

First, and most simply, the Presocratics invented the very idea of science and philosophy. They hit upon that special way of looking at the world which is the scientific or rational way. They saw the world as something ordered and intelligible, its history following an explicable course and its different parts arranged in a comprehensible system. The world was not a random collection of bits, its history was not an arbitrary jumble of events.

Nor was it a series of events determined by the will or the caprice of the gods. The Presocratics were not atheists: they allowed the gods into their brave new world, and some of them attempted to produce an improved and rationalized theology in place of the anthropomorphic divinities of the Olympian pantheon. But their theology had little to do with religion, and they removed most of the traditional functions from the gods. Thus thunder was no longer the growling of a minatory Zeus. Iris or Rainbow was no longer a goddess – what is a rainbow but a multicoloured cloud? The Presocratic gods – like the gods of Aristotle and of that arch theist Plato – do not interfere with the natural world.

The world is orderly without being divinely run. Its order is intrinsic: the internal principles of nature are sufficient to explain its structure and its history. For the happenings which constitute the world's history are not mere brute events, to be recorded and admired: they are structured events, they fit together and interconnect. And the patterns of their interconnections yield an explanatory account of the ways of the world.

In the first book of his *Metaphysics* Aristotle wrote a short account of the early history of Greek philosophy. He discussed the subject exclusively in terms of explanations or causes. He himself held that there were four different types of explanation (or 'four causes') and he thought that the four had been slowly discovered, one by one, by his predecessors. The history of philosophy was thus the history of the conceptual understanding of explanatory schemes. Aristotle's account of this history has been criticized for bias and partiality. But in essence Aristotle is right; at any rate, it is in the development of the notion of explanation that we may see one of the primary features of Presocratic philosophy.

Presocratic explanations, as I have said, are internal: that is to say, they explain the universe from within, in terms of its own constituent features, and they do not appeal to arbitrary intervention from without. Secondly, Presocratic explanations are systematic: they explain the whole sum of natural events in a single set of terms and by a single set of methods. The general principles which are adduced to account for the origins of the world are also invoked, in particular forms, in order to explain earthquakes or hailstorms or eclipses or diseases or monstrous births.

Finally, Presocratic explanations are economical: they use few terms, invoke few operations, assume few 'unknowns'. Anaximenes, for example, thought to explain everything in terms of a single material element (air) and a pair of co-ordinated operations (rarefaction and condensation). If the natural world exhibits an extraordinary variety of phenomena and events, this variety must be reduced to order, and the order made simple – for that is the way to intelligibility. And most of the Presocratics were niggardly in the extreme. If their attempts look comic or infantile when they are compared with the refined and esoteric theories of modern science, none the less the same desire underlies and informs both the ancient and the modern endeavours – the desire to explain as much as possible in terms of as little as possible.

Science has its jargon and its set of specialized concepts – mass, force, atom, element, tissue, nerve, parallax, ecliptic, and so on. The terminology and the conceptual equipment were not god-given, nor did they lie to hand in the speech and thought of ordinary life: they had to be invented. The Presocratics were among the first inventors. Plainly, the very attempt to provide scientific explanations presupposes the mastery of certain concepts; equally plainly, the prosecution of the attempt will demand further conceptual development. The process will not always be self-conscious. The scientists will not often say to themselves: 'Here is a curious phenomenon; we must elaborate new concepts to understand it and devise new names to express it.' But concept formation, and the consequent elaboration of a technical vocabulary, are constant corollaries of scientific struggle.

The point may be illustrated by four examples.

First, there is the concept of the universe or the world itself. The Greek word is *kosmos*, whence our 'cosmos' and 'cosmology'. The word was certainly used by Heraclitus, and it may have been used by the first Milesian philosophers.

It is remarkable enough that these thinkers should have felt the need for a word to designate the world as a whole. Normal conversation and normal business hardly require us to talk about everything, or to form the concept of a totality or universe of all things. Far more noteworthy, however, is the choice of the word *kosmos* to designate the universe. The noun *kosmos* derives from a verb which means 'to order', 'to arrange', 'to marshal' – it is used by Homer of the Greek generals marshalling their troops for battle. Thus a *kosmos* is an orderly arrangement. Moreover, it is a beautiful arrangement: the word *kosmos* in ordinary Greek meant not only an ordering but also an adornment (hence the English word 'cosmetic'), something which beautifies and is pleasant to contemplate. The cosmos is the world, the totality of things. But it is also the elegant world, and it is the orderly world. And if the cosmos is by definition ordered, then it must in principle be explicable.

The second term is *phusis* or 'nature'. The Presocratics, as I have said, were later regarded as *phusikoi*, and their works were often given the title *Peri Phuseôs* or 'On Nature'. They themselves used the term *phusis*: it is present in several of the fragments of Heraclitus, and it is plausible to suppose that it was also used by the Milesians.

The noun derives from a verb meaning 'to grow'; and the significance of the concept of nature lies partly in the fact that it introduces a clear distinction between the natural and the artificial world, between things which have 'grown' and things which have been made. Tables and carts and ploughs (and perhaps societies and laws and justice) are artefacts: they have been made by designers (in these cases, by human designers). They are not natural: they do not belong to the world of nature, and they themselves have no nature – for they do not grow. Trees and plants and snakes (and perhaps also rain and clouds and mountains), on the other hand, have not been made: they are not artefacts but natural objects – they grew, they have a nature.

But the distinction between nature and artifice (in Greek, between *phusis* and *technê*) does not exhaust the significance of the notion of nature. In one sense the word 'nature' designates the sum of natural objects and natural events; in this sense to discourse on nature or *peri phuseôs* is to talk about the whole natural world – *phusis* and *kosmos* come to much the same thing. But in another sense the word serves to denote something within each natural object: in the first fragment of Heraclitus, the term *phusis* designates not the cosmos as a whole but rather a principle within each natural part of the cosmos. When the Presocratics inquired into 'nature', they were not only inquiring into the natural world – they were inquiring into 'the natures of things'.

Any natural object – anything which grows and is not made – has, it was assumed, a nature of its own. Its nature is an intrinsic feature of it, and it is an essential feature – not an accidental or chance fact about it. Moreover, it is an explanatory feature: the nature of an object explains why it behaves in the ways it does, why it has the various accidental properties it does.

All scientists are interested, in this sense, in the *phusis* of things. A chemist investigating gold is concerned to find out the underlying or basic properties of gold, in terms of which its other properties can be explained. Perhaps the basic properties of gold are those associated with its atomic weight. These properties will then explain why gold is, say, malleable and ductile, why it is soft and yellow, why it dissolves in sulphuric acid, and so on. The chemist is looking for the 'fundamental properties' of gold, for its 'essence' – for its 'nature' or *phusis*. This indispensable scientific concept was first established by the Presocratics.

Nature is a principle and origin of growth; and the notions of principle and origin introduce a third Presocratic term: *archê*. The word, we are told, was first used by Anaximander. It is a difficult term to translate. Its cognate verb can mean either 'to begin', 'to commence', or else 'to rule', 'to govern'. An *archê* is thus a beginning or origin; and it is also a rule or a ruling principle. (*Archê* is in fact the normal Greek word for a public office or magistracy.) Writers on ancient philosophy often use the word 'principle' or the phrase 'first principle' to render *archê*, and I shall follow the practice. The term is apt, providing that the reader keeps in mind the Latin etymology of the English word: a principle is a *principium* or a beginning.

The inquiry into the natures of things leads easily to a search for principles. Nature is growth: what, then, does growth start from? What are the principles of growth, the origins of natural phenomena? The same questions were readily asked of the cosmos as a whole: how did it begin? What are its first principles? What are the fundamental elements from which it is made and the fundamental operations which determine its structure and career?

The inquiry into principles was in this way closely associated with cosmology, and also with abstract physics or chemistry. The 'principles' of the universe will include its basic stuff or stuffs. And since everything must, in the last analysis, be made out of the basic stuff or stuffs of the universe, an inquiry into the principles of the cosmos is thereby an inquiry into the fundamental constituents of all natural objects.

The first Presocratic accounts of such principles were, unsurprisingly, rum. Thales proposed that everything is made of water. The basic stuff or first principle of the universe – the *archê* of the *kosmos* – is water, and in consequence everything in the universe is, at bottom, made of water. Cucumbers and courgettes, for example, are all water – 100 per cent water, not 99 per cent as modern pundits allege. And in just the same way the sands of the Sahara are water, nothing but water. Of course, we see and feel and taste and touch a variety of apparently different stuffs: a heap of sand, for example, does not look or taste – or behave – much like a slice of cucumber. None the less, these apparent differences are superficial; for all the different stuffs are, in Thales' view, mere modifications of water. If this seems insane, think how utterly different diamonds are from coal – and then recall that they are merely two different forms of the same stuff, carbon.

Thales' suggestion is false in fact; but it is not foolish – on the contrary, it is thoroughly scientific in spirit.

The fourth illustrative example is the concept of *logos*. The word *logos* is even harder to translate than *archê*. It is cognate with the verb *legein*, which normally means 'to say' or 'to state'. Thus a *logos* is something said or stated. When Heraclitus begins his book with a reference to 'this *logos*', he probably means only 'this statement' or 'this account': his *logos* is simply what he is going to say. But the word also has a richer meaning: to give a *logos* or an account of something is indeed to describe it, to say what it is; but it is also to explain it, to say why it is what it is. Thence, by an intelligible transference, *logos* comes to be used of the human faculty which enables us to offer explanations or reasons for things: *logos* may mean 'reason'. In this sense *logos* may be contrasted with perception, so that Parmenides, for example, can urge his readers to test his argument not by their senses but by *logos*, by reason. (The English term 'logic' derives ultimately from this sense of the word *logos*, by way of the later Greek term *logikê*.)

The Presocratics never imposed a single and clear sense on the term *logos*, and it would be exaggerated to contend that they invented the concept of reason or of rationality. But their use of *logos* constituted the first step towards the delineation of a notion which is central to science and philosophy.

The term *logos* brings me to the third of the three great achievements of the Presocratics. I mean their emphasis on the use of reason, on rationality and ratiocination, on argument and inference.

The Presocratics were not, on the whole, dogmatists. That is to say, they did not usually rest content with mere assertion. Determined to explain as well as describe the world of nature, they realized that explanations needed rational support. This is evident even in the earliest of the Presocratic thinkers and even when their claims seem most strange. Thales held that all things possess souls or are alive. He did not merely assert this bizarre doctrine: he argued for it by appealing to the case of the magnet. Here is a piece of stone – what could appear more lifeless? Yet the magnet possesses a power to move other things: it attracts iron filings, which move towards it without the intervention of any external pushes or pulls. Now it is a noticeable feature of living things that they are capable of producing motion. (Aristotle later took it as one of the defining characteristics of things with souls that they possess such a motive power.) Hence Thales concluded that the magnet, despite appearances, has a soul.

Thales' argument is perhaps unimpressive: certainly we do not believe that magnets are alive, nor should we regard the attractive powers of a piece of stone as evidence of life. But I do not claim that Thales in particular or the Presocratics in general offered good arguments for their theories; rather, I claim that they offered arguments for their theories. And with the thinkers of the second Presocratic phase, this love of argument and justification becomes more obvious and more pronounced. For them, indeed, reasoned argument is the sole pathway to truth, and the writings of Parmenides, Melissus and Zeno are nothing other than chains of arguments.

The Presocratic achievement is evident in their language. Ordinary Greek is peculiarly suited for rational discourse and the expression of argument. In particular, it is a language rich in particles which conspire to express nuances of thought which in English (and in most other languages) are normally conveyed by such things as emphasis or tone of voice or manner of delivery. That is to say, the Greek particles make explicit and obvious what other languages normally leave implicit and sometimes leave obscure. Little words like 'so', 'therefore', 'for', which English frequently omits (or includes at the cost of tedious pedantry), are normally expressed in a Greek text. The fragments of Melissus, for example, are peppered with such inferential particles. Presocratic writing wears its rationality on its sleeve.

It is important to see exactly what this rationality consisted in. First, it is not a matter of getting things right; I do not affirm that the Presocratics were peculiarly good at arguing or that they regularly produced sound arguments. On the contrary, most of their theories are false, and most of their arguments are unsound. (This is not deep damnation – the same could be said of virtually every scientist and philosopher who has ever lived.) Secondly, it is not that the Presocratics made a study of logical technique or developed a theory of inference and argument. Some of them, it is true, did reflect on the powers of the mind and on the nature, scope and limits of human knowledge. But the study of logic was invented by Aristotle, and Aristotle rightly boasted that no one before him had attempted to make explicit and systematic the rules and procedures which govern rational thought.

Nor, thirdly, is it that the Presocratics were consistently critical thinkers. It is sometimes said that the essence of science is criticism, that science lives by the constant critical appraisal of theories and arguments. Whether or not that is so, the Presocratics were not avid critics. Although we may reasonably talk of the influence of one Presocratic on another, and although it is immensely tempting to imagine that each thinker probed and tested the arguments of his predecessors, nevertheless no Presocratic (so far as we know) ever set down in writing an analysis or a detailed criticism of an earlier theory. Parmenides urged his readers to test with their reason what he had said: his urgings went unanswered. Presocratic reasoning was constructive rather than critical. Critical reflection did not become a normal part of philosophical discourse until the fourth century BC.

What, then, is the substance of the claim that the Presocratics were champions of reason and rationality? It is this: they offered reasons for their opinions, they gave arguments for their views. They did not utter *ex cathedra* pronouncements. Or rather, and more modestly: most of the Presocratic thinkers were, for most of the time, concerned not to advance opinions but to advance reasoned opinions.

That may seem an unremarkable achievement. It is not. On the contrary, it is the most remarkable and the most praiseworthy of the three achievements I have rehearsed. Those who doubt the fact should reflect on the maxim of George Berkeley, the eighteenth-century Irish philosopher: All men have opinions, but few think.

The Evidence

A few Presocratics wrote nothing, but most put their thoughts down on paper. Some wrote in verse and some in prose. Some wrote a single work, others several – and Democritus allegedly composed some fifty books. The collected works of the Presocratic thinkers would have filled a few shelves in the library.

Of all these works not one has survived intact. Some endured for a thousand years or so. The philosopher and scholar Simplicius, who worked in the first half of the sixth century AD, was able to consult texts of Parmenides, Melissus, Zeno, Anaxagoras, Diogenes of Apollonia and others. But Simplicius himself remarks that Parmenides' book was a rarity, and by his time many other Presocratic works had surely disappeared. The Presocratics were never best-sellers. And books were easily destroyed.

Our knowledge of the Presocratics, then, unlike our knowledge of Plato or of Aristotle, is not gained directly from the books they wrote. Rather, it depends upon information of two different sorts.

First, there survive several fragments of the original works of the Presocratics. The word 'fragment' may mislead. Insofar as it suggests a scrap of paper, torn from a Presocratic book and preserved by some accident of time, then we possess only one meagre collection of Presocratic fragments – the broken remains of a copy of Empedocles which was written in about AD 100. But scholars customarily use the term 'fragment' in a more generous sense: it comprehends not only torn scraps but also, and especially, passages from the Presocratics' own writings – words, phrases, sentences, paragraphs – which were quoted by later authors and survive embedded in their writings.

Such 'fragments' constitute our most precious testimony to the views of the Presocratics. Their number and their extent vary from one thinker to another. For a few Presocratics they are non-existent. For most they are short and sparse. But in some happy cases they are sufficiently extensive to convey a tolerably determinate idea of some part of the original work from which they were quoted.

Secondly, in addition to the fragments there are numerous references to Presocratic thought in the works of later authors – allusions or reports or paraphrases or assessments of ideas or of arguments or of doctrines. Some of the references are brief and casual, mere embellishments to a text whose chief aim was never the transmission of historical information about early philosophy. Many of the references are embedded in philosophical texts where they have an historical purpose and were written with a philosophical intention. And some of the references represent genuine attempts at the history of philosophy – attempts which exist in a variety of forms: there is the ambitious but uncritical *Lives of the Philosophers* by Diogenes Laertius; there are handbooks and compendia, such as the *History of Philosophy* which goes under Galen's name, or the *Opinions of the Philosophers on Nature* falsely attributed to Plutarch; there are historical essays incorporated in the scholarly writings of late antiquity, most notably in the commentary on Aristotle's *Physics* by Simplicius; there are pertinent passages in works of Christian polemic, most notably in the *Refutation of All Heresies* of Hippolytus.

These references or testimonies have been the subject of subtle scholarly investigation. They are of disparate value. They were written centuries after the thoughts which they chronicle, and they were written by men with different interests and different outlooks. They must be read with caution, if not with scepticism. When Bishop Hippolytus ascribes a certain view to Heraclitus, he should not be believed before he has answered two questions. First, from what source did he draw his information? For the channel which wound from Heraclitus to Hippolytus is long, and we must wonder if the information flowing down it was not contaminated with falsehood or poisoned by inaccuracy. Secondly, what were Hippolytus' own philosophical predilections, and what were the aims of his own book? For these may have biased him – consciously or unconsciously – in his reporting. The arguments on these issues are intricate.

Nor should it be thought that the fragments offer a clear and easy path to the truth about their authors. There is a sequence of difficulties of which every student of early Greek philosophy becomes quickly aware. It may be useful to say a little about these difficulties here (which have, in any case, their own intrinsic interest); and it will be best to consider the general issues through the medium of a particular example.

Take the following passage (which will reappear in the chapter on Anaxagoras):

In the first book of the *Physics* Anaxagoras says that uniform stuffs, limitless in quantity, separate off from a single mixture, all things being present in all and each being characterized by what predominates. He makes this clear in the first book of the *Physics* at the beginning of which he says: Together were all things, limitless both in quantity and in smallness. [59 B 1]

(Simplicius, *Commentary on the* Physics 155.23–27)

Simplicius was born in Cilicia in the latter part of the fifth century AD. He studied philosophy first at Alexandria and then at Athens, where he became one of the leading figures of the Platonist school. After Justinian's edict he left Athens and went, with some of his associates, to the royal court in Persia; but the Eastern life proved unattractive and he returned to Athens a few years later. There he continued his researches, writing long and learned commentaries on Aristotle's works and using the resources of the Athenian libraries. His *Commentary on the* Physics was probably completed in about 540. It is a huge work, running to more than a thousand large pages; in it Simplicius cites numerous Presocratic texts and in addition presents valuable accounts of early Greek thought.

Simplicius wrote more than a millennium after Anaxagoras. But that is not the full measure of our distance from Anaxagoras as we read Simplicius' texts; for we do not possess Simplicius' own autograph copy of his commentary. Some sixty manuscript copies of the work are extant, the earliest of which dates from the twelfth century and is therefore some six hundred years later than Simplicius' own copy. All these manuscripts derive ultimately from Simplicius' autograph; but they are copies of copies of copies. Each act of copying introduces errors (for however careful a scribe may be, he will certainly make mistakes), and no two manuscripts agree word for word with one another.

The first task, then, is to determine, on the evidence of these late and conflicting manuscripts, which words Simplicius himself wrote. (In our illustrative text some of the manuscripts give the Greek for 'a single mixture', and that is the Greek I have translated; other manuscripts give the Greek for 'some mixture'. Here the variants differ little in sense, and the choice between them is not of great moment.

In many cases, however, the readings of different manuscripts give radically different senses.) The discipline of textual criticism has procedures and techniques whose aim is to produce the best text or the text closest to what the author originally wrote. Often it is possible to decide which of several variant readings offered by the different manuscripts is the original reading. Sometimes it is clear that none of the manuscript readings can be correct, and conjectural emendation may restore the original text. Occasionally – more often than scholars like to admit – we should confess that we do not know what Simplicius wrote.

Once Simplicius' text is established, we may turn to the Anaxagorean material embedded in it. Here the first question is whether or not Simplicius purports to be quoting Anaxagoras. This question is easy in the case of those Presocratics who wrote in verse, as Parmenides and Empedocles did; for if Simplicius remarks that 'Parmenides says this . . .' and then breaks into verse, we can be sure that he is purporting to quote Parmenides and not merely to paraphrase him. With prose authors the question is harder. Occasionally Simplicius will say 'X says, in these very words, that . . .', and then he claims to quote. But such explicitness is rare. Far more often he will simply say 'X says that . . .'. In Greek as in English, phrases of this sort may as well introduce a paraphrase – even a remote paraphrase – as a *verbatim* citation. To distinguish citations from paraphrase we must rely on various linguistic signs. For example, if Simplicius writes 'Anaxagoras says that . . .', and follows it with a paragraph of prose in an archaic style, it is plausible to infer that he thinks he is quoting Anaxagoras. (So it is in our illustrative text.) But if the saying is short there may be nothing to distinguish quotation from paraphrase.

Suppose, then, that we have established Simplicius' text and have determined that he claims to quote Anaxagoras. Not all purported quotations are actual quotations. (And not all actual quotations are purported quotations. But in this context the possibility of disguised or unannounced quotations need not exercise us.) When Simplicius purports to quote from a work written a thousand years before his time, he may be mistaken. The work he cites could be a forgery: the counterfeiting of early texts was a popular pastime in the ancient world, and among the Presocratics Pythagoras and his immediate followers had numerous works falsely fathered on them. Again, the book from which Simplicius quotes may have been wrongly labelled or misidentified. Some scholars have thought that Simplicius did not have a genuine text of Anaxagoras available to him; and his quotations, they think, come from a later epitome of Anaxagoras' book, not (as he thought) from the book itself.

Suppose, now, that we have a genuine quotation of Anaxagoras before us: the next questions concern its contents – and first, its contents in the most literal sense of the term. What words did Anaxagoras use? For we cannot assume that Simplicius' words accurately represent Anaxagoras' words. Simplicius may be quoting from memory – and misremembering; or he may be quoting from a text he has in front of his eyes – and miscopying. Errors of both sorts are easy and common. More importantly, even if Simplicius is accurately transcribing the text he has in front of him, there is no guarantee that his text is faithful to the original. During the millennium separating Simplicius from the Presocratics, the works of Anaxagoras will have been copied many times over. Just as we read copies of copies of Simplicius' autograph, so Simplicius will have read a copy of a copy of Anaxagoras' autograph. The probability that Simplicius read a pure text of Anaxagoras is zero.

What can a modern scholar do? Some Presocratic passages are quoted more than once. The first phrase of the quotation in our illustrative text became the 'To be, or not to be' of Presocratic thought: it is cited some sixty times by some twenty authors. In such cases there are always variant versions of the text, but there is often reason to prefer one version to another. For example, an author who quotes a brief passage was probably quoting from memory, and he is therefore more likely to have made an error than an author who quotes a long portion of the original and who was presumably transcribing it from his copy of the text. Or again, we may be able to construct a plausible story to account for the different readings in the different citations, and hence to establish the genuine Presocratic text. In our illustrative case we can, by these means, be reasonably confident that we know what words Anaxagoras himself wrote.

But most surviving fragments are quoted only once. Here there is less chance of getting back to the original text. Various philological techniques can be applied. Sometimes, for example, a linguistic anachronism will betray itself, and we may suspect that an explanatory note or gloss has insinuated itself into the text. Sometimes we may conjecture that the old text was retailored to fit its later context – and plausible guesses may sometimes hit upon the original readings. The case is rarely hopeless, but it always requires expert diagnosis and sometimes demands subtle therapy.

Once we have before us the words of Anaxagoras, or as close an approximation to them as we can reach, we must next try to understand them. This task has two distinct but closely connected aspects. First, and most obviously, there is the elementary matter of grasping the sense of the words and phrases which the text contains. Sometimes this is surprisingly hard. Anaxagoras, it is true, is on the whole an intelligible author; but the same cannot be said for all the Presocratics, and some of them (Heraclitus and Empedocles, for example) are often highly obscure. Their obscurity is due in part to the ravages of time: had more Greek of the early period survived, we should possess more comparative material and so have less difficulty in understanding Empedocles. But in part the obscurity is intrinsic to the texts themselves: Empedocles was writing in a new idiom on a new subject – it is only to be expected that he should sometimes have been less than pellucid.

Secondly, even if we can grasp what, at a literal level, the words of a fragment mean, we may still be far from understanding the passage. Sentences taken out of context are rarely easy to interpret, and isolated phrases, which are sometimes all we have, may be virtually senseless. We need, in other words, to ask what sense the fragment had in its original context, what contribution it made to the general economy of the philosopher's work, how it fitted into his argument or into the exposition of his views.

This is the point at which serious philosophical interpretation begins. It is a testing and an elusive business. There are some external aids. In particular, there is the context in which the fragment is cited. Sometimes, it is true, this context is of little use: for the fragments cited by John Stobaeus, for example, all we have to go on are the section headings under which he arranged them in his anthology. Sometimes the context may be actually misleading. Clement of Alexandria, for example, cites the Presocratic pagans for his own Christian ends, and he does not purport to preserve the original settings of the passages he adduces (why should he?). None the less, the context is sometimes helpful, especially so in the case of Simplicius, who was an able scholar of great learning. (A good example of this is the long passage from the commentary on Aristotle's *Physics* which contains all the surviving fragments of Zeno.) At the very least, the context of citation will give us an idea of how a fragment might have functioned in its original home.

Again, comparison of one fragment with another, and comparison of the fragments with the testimonies, will yield further evidence. This is often a risky matter: it is all too easy to imagine that we have enough bits and pieces to reconstruct the original picture when in fact we may possess only enough to give one small part of it. (This is certainly true of Anaxagoras, where almost all the surviving fragments appear to come from the early part of his book.) The dangers need to be acknowledged. They can sometimes be overcome.

In sum, the task of interpretation is full of difficulty. (That is one reason why it is full of excitement.) Sometimes we may fairly claim success. Frequently we should be content with a Scottish verdict: *non liquet*, 'It is not clear'. But these questions go beyond the scope of the present book, whose function is not to offer an exegesis of Presocratic thought but to exhibit the material on which any exegesis must be based.

The Texts

This book contains English translations of all the surviving philosophical fragments of the Presocratic thinkers. In each chapter the fragments have been supplemented by extracts from the secondary material. This material is vast and repetitive. A comprehensive translation would fill several tedious volumes. My selection of texts does not pretend to convey all we can glean; but I mean it to include all the most important items – and to give a fair sample of the unimportant.

The main chapters of the book thus present a partial view of their subjects relative to the evidence we possess. They also, and inevitably, present a partial view relative to the sum total of the original evidence; for it is not to be supposed that the surviving information represents a balanced account of the original works. Some parts of the Presocratic writings happen to have been well reported; others were only sketchily described; still others were entirely forgotten. We can do little to redress things.

The information which we do possess is contained in a large number of different and disparate texts, and it cannot readily be set out in a manner which reveals the general drift and tenor of the philosophies it describes. From the material exhibited in the chapter on Heraclitus, for example, it is no easy business to form a general impression of the overall shape and intention of his thought. The Synopsis which follows this Introduction is designed to mitigate the difficulty. It contains a sequence of sketches of the main views of each thinker, insofar as they can be known. The sketches are not substitutes for the texts in the main chapters, nor do they claim to convey definitive interpretations. Rather, they are intended to provide a moderately intelligible framework within which the texts may first be read. They are fixed ropes on a difficult rock face, placed there for the inexperienced climber. Use them once or twice and then climb free. Read them, and forget them.

The fragments are presented in the contexts in which they have been preserved. This mode of presentation, which is not customary, has certain disadvantages: it makes for occasional repetition, and it means that the texts often appear in a different order from that of the standard modern editions. But those disadvantages are, I think, decisively outweighed by the advantages. A presentation of the texts shorn of their contexts gives a wholly misleading impression of the nature of our evidence for Presocratic philosophy. Translation in context avoids that erroneous impression, and at the same time it enables the English reader to see how difficult it often is, especially in the case of prose fragments, to distinguish genuine citations from paraphrases or mere allusions. In addition, as I have already remarked, the context of a quotation often helps us to understand the fragments better – or at least to see how the ancient authors understood them. And in any case, the contexts are interesting in their own right.

Every translator, and in particular every translator of philosophical texts, has two desires. He wants to be faithful to his original: he wants to convey all and only what it conveys, and he wants to reproduce something of the form, as well as the content, of the original. But he also wants to produce readable and tolerably elegant sentences of his own language. These two desires usually conflict; for different languages have different idioms and different modes of expression. Fidelity, if pressed to the limit, will result in barbarous or even in unintelligible English. Elegance will disguise the sense and the argumentative flow of the original. Moreover, the first desire is essentially unsatisfiable. It is a commonplace that 'something is lost in translation' – a commonplace which applies to prose no less than to poetry. It is equally true that any translation will add something to the original, if only by virtue of the different resonances and overtones of synonymous expressions in different languages.

In the face of these difficulties a translator must adopt some working principle. On the whole I have chosen to give more weight to the first desire than to the second. I have put fidelity above elegance, being more concerned to transmit the sense of the Greek texts than to provide an aesthetic feast for the English reader. Some Presocratics, as I have said, wrote in verse: their fragments have been put into English prose, but the prose is printed in broken lines, each line corresponding in principle to a single Greek verse.

My translations are sometimes contorted, and often obscure or ambiguous. But such infelicities are not invariably faults in the translation. Presocratic Greek is itself sometimes contorted, and it is often obscure or ambiguous. It is no duty of a translator to polish his authors' work. On the contrary, fidelity demands that the translation be as uncouth as the original.

The translated texts are linked by bridge passages, and each chapter is introduced by a paragraph or two of commentary. But I have tried to keep such editorial matter to a minimum. There are numerous commentaries on, and interpretations of, the Presocratics in print: this book is not an addition to that large literature.

The source of each translated passage is given, and the Appendix offers some elementary information about the authors to whom we owe our knowledge of Presocratic philosophy. In addition, the fragments are equipped with 'Diels-Kranz numbers' (these are the ciphers which appear in square brackets after the texts). The numbers key the passages to the standard edition of the Greek texts, edited by Hermann Diels and Walther Kranz: *Die Fragmente der Vorsokratiker* (10th edn; Berlin, 1952). Diels-Kranz numbers are invariably used by scholars who write about early Greek thought: anyone who wants to chase up a fragment in the modern literature will find that a Diels-Kranz number simplifies the task.

Readers of this book will, I suspect, be frequently perplexed and sometimes annoyed. It is as though one is presented with a jigsaw puzzle (or rather, with a set of jigsaw puzzles) in which many of the pieces are missing and most of the surviving pieces are faded or torn. Or, to take a closer analogy, it is as though one were looking at a museum case containing broken and chipped fragments of once elegant pottery. Many of the pieces are small, some of them do not seem to fit at all, and it is difficult to envisage the shape and form of the original pot.

But the vexation which this may produce will, I hope, be accompanied by other, more pleasing, emotions. Fragments of beautiful pottery may, after all, be themselves objects of beauty; and certainly many of the Presocratic texts are fascinating and stimulating pieces of thought. Moreover, parts are challenging in a way in which wholes are not: they appeal to the intellectual imagination, and they excite readers to construct for themselves some picture of the whole from which they came.

For my part, I find the Presocratic fragments objects of inexhaustible and intriguing delight. I like to think that readers of this book may come to find a similar pleasure in contemplating the battered remains of the first heroes of Western science and philosophy.

SYNOPSIS

I

Greek philosophy began with three men from Miletus. THALES was a practical statesman, and perhaps something of an astronomer. What he did in philosophy is uncertain: he suggested that the earth floats on a vast water-bed; he conjectured that everything was made from water – or perhaps that everything is made of water; he is said to have argued that magnets 'have souls' (that they are alive), and that everything is full of gods. No doubt he made further inquiries 'On Nature' – at any rate, tradition counts him the first *phusikos* or natural scientist.

ANAXIMANDER was a full-blooded *phusikos*, and he certainly spoke of the material principle or *archê* of all natural things. He did not identify this principle with any familiar sort of stuff; rather, he described it simply as 'the limitless', infinite in extent and indefinite in its characteristics. From this characterless material the familiar stuffs of the world – earth, air, water, and so on – were generated by a process in which the twin powers of heat and cold played some part. The generated stuffs encroach on one another and have in the course of time to pay compensation for their 'injustice'. (We might think of the alternating encroachments of summer and winter, of the hot and dry and the cold and wet.) Thus the world is law-governed. Anaximander also gave a detailed account of natural phenomena, two of the more remarkable features of which concern biology (where he speculated on the origins of mankind) and astronomy (where he developed an ingenious theory of the celestial system and suggested that the earth remains where it is, motionless, because, in a symmetrical universe, there is no reason for it to move in one direction rather than in another).

ANAXIMENES, a pupil of Anaximander, also provided a detailed account of nature, in which he ventured to correct his master on certain points; and he also proposed a cosmogony. His *archê* was limitless, like Anaximander's, but it was not indeterminate; rather, the primal stuff was air. And Anaximenes maintained that a pair of operations – rarefaction and condensation – was sufficient to generate all the world's familiar substances from thin air.

A different speculative tradition was initiated by PYTHAGORAS. He attracted a band of disciples who followed a 'Pythagorean way of life'; he was a political figure of some importance; and legends soon collected around his name. He had a reputation for vast learning; but he seems not to have concerned himself particularly with nature. Moreover, scholars are generally sceptical of the ancient tradition which associates him with various mathematical and musical discoveries. (Pythagoras' theorem was not discovered by Pythagoras.) Rather, his first interest was the soul: he held that the soul was immortal, and that it undergoes a sequence of incarnations (a thesis which was later known as the theory of 'metempsychosis'). This process – and the whole history of the world – is endless and unchanging, the same things repeating themselves in cycles of eternal recurrence. The theory of metempsychosis suggested that all living things are fundamentally the same in kind, inasmuch as they are hosts to the same souls; Pythagoras probably made this the ground for certain dietary recommendations.

ALCMAEON, who had Pythagorean connections, also held that the soul was immortal; and he advanced a new argument for this tenet. He was a doctor with an interest in nature, and especially in human nature: he speculated, for example, on the structure and functioning of the sense-organs. He seems to have held that all things – or at least all things in human life – are to be explained in terms of pairs of opposites: hot and cold, light and dark, wet and dry, etc.

The poet XENOPHANES, long-lived and peripatetic, knew something about Pythagoras and the other early philosophers; and he engaged in inquiries into nature, even if he did not write 'On Nature' in the thorough-going Milesian way. His most original ideas concern other matters. First, impressed by the pretensions of the new science of *phusiologia*, he came to reflect on the nature and limits of human knowledge. Later tradition held him to have been a sceptic; but although one fragment appears to entertain a sceptical position, other texts suggest that he was a 'gradualist': knowledge is difficult to come by, but not beyond all endeavour.

Xenophanes' second claim to originality lies in the field of natural theology. He criticized the immoral gods of Homer and the poets; and, more generally, he regarded customary religious beliefs as groundless. Instead, he offered a rational theology. The later tradition ascribes to him a highly articulated system; and if the tradition exaggerates, the fragments show that Xenophanes believed in a single or supreme god, who was moral and motionless, all-knowing and all-powerful. Nor was the god anthropomorphic: rather, he was an abstract and impersonal force, not a god from the Olympian pantheon, but a god accommodated to the new world of the Ionian philosophers.

The major figure in the first phase of Presocratic philosophy is HERACLITUS. He is a baffling thinker, whose writings won him an early reputation for obscurity and whose disdain for the folly of his fellows cannot have won him popularity. Not all his work was newfangled or riddling. He stood in the Ionian tradition, making fire the *archê* of the universe and offering an account of nature and the natural world. That account included a novel astronomy, and it made much use of 'exhalations'; but it followed the Milesian model, and, like Anaximander, Heraclitus stressed that the universe of nature was law-governed. He also had what might be called a Pythagorean side: the fragments betray an interest in the soul and in human psychology, some of them hinting at an existence for the soul after death. He also advanced some moral and political ideas. In addition, Heraclitus, like Xenophanes, criticized received religious practices and offered the world a new and more scientific god, now identified with the cosmic fire. And, again like Xenophanes, he reflected on the possibility of knowledge: he thought that knowledge about the nature of things was not easy to come by; but he believed that he had himself hit upon the truth of things, and he supposed that the book of nature could be read by men who made proper use of their senses and their understanding.

The novelty of Heraclitus lies in what might be called his metaphysical views. Here three features are worth emphasizing. First, he rejected cosmogony: the Milesians had told stories about the origins of the world: Heraclitus held that the world had always existed, and that there was therefore no cosmogonical story to tell. Secondly (his most celebrated notion), he held that 'everything flows': the world and its furniture are in a state of perpetual flux. What is more, things depend on this flux for their continuity and identity; for if a river ceases to flow it ceases to be a river. Finally – and most strangely – Heraclitus believed in the 'unity of opposites'. The path up is the same as the path down, and in general, existing things are characterized by pairs of contrary properties, whose bellicose coexistence is essential to their continued being.

The fundamental truth about nature is this: the world is an eternal and ever-changing modification of fire, its various contents each unified and held together by a dynamic tension of contrarieties. This truth is the account in accordance with which everything happens, and it underlies and explains the whole of nature.

II

The early philosophers had taken the first tottering steps down the road to science. The sceptical suggestions of Xenophanes cast a small shadow over their inquiries, but the sun of Heraclitus soon burned it away. In the second phase of philosophy, a thicker and darker cloud loomed; it threatened to cut off all light from empirical science, and it seemed impenetrable. The cloud blew in from Elea.

PARMENIDES wrote at some length on nature. He developed a novel system invoking a co-ordinated pair of principles, and he spoke in detail on biology and on astronomy. (He was the first Greek to say that the earth is spherical, that the moon shines with a reflected light, that the Evening and the Morning Star are one and the same.) But the discourse on nature occupied the second half of his poem, the half which described the Way of Opinion and which was self-confessedly false and 'deceitful'. The first part of the poem was a guide to the Way of Truth, and that Way led through strange and arid territory.

Parmenides began by considering the possible subjects of inquiry: in principle, you might think to inquire into what exists, or you might think to inquire into what does not exist. But the latter is not a genuine possibility, for you cannot think of, and hence cannot inquire into, the non-existent. So every subject of inquiry must exist. But everything which exists must, as Parmenides proceeds to argue, possess a certain set of properties: it must be ungenerated and indestructible (otherwise it would, at some time, not exist – which is impossible); it must be continuous, without spatial or temporal gaps; it must be entirely changeless – it cannot move or alter or grow or diminish; and it must be bounded or finite, like a sphere. Reason, or the logical power of ineluctable deduction, shows that anything which exists must be as Parmenides describes it: if sense-perception suggests a world of a different sort, then so much the worse for sense-perception.

MELISSUS rewrote the Parmenidean system in plain prose. But he was not without originality. He produced new arguments for Parmenides' old positions – most notably, he urged that empty space is a logical impossibility, that the world is therefore full, and that in a tightly packed world nothing can budge. And on two matters he differed from Parmenides: first, whereas Parmenides' world was a limited sphere, Melissus held that whatever exists must be infinitely extended in all directions; secondly, Melissus argued that, since everything which exists must be infinitely extended, there can be at most one thing in existence – that is to say, he argued for a theory of 'monism'. Melissus also presented an explicit argument to show that sense-perception is illusory and that the world is utterly different from the way it appears to our senses.

ZENO produced no systematic philosophy. He contrived a series of arguments (forty in all, we are told), each of which concluded that plurality is paradoxical: if more things than one were to exist, then contradictions would follow. Two of the forty arguments survive; in them Zeno argues that if more things than one exist, then they must be both large and small, and that if more things than one exist, then they must be both limited in number and limitlessly many. Zeno also devised four celebrated arguments proving the impossibility of motion; it is not clear whether these are to be numbered among the forty arguments against plurality.

Zeno's puzzles are both entertaining and serious. For if at first sight they may seem Christmas-cracker conundrums, they all involve concepts – notably the concept of infinity – which continue to perplex and to exercise philosophers. Zeno's own purpose in propounding his puzzles is uncertain. Plato regarded him as a supporter of Eleatic monism who meant to show that the consequences of pluralism were 'more ridiculous' than those of monism. Others have suspected that Zeno was an intellectual nihilist.

III

The third phase of Presocratic philosophy is best understood as a reaction against the Parmenidean position. If the Eleatics were right, then science was impossible. The post-Eleatics tried in their different ways to do justice to the force of Parmenides' arguments while retaining the right to follow the pathways of science. The period produced three major figures (Empedocles, Anaxagoras, Democritus) and some interesting minor characters.

EMPEDOCLES promised his audience knowledge (and with it some magical powers). He insisted, against the Eleatics, that the senses, if properly used, are routes to knowledge. He agreed with Parmenides that nothing could come into existence or perish, and he agreed with Melissus that empty space is impossible. None the less, Empedocles argued, motion is possible, and hence change too is possible; for the eternal stuffs can move and intermingle with one another, thereby effecting the changes which we observe in the world about us.

The basic stuffs of the universe, according to Empedocles, are four: earth, air, fire, water. Everything in the world is made up from these four 'roots' or elements. In addition there are two opposing powers,

Love and Strife, or attraction and repulsion, whose operations are manifested in the natural powers of the stuffs themselves and are governed by chance and necessity. The powers determine the development of the universe, a development which is cyclical and eternal. In the joust between Love and Strife, each champion periodically dominates the lists: under the dominion of Love, all the elements come together into a unity, a homogeneous sphere. As Strife regains power, the sphere breaks up, the elements begin to separate, various bodies, including those of our familiar world, come to be articulated, and eventually the four 'roots' are entirely distinct in four concentric spheres. Then the process reverses itself: from the separated elements, through several stages of articulation, back to the homogeneous sphere. The infinite alternations between sphere and separation, separation and sphere, are the eternal and unchanging history of the universe.

A notorious feature of Empedocles' poem *On Nature* was his account of the various monstrosities which come into existence at certain stages of the cosmic history. But much of the poem gave a detailed description of the articulated world we live in. The description covered every subject from astronomy to human psychology. Long accounts of the structure of the eye and of the mechanism of breathing survive. Empedocles' major contribution here lies less in matters of detail than in one general and unifying notion. He believed that all things give off 'effluences' and are perforated by channels or pores. Different effluences fit different pores; and their matches and mismatches account for physical and chemical reactions, for biological and psychological phenomena – for perception, for magnetism, for the sterility of mules.

Alongside the science there is a story about souls. There were once spirits who enjoyed a life of bliss; but they erred (the error is unspecified, but it is usually supposed to have involved bloodshed) and their punishment was a sequence of mortal incarnations. We are all such fallen spirits, clothed temporarily and punitively in human flesh. Animals and some plants are also fallen spirits. (Empedocles himself has already been a bush, a bird and a fish. But he has now reached the highest point in the cycle of incarnations – he is not only a human, but a seer and a god.) For Empedocles, as for Pythagoras, metempsychosis had moral implications: animals (and certain plants) are our kin; eating them is therefore a sort of cannibalism, and must be assiduously avoided. If we follow Empedocles' advice we too may hope to become fellow feasters at the table of the gods.

Most readers are struck by the difference between Empedocles' scientific speculations and his romantic stories of spirits and souls. Some have accused him of inconsistency, or at least of a form of schizophrenia, and modern scholars have generally supposed that the romantic story was told not in *On Nature* but in Empedocles' second poem, *Purifications*. However that may be, it is now plain that Empedocles himself presented his science and his story of souls as parts of a single and unitary philosophical system.

Empedocles is sometimes called a Pythagorean, and his views have Pythagorean connections. The fifth-century PYTHAGOREANS divided into two groups, the Aphorists and the Scientists. The Aphorists believed that wisdom – the wisdom of Pythagoras – could be captured in gnomic utterances, and they had no desire to inquire or to reason. Their aphorisms were for the most part religious or ritualistic in content – they concerned diet, or sacrifice, or burial. The Scientists fell into different factions; but they were united by a belief in the importance of mathematics. Not technical mathematicians themselves, they hypothesized that the world was fundamentally composed of numbers: numbers, or rather the principles of numbers, were the principles of all things. Such a hypothesis either falls into mystical nonsense or else represents the insight that science is essentially applied mathematics. In the case of the Pythagoreans, sense and nonsense were present in equal measure.

The only Pythagorean of this period who has a face is PHILOLAUS (for HIPPASUS is little more than a name). The surviving fragments suggest that Philolaus was attempting to produce a Pythagorean version of natural science, a version which would be invulnerable to the Eleatic objections. He held that, although we can know little enough about the world, we can at least see that it must have been made up out of two types of thing – limitless items and limiting items. (Roughly, stuffs and shapes: a pond, for example, consists of limitless stuff, water, determined by a limiting item, its shape.) Something – it is unclear exactly what – was required to harmonize limiting and limitless items in order to generate the world.

So far the scheme is essentially Milesian in style. Pythagorean elements enter at the next stage of the argument: when the world is generated, it is determined by numbers, in the sense that it is describable in quantitative terms – otherwise it could not be known by us. On such foundations Philolaus hoped to erect the structure of natural science. Few details of his views are reported; we know, however, that he had views on astronomy which embraced the theory of the 'counter-earth' (another planet, balancing the earth, and bringing the heavenly bodies up to the perfect number, ten). He also interested himself in biology, where he presented an account of the nature of diseases. In addition, he expressed an opinion about the nature and future of the soul.

Like Empedocles, ANAXAGORAS accepted the Eleatic ban on generation and destruction, but maintained that motion is none the less possible, and hence that change can take place in the world. Again like Empedocles, he believed that our faculties, if properly used, would yield reliable information about the natural world; and he offered explanations and descriptions – none of which survives in his own words – of a vast number of natural phenomena. But in his conception of the nature of things, Anaxagoras differed fundamentally from Empedocles.

He held that every substance or stuff is eternal – that is to say, he had no theory of basic stuffs, no 'elements'. In the beginning 'everything was together' in an infinite gaseous tohu-bohu, wherein all things were present and no thing was clear. (By 'everything' Anaxagoras probably meant 'all stuffs and all qualities' – stuffs such as earth, gold, flesh, cheese; qualities, themselves conceived of as stuffs, such as the hot and the cold, the sweet and the bitter.) The cosmos formed when distinct stuffs and things gradually separated out from this undifferentiated mass. And here come Anaxagoras' two most novel doctrines.

First, he held that the original cosmogonical force was mind or thought. Thought, although different from all other things and not mixed with them, none the less pervades everything and knows everything and is responsible for the initial 'revolution' by which stuffs separated out. Later thinkers saw this as a great leap forward: Anaxagoras, they believed, had seen that the universe was planned by an intelligent designer. But they then found fault with him, complaining that he had not invoked mind at the level of particular scientific explanations – there he had remained content with explanations in terms of material forces. Other readers have judged Anaxagoras in other ways. It is in any case uncertain to what extent Anaxagoras considered cosmic thought a personal, planning faculty which determined the history of the world in an intentional – and perhaps a benevolent – fashion: perhaps it was an impersonal force, like the Love and Strife of Empedocles.

Anaxagoras' second innovation concerns his conception of stuffs. As stuffs separate out, none is ever entirely segregated, no pure stuff ever comes into being. Indeed, every piece of stuff always contains a portion of every other stuff. What we call 'gold' is not wholly golden: rather, 'gold' is the name we give to lumps of stuff which are predominantly gold. If Anaxagoras' grounds for holding this doctrine are disputed, two of its consequences are clear. First, there is no smallest piece of stuff of any sort – however small a piece of gold you may take, there is always a smaller bit; for within your piece of gold there is a portion of, say, blood – and that blood will itself contain a smaller portion of gold. The second consequence is not explicitly drawn in the fragments: stuffs cannot consist of particles or be 'in' one another in the way in which different sorts of seeds may be mixed in a packet; rather, Anaxagoras' view demands that stuffs be mixed through and through – that they be associated in something more like chemical combination than physical juxtaposition.

Anaxagoras' views were largely adopted by ARCHELAUS, who stood to him as Anaximenes had stood to Anaximander. But Archelaus has the reputation of being one of the first thinkers to reflect in a philosophical fashion on ethics; at any rate, he maintained – we no longer know on what grounds – that moral qualities are conventional and not natural.

In the long run, the physics of Anaxagoras proved infertile. Far more influential were the views of LEUCIPPUS and DEMOCRITUS, the two Atomists. Democritus, the younger of the two, eclipsed Leucippus: there is virtually nothing which our texts ascribe to Leucippus alone; and most aspects of Atomism are attached to the name of Democritus.

The Atomists tackled Parmenides head on. For they denied that what does not exist cannot be thought of – indeed, they maintained, paradoxically, that what does not exist is no less real than what does exist. What does not exist is empty space. What exists are bodies, the things which occupy space and move through its emptinesses. Empty space is infinite in extent, bodies are infinite in number. Moreover, bodies, in the proper sense of the word, are atomic or indivisible. The Atomists argued that there must be indivisible bodies, for they thought that the supposition that bodies can be divided *ad infinitum* led to paradox. These indivisibles were small, solid and without any 'qualities'. That is to say, they have size and shape and hardness or solidity (the so-called 'primary' qualities), but they lack the 'secondary' qualities – colour, smell, taste, etc. The atoms exist for ever and are unchangeable. To that extent each atom is a Parmenidean entity. But atoms move. Indeed, they move constantly and have been moving for all eternity.

Atomic movements create the world. For atoms sometimes collide, and after some collisions they stick together, when the hooks on one atom happen to lock with the eyes on another. In this way compound bodies are eventually formed. Everything happens by mechanical chance; but given infinite space and infinite time, it is only to be expected that the complex structure of the world about us will somewhere and somewhen be formed.

Democritus was an enthusiastic and prolific scientist. He wrote on an immense variety of topics, and he generally attempted to use his atomism in the service of detailed scientific explanations. The best examples of this are perhaps to be found in his account of perception and the objects of perception. One of the most interesting portions of his work dealt with anthropology – with the history and description of the human race as a social and cultural object. Democritus discussed, among other things, the origins of religion and the nature of language. His remarks here are entirely speculative – and the speculations began a long tradition of armchair anthropology.

Democritus also offered opinions on the possibility of human knowledge. Despite his scientific aspirations, he appears to have entertained some form of scepticism. His reasons for this are mostly missing, but some of them at least were closely connected with his atomism. If the only real things are atoms and empty space, and if neither empty space nor atoms are coloured, then colours – and all other secondary properties – are illusory. Hence the world is very different from the way our senses take it to be, and our senses are fundamentally misleading. But if we distrust our senses, how can we say anything about the structure of reality? The atomist theory itself, though largely an a priori construction, seemed to presuppose the validity of sense-perception and to gain support from its capacity to explain the phenomena of perception. If atomism is right, perception is illusory; but if perception is illusory, why embrace atomism? Democritus was aware of this puzzle. How he attempted to solve it we do not know.

Finally, Democritus wrote at length on matters of moral and political philosophy. Some scholars have attempted to find connections between his ethics and his atomism, and some have discerned a moral system behind the fragments. It is reasonably clear that Democritus was a hedonist of sorts: the goal of life is contentment, or imperturbability, and this is somehow equated with joy or pleasure. Democritean pleasures, however, are on the whole dry – Democritus was no advocate of a life of Riley. It is probably a mistake to look for anything more systematic than this in the fragments, which are presented as independent maxims. Some of them are sane, some are droll, some are banal, some are outrageous – a typical collection of moralistic aphorisms.

The last of the Presocratics was DIOGENES of Apollonia. His was not an original genius, and he is often, with some justice, described as an eclectic. His treatment of nature was in many respects close to that of the early Milesians: he postulated a single material principle – air – and generated the world from it by rarefaction and condensation. He explained the various natural phenomena by reference to this original stuff and its manifold modifications. If there is novelty in his physics, it must lie in his argument for positing a single underlying stuff: unless all things were fundamentally the same, he claimed, the changes which we observe in the world could not come about. In addition, he adopted Anaxagoras' cosmic thought. But in Diogenes' system, thought was identified with eternal, all-knowing and divine air, and it was the controlling and governing force of the universe: Diogenes held that the world was well designed.

The most remarkable fragment of Diogenes' work is a detailed description of the blood vessels of the human body. Here we can read at first hand what in the case of the other Presocratics we learn only indirectly: an attempt to describe in scientific detail the structure and organization of the physical world. The Presocratics were philosophers, and they concerned themselves with the most general questions about the nature and origins of the universe. But they were also scientists. The abstractions of their cosmogonical thought were complemented and completed by the concrete detail of their particular descriptions and explanations. In this way they were the forerunners of Aristotle – and through him of modern science and philosophy.

NOTE TO THE READER

The main chapters of this book employ a number of typographical devices. Italics have the normal functions of marking stress, identifying book-titles, and so on. In addition, all editorial comments on the ancient texts are set in italics. Bold is used for all purported citations from the Presocratics – for all 'fragments'. Roman type marks all quotations from ancient authors except such citations. Thus the contexts of citations will be set in roman, and so too will allusions to and paraphrases of Presocratic views.

Three different styles of brackets appear in the quoted material. Ordinary parentheses, '(. . .)', are used in the normal way as punctuation signs. Square brackets, '[. . .]', enclose trivial editorial alterations to the quoted texts (e.g. an unspecific pronoun, 'he', in the original is sometimes replaced by the appropriate proper name). They also enclose editorial comments (for example, they enclose the modern equivalent of the ancient system of dating by Olympic years). Angled brackets, '<. . .>', mark lacunae in the Greek text, i.e. places where the ancient scribes have accidentally omitted something. Where the pointed brackets enclose words, these represent what we may guess to have been omitted.

Daggers, '†. . .†', surround passages where either the translation or the text itself is wholly uncertain. Words between the daggers are at best an optimistic guess.

Each quoted passage is identified by the author's name, the title of the work in which it appears and sufficient auxiliary information to enable the passage to be located in any standard edition. Square brackets around an author's name are a sign of spuriousness (e.g. '[Aristotle], *Problems*' refers to the book called *Problems* which the manuscript tradition falsely ascribes to Aristotle). I have generally translated the text as it is printed in the best or most recent modern edition; but sometimes, and without any indication of the fact, I have preferred a different reading.

To each Presocratic fragment quoted there is appended a Diels-Kranz reference, enclosed in square brackets. This normally consists of the letter 'B' followed by a number. The number is the number of the fragment in H. Diels and W. Kranz, *Die Fragmente der Vorsokratiker* (10th edn; Berlin, 1952). The first Diels-Kranz reference in any chapter prefixes a number to the letter 'B'. This is the number of the relevant chapter in Diels-Kranz. Thus '[59 B 1]' refers to fragment 1 in chapter 59, the chapter on Anaxagoras, of Diels-Kranz. A subsequent '[B 21a]' refers to fragment 21a in the same chapter. In principle, the 'B' passages in Diels-Kranz are genuine fragments (in contrast to paraphrases and allusions which appear in separate sections labelled 'A'). In fact Diels-Kranz often include passages among their 'B' texts which are certainly not fragments. When the following pages give a Diels-Kranz reference for a passage which is not set in bold type, it should be inferred that Diels-Kranz falsely present the passage as a fragment.

PART I

1

Precursors

*Thales, the first of the canonical line of Presocratic philosophers, did not
start from scratch. Scholars have speculated on the sources from which
he may have drawn, and two possible lines of influence have been
discerned.*

*First, there are native Greek antecedents. Homer's poems, the earliest
surviving works of Greek literature, contain occasional references to what
were later to become scientific and philosophical topics. The poems
presuppose a certain conception of the nature and origins of the universe,
and that conception finds echoes, both verbal and substantial, in Presocratic thought. More influential, because more explicit, was the view of
the universe expressed by the seventh-century BC poet Hesiod. A short
passage from his* Theogony – 'The Birth of the Gods' – *may be quoted.*

> Hail, children of Zeus, grant a sweet song
> and tell of the holy race of the immortals who exist forever,
> those who came from Earth and from starry Heaven
> and from dark Night, and those whom the salt Sea reared,
> and the gods, givers of good things, who came from them.
> And say how they divided their wealth and shared their
>   honours,
> and also how they first took rugged Olympus.
> Tell me this, you Muses who have your home on Olympus,
> from the beginning, and tell which of them first came into
>   being.
>   In truth, first of all came Expanse; and then
> wide-bosomed Earth, seat ever safe of all
> the immortals who hold the heights of snowy Olympus,

and murky Tartarus in the recesses of the wide-pathed land,
and Love, who is fairest among the immortal gods,
loosener of limbs, who in the breasts of all gods and all men
overcomes thought and prudent purposing.

    From Expanse came Darkness and black Night;
and from Night came Ether and Day
whom she conceived and bore after joining with Darkness in
    love.

    Earth bore first, equal to herself,
starry Heaven, to enclose her all about
that there might be a seat ever safe for the blessed gods.
And she gave birth to tall Mountains, graceful haunts of
    goddesses –
of the Nymphs who live in the wooded mountains.
And she also bore the restless deep with its seething swell,
Sea, without the ardours of love; and then
she lay with Heaven and bore deep-eddying Ocean
and Coius and Creius and Hyperion and Iapetus
and Theia and Rheia and Right and Memory
and golden-crowned Phoebe and alluring Tethys.
And after them, the youngest, came wily Cronus,
most terrible of her children; and he hated his strong father.

                                           (Hesiod, *Theogony* 104–138)

This is not science; but it is, as it were, a scientific story: many of Hesiod's gods and goddesses are, as their names indicate, personifications of natural features or phenomena, and in telling the birth of 'the gods' Hesiod is telling, in picturesque form, the origins of the universe.

Thus the Sicilian comic poet Epicharmus, who wrote at the beginning of the fifth century BC, dramatizes a mock philosophical discussion of Hesiod's story:

    – The gods were always there: they were never missing;
and these things are always there, the same and in the same
    way always.
– But Expanse is said to have been the first god to be born.

– How could that be? He had nothing to come from and
   nowhere to go to at first.
– Then didn't anything come first? – No, nor anything
   second, by Zeus,
of the things we're now talking about: these things existed
   always. [23 B 1]
                           (Diogenes Laertius, *Lives of the Philosophers* III 10)

An anecdote from a later century is worth retelling:

The man who said

   In truth, first of all came Expanse; and then
   wide-bosomed Earth, seat of all . . .

refutes himself. For if someone asks him what Expanse came from,
he will not be able to answer. Some say that this is the reason why
Epicurus turned to philosophy. When he was still very young he asked
his schoolmaster who was reading out

   In truth, first of all came Expanse . . .

what Expanse came from if it came first. The schoolmaster replied
that it wasn't his job, but the job of the so-called philosophers, to
teach that sort of thing. 'Well, then,' said Epicurus, 'I must go to
them, if they are the ones who know the truth about the things which
exist.'   (Sextus Empiricus, *Against the Mathematicians* X 18–19)

In the final book of his Metaphysics *Aristotle discusses the place of
'the good and the beautiful' in the world. Some thinkers, he says, hold
that goodness and beauty only make their appearance as the world
progresses,*

and the early poets say something similar insofar as they hold not that
the first comers – Night and Heaven, or Expanse or Ocean – rule and
govern, but rather that Zeus does. But they are led to say this because
their world-rulers change: the hybrids among them – hybrids inasmuch as they do not express everything in a mythical vein – (I mean
Pherecydes and some others) do make the first generating principle
the best thing.   (Aristotle, *Metaphysics* 1091b4–10)

Pherecydes of Syrus, whom Aristotle here distinguishes from Hesiod and his fellows, is probably to be dated to the middle of the sixth century BC. He was therefore a contemporary of the first philosophers.

Aristotle's judgement that he was a hybrid, part mythologist and part natural philosopher, is scarcely borne out by the surviving remnants of his writings. Here are the two most 'philosophical' pieces:

The book which [Pherecydes] wrote has been preserved; it begins like this:
Zas and Time always existed, and so did Chthonie; and Chthonie gained the name Earth when Zas honoured her with the gift of the earth. [7 B 1]   (Diogenes Laertius, *Lives of the Philosophers* I 119)

Pherecydes of Syrus says that Zas and Time and Chthonie existed always as the three first principles (the one before the two, I mean, and the two after the one). Time from his own seed made fire and breath and water (I take this to be the threefold nature of the intelligible): they were set apart in five recesses and from them were constituted another and numerous generation of gods, which is called the generation of the five recesses (meaning, perhaps, of the five worlds).   (Damascius, *On First Principles* III ii 2.3)

The other reports of Pherecydes' work – a hundred passages or so – contain nothing but fanciful mythology.

Many of the Greeks believed that philosophy began among 'the barbarians' – in Egypt, in Persia, in Babylonia. They credited the early Presocratics with journeys to Egypt and the Near East, and supposed that they returned with philosophy among their souvenirs.

There was no doubt some intellectual contact between the Greeks and their eastern neighbours. But in philosophy, and in the more theoretical aspects of science, it is difficult to find a single clear case of influence. (And where one scholar sees striking parallels between a Greek and an Eastern text, others merely acknowledge superficial and coincidental resemblances.) Here are two brief passages from Eastern creation stories, one from Babylonia and the other from Egypt.

The Enuma Elishu, *the Babylonian creation epic, was probably composed early in the second millennium* BC. *It is written in Akkadian, and the translation is in many places uncertain – at all events, different scholars have produced remarkably different versions. The epic begins as follows:*

> When on high the heaven had not been named,
> firm ground below had not been called by name,
> nothing but primordial Apsu, their begetter,
> and Mummu-Tiamat, she who bore them all,
> their waters commingling as in a single body:
> no reed hut had been matted, no marsh land had appeared,
> when no gods whatever had been brought into being,
> uncalled by names, their destinies undetermined –
> then it was that the gods were formed within them.
> Lahmu and Lahamu were brought forth, they were called by
>   name.
> Before they had grown in age and stature,
> Anshar and Kishar were formed, surpassing the others.
> They prolonged the days, added on the years.
> Anu was their heir, the rival of his fathers;
> indeed, Anshar's first-born, Anu, was his equal.
> Anu begot in his image Nudimmud.
>   (J. B. Pritchard, *Ancient Near Eastern Texts*
>   (3rd edn; Princeton, 1969), p. 61)

Anu and Nudimmud are the sky and the earth; Apsu and Mummu-Tiamat are primordial waters, the fresh waters and the sea. Identification of the other divinities is uncertain.

The Egyptian creation myth is known in a number of variant forms. The following text probably dates from about 2,000 BC:

I am he who came into being as Khepri. When I had come into being, being came into being, and all beings came into being after I came into being. Many were the beings which came forth from my mouth, before heaven came into being, before earth came into being, before

7

the ground and creeping things had been created in this place. I put together some of them in Nun as weary ones, before I could find a place in which I might stand. It seemed advantageous to me in my heart; I planned with my face; and I made every form when I was alone, before I had spat out what was Shu, before I had sputtered out what was Tefnut, and before any other had come into being who could act with me.

I planned in my own heart, and there came into being a multitude of forms and beings, the forms of children and the forms of their children. I was the one who copulated with my fist, I masturbated with my hand. Then I spewed with my own mouth: I spat out what was Shu, I sputtered out what was Tefnut. It was my father Nun who brought them up . . .

Then Shu and Tefnut brought forth Geb and Nut. Then Geb and Nut brought forth Osiris, Horus Khenti-en-irti, Seth, Isis, and Nephthys from the body, one of these after another; and they brought forth their multitudes in this land.

(Pritchard, *Ancient Near Eastern Texts*, p. 6)

Khepri is the morning sun-god; Nun is the primordial water; Shu and Tefnut are the air-god and the moisture-goddess; Geb and Nut are earth and sky.

Both the Babylonian and the Egyptian stories bear comparison with Hesiod as examples of mythical cosmogony. Many scholars compare the stories more directly with Greek philosophy, suggesting (for example) that Thales' ideas about the importance of water may derive from the primordial significance of Mummu-Tiamat and Nun. To me Thales seems to live in a different and a more luminous world.

2

Thales

According to Aristotle, Thales of Miletus was 'the founder of natural philosophy'. He is dated by the eclipse of the sun which he observed and which modern astronomers place on 28 May 585 BC. The other known facts about his life suggest that he was born in about 625 and died in about 545. Simplicius reports that

Thales is said to have been the first to introduce the study of nature to the Greeks: although many others came before him, as Theophrastus thinks, yet he so far excelled them as to eclipse all his predecessors. But he is said to have left nothing behind in writing except the so-called *Nautical Astronomy*.

> (Simplicius, *Commentary on the* Physics 23.29–33)

Other sources ascribe other writings to him, and there were books circulating under his name in antiquity. But it is probable that he wrote nothing – or at least nothing which survived even to the time of Aristotle. Our knowledge of his views therefore depends entirely on later reports; and those reports were themselves based on oral tradition.

Thales was a man of practical wisdom, one of the so-called Seven Sages of early Greek history, and he was regarded by posterity not only as an original contributor to science and philosophy, but also as an astute statesman.

Herodotus, the fifth-century BC historian, tells several stories which illustrate his political sagacity.

Useful advice had been given before the destruction of Ionia by Thales, a Milesian whose family originally came from Phoenicia: he urged that the Ionians establish a single council-chamber, that it be located on Teos, which was the centre of Ionia, and that the other cities be governed and treated as though they were cantons.

(Herodotus, *Histories* I 170.3)

When Croesus came to the River Halys, then – according to my account – he crossed his army by way of the existing bridges; but according to a common account given by the Greeks, Thales of Miletus crossed the army for him. For it is said that Croesus was at a loss how his army should cross the river, since these bridges did not yet exist at that time, and that Thales, who was in the camp, made the river which flowed to the left of the army flow to its right as well, and that he did so in the following way. Beginning upstream of the camp, he dug a deep channel which he drew in the shape of a crescent so that the river should bend round the rear of the camp, being diverted down the channel away from its original course, and then, having passed the camp, should debouch again into its original course. Thus as soon as the river was divided it became fordable in both its parts.

(Herodotus, *Histories* I 75.3–5)

Herodotus also reports the eclipse:

The war [between the Lydians and the Persians] was equally balanced, until in the sixth year an engagement took place in which, after battle had been joined, the day suddenly turned to night. This change in the day had been foretold to the Ionians by Thales of Miletus, who had fixed as its term the very year in which it actually occurred.

(Herodotus, *Histories* I 74.2)

Note also the following snippet:

Thales said that the sun is eclipsed when the moon is in front of it, and he indicated the day on which it is eclipsed, which some call the thirtieth and others the new moon.

(anonymous *Commentary on the* Odyssey, Oxyrhynchus Papyrus 3710, col. II 37–43)

Modern scholars conjecture that Thales had learned something of Baby-lonian astronomy; even so, it is generally doubted that he could have predicted his eclipse.

Of Thales' philosophico-scientific doctrines, the most celebrated con-cern water. First, he held that the earth rests upon water. Here is Aristotle's report:

Some say that [the earth] rests on water. This in fact is the oldest view that has been transmitted to us, and they say that it was advanced by Thales of Miletus who thought that the earth rests because it can float, like a log or something else of that sort (for none of these things can rest on air, but they can rest on water) – as though the same does not hold of the water supporting the earth as holds of the earth itself (water cannot rest in mid-air – it must rest on something).

(Aristotle, *On the Heavens* 294a28–b1)

(Note Aristotle's non-committal 'they say': his cautious approach to Thales is yet more pronounced in the next three extracts.)

In addition, and more strikingly, Thales held that everything was made from water, or that water, in a later jargon, was the 'material principle' of the world. Aristotle again:

Most of the first philosophers thought that material principles alone were principles of all things. For they say that the element and principle of the things which exist is that from which they all are and from which they first come into being and into which they are finally destroyed, the substance remaining and its properties changing ... There must be some nature – either one or more than one – from which, being preserved itself, the other things come into being. But as to the number and form of this sort of principle, they do not all agree. Thales, the founder of this kind of philosophy, says that it is water (that is why he asserted that the earth rests on water). He perhaps came to acquire this belief from seeing that the nourishment of everything is moist and that all hot things come from water and live by water (for that from which anything comes into being is its principle) – he came to his belief both for this reason and because the seeds of all things have a moist nature, and water is the natural principle of moist things.   (Aristotle, *Metaphysics* 983b6–11, 17–27)

Aristotle elsewhere reports something of Thales' views on the nature of the soul:

Thales, judging by what they report, seems to have believed that the soul is something which produces motion – if indeed he said that magnets have souls because they move iron.

(Aristotle, *On the Soul* 405a19–21)

Some say that [soul] is mixed in the whole universe. Perhaps that is why Thales thought that everything was full of gods.

(Aristotle, *On the Soul* 411a7–8)

Eudemus, a pupil of Aristotle, ascribed various geometrical discoveries to Thales. Scholars are generally sceptical – but the passages may none the less be set down.

They say that Thales was the first to prove that a circle is bisected by its diameter.   (Proclus, *Commentary on Euclid* 157.10–11)

We are indebted to old Thales for many discoveries and for this theorem in particular: he is said to have been the first to have recognized and stated that in every isosceles triangle the angles at the base are equal, and to have called the equal angles 'similar' in the archaic style.   (Proclus, *Commentary on Euclid* 250.20–251.2)

This theorem proves that when two straight lines intersect with one another the angles at the vertex are equal: it was first discovered (according to Eudemus) by Thales and given a scientific proof by [Euclid].   (Proclus, *Commentary on Euclid* 299.1–5)

Eudemus in his *History of Geometry* ascribes this theorem [that a pair of triangles with one equal side and two equal angles are equal] to Thales; for he says that he must have made use of it in the procedure

by which they say he determined the distance of ships out at sea.
(Proclus, *Commentary on Euclid* 352.14–18)

*The account of Thales in Diogenes Laertius' Lives of the Philosophers
contains many dubious and some false statements. It should be read as
a specimen of one sort of material on which our knowledge of the
Presocratics depends.*

According to Herodotus, Duris and Democritus, Thales' father was
Examyes and his mother Cleobulina, from the family of Theleus (they
were Phoenicians, the best-born of the descendants of Cadmus and
Agenor). <He was one of the Seven Sages,> according to Plato, and
he was the first to be called a Sage – during the archonship of Damasias
at Athens [582–580 BC], at which time, according to Demetrius of
Phaleron in his list of archons, the Seven Sages were in fact named.
He was enrolled as a citizen at Miletus when he came there with
Neileus who had been expelled from Phoenicia. But most authorities
say that he was a native Milesian of a famous family.

After his political activities he turned to the study of nature. According to some, he left no writing behind; for the *Nautical Astronomy*
ascribed to him is said to be by Phocus of Samos. But Callimachus
knows him as the discoverer of the Little Bear and writes as follows
in his *Iambi*:

And he is said to have plotted the stars of the Wain
by which the Phoenicians sail.

According to some, he wrote just two works, *On the Solstice* and *On
the Equinox*, deeming that everything else was inapprehensible.

He is thought by some to have been the first to study astronomy
and to have predicted eclipses of the sun and solstices, as Eudemus
says in his *History of Astronomy* – that is why Xenophanes and
Herodotus admire him. Heraclitus and Democritus also mention him.
Some (among them the poet Choerilus) say that he was also the first
to say that souls are immortal. He was the first to discover the period
from one solstice to the next, and the first, according to some, to state
that the size of the sun is one seven hundred and twentieth part <of
the solar orbit, just as the size of the moon is a seven hundred and

13

twentieth> of the lunar orbit. He was the first to call the last day of the month the thirtieth. And he was the first, according to some, to discourse about nature.

Aristotle and Hippias say that he ascribed souls to lifeless things too, taking the magnet and amber as his evidence.

Pamphila says that he learned geometry from the Egyptians and was the first to inscribe a right-angled triangle inside a circle, for which he sacrificed an ox. (Others, including Apollodorus the calculator, ascribe this to Pythagoras, who greatly advanced the discoveries which Callimachus in his *Iambi* attributes to Euphorbus the Phrygian – for example, 'scalenes and triangles' and what belongs to the study of geometry.)

He is also thought to have given excellent advice in political affairs. For example, when Croesus sent envoys to the Milesians to make an alliance he prevented it – which saved the city when Cyrus came to power. But Clytus says, as Heraclides recounts, that he lived a solitary life as a private citizen. Some say that he married and had a son, Cybisthus, others that he remained a bachelor but adopted his sister's son – so that when he was asked why he had no children he replied, 'Because I love children.' And they say that when his mother pressed him to marry he said, 'It's too early,' and that then, when he had passed his prime and she insisted, he said, 'It's too late.' Hieronymus of Rhodes, in the second book of his *Miscellanies*, says that, wanting to show how easy it is for a philosopher to be rich, he foresaw that there was about to be a good crop of olives, hired the olive presses, and made a large sum of money.

He held that water is the principle of all things, and that the world has a soul and is full of spirits. They say he discovered the seasons of the year, which he divided into three hundred and sixty-five days.

No one taught him, except that he went to Egypt and spent time with the priests there. Hieronymus says that he actually measured the pyramids from their shadows, having observed the time when <our shadows> are the same size as we are. He lived with Thrasybulus, the ruler of Miletus, according to Minyes.

There is a celebrated story about the tripod which was discovered by some fishermen and sent round to the Sages by the people of

Miletus. They say that some young men from Ionia bought a catch from a Milesian fisherman. Since the tripod had been fished up in it, there was a dispute until the Milesians sent to Delphi. The god gave this oracle:

Offspring of Miletus, do you ask Apollo about a tripod?
I declare that the tripod belongs to him who is first in wisdom.

So they gave it to Thales. But he gave it to someone else, who passed it on until it reached Solon. Solon said that the god was first in wisdom and sent it to Delphi.

[*There follow a number of different versions of the tripod story.*]

Hermippus in his *Lives* ascribes to Thales what others say of Socrates. He used to say, they report, that he thanked Fortune for three things: first, that I am a man and not a beast; secondly, that I am male and not female; thirdly, that I am Greek and not foreign.

He is said to have been taken from his house by an old woman to look at the stars, and to have fallen into a ditch: when he cried out, the old woman said: 'Do you think, Thales, that you'll learn what's in the heavens when you can't see what's in front of your feet?' Timon knows him as an astronomer and praises him in his *Silli* in the following words:

Like Thales of the Seven Sages, that sage astronomer ...

Lobon of Argos says that his writings stretched to two hundred lines and that the following epigram was inscribed on his statue:

This is Thales whom Ionian Miletus bred and showed
an astronomer, the highest of all in wisdom.

He adds that his poems include these verses:

It is not many words which show an intelligent opinion:
search out one wise thing,
choose one good thing;
for thus you will stop
the ceaseless tongues of babbling men.

The following aphorisms are ascribed to him. Of existing things, god is the oldest – for he is ungenerated. The world is the most beautiful – for it is god's making. Space is the greatest – for it includes everything. Mind is the swiftest – for it runs through everything. Necessity is the strongest – for it controls everything. Time is the wisest – for it discovers everything. He said that death is no different from life. 'Then why don't you die?' someone asked him. 'Because death is no different,' he replied. When someone asked him which came first, night or day, he answered, 'Night came first – by a day.' When someone asked him whether a man can escape the notice of the gods if he does wrong, he replied: 'Not even if he thinks of doing wrong.' An adulterer asked him if he should swear that he had not committed adultery: he replied, 'Perjury is no worse than adultery.' When asked what is difficult, he said, 'To know yourself'; what is easy, 'To give advice to someone else'; what most pleasant, 'Success'; what divine, 'What has neither beginning nor end'. When asked what was the strangest thing he had seen, he said: 'An old tyrant.' How can we bear misfortune most easily? – If we see our enemies faring worse. How can we live best and most justly? – If we do not ourselves do the things we blame others for doing. Who is happy? – One who has a healthy body, a well-stocked soul and a cultivated nature. He says that we should remember our friends both present and absent, and that we should not beautify our appearance but be beautiful in our practices. 'Do not be rich by evil means,' he says, 'and let not words set you against those who have had your trust.' 'Expect from your children the same provision you made for your parents.'

He said that the Nile floods when its streams are checked by the contrary etesian winds.

Apollodorus in his *Chronicles* says that he was born in the first year of the thirty-ninth Olympiad [624 BC]. He died at the age of seventy-eight (or, as Sosicrates says, at ninety); for he died in the fifty-eighth Olympiad [548–545 BC]. He was a contemporary of Croesus, whom he undertook to transport across the Halys without a bridge by diverting its course.

There were other men called Thales, according to Demetrius of Magnesia in his *Homonyms* – five in all: an orator from Callatis, who had an affected style; a painter from Sicyon, of great talent; third, a very early figure, a contemporary of Hesiod, Homer and Lycurgus; a fourth is mentioned by Duris in his work *On Painting*; a fifth, more recent and obscure, is mentioned by Dionysius in his *Critical Essays*.

The Sage died of heat and thirst and weakness while watching a gymnastic contest. He was by then an old man. On his tomb is inscribed:

> His tomb is small, his fame is heaven-high:
> behold the remains of wise Thales.

In the first book of my *Epigrams, or Poems in All Metres* there is an epigram on him:

> When once he was watching a gymnastic contest, O Zeus of
>   the Sun,
> you stole Thales the Sage from the stadium.
> I praise you for taking him near to you; for the old man
> could no longer see the stars from the earth.

The motto 'Know Thyself' is his, though Antisthenes in his *Successions* says that it was Phemonoe's and that Chilon appropriated it.   (Diogenes Laertius, *Lives of the Philosophers* 1 22–28, 33–40)

3

Anaximander

Anaximander, like Thales, came from Miletus.

Apollodorus of Athens . . . says in his *Chronicles* that [Anaximander] was sixty-three in the second year of the fifty-eighth Olympiad [547/6 BC] and that he died shortly afterwards.

(Diogenes Laertius, *Lives of the Philosophers* II 2)

If Apollodorus is right, Anaximander was born in 610 and died in about 540 BC. He wrote a book, which circulated under the title On Nature. *He also produced a star-map and a map of the world:*

Anaximander of Miletus, a pupil of Thales, was the first to try to draw the inhabited world on a tablet; after him, Hecataeus of Miletus, a great traveller, made it more accurate so that the thing was greatly admired.

(Agathemerus, *Geography* I i)

The leading ideas of Anaximander's work On Nature *are summarized in the following extract:*

Anaximander was a pupil of Thales. Anaximander, son of Praxiades, a Milesian. He said that a certain nature, the limitless, is the principle of the things which exist. From it come the heavens and the worlds in them. It is eternal and ageless [12 B 2], and it contains all the worlds. He also calls it time, since the generation and the destruction of the things which exist are determinate.

He said that the limitless is the principle and element of the things which exist, being the first to call it by the name of principle. In addition, there is an eternal motion by which the heavens come into being.

The earth is aloft, not supported by anything but resting where it is because of its equal distance from everything. Its shape is rounded, circular, like a stone pillar. Of its surfaces, we stand on one while the other is opposite. The heavenly bodies are a circle of fire, separated off from the fire in the world and enclosed by air. There are vents – tubular channels – at which the heavenly bodies appear; hence eclipses occur when the vents are blocked, and the moon appears now waxing and now waning according to the blocking or opening of the channels. The circle of the sun is twenty-seven times greater <than the earth and the circle> of the moon <eighteen times greater>. The sun is highest, the circles of the fixed stars lowest.

Animals come into being <from moisture> evaporated by the sun. Men originally resembled another type of animal, namely fish.

Winds occur when very fine vapours of air are separated off, collect together and move. Rain comes from vapour drawn up from the earth by the sun. Lightning occurs when wind breaks out and parts the clouds.

He was born in the third year of the forty-second Olympiad [610/ 609 BC]. (Hippolytus, *Refutation of All Heresies* I vi 1–7)

A second report contains some supplementary material:

Anaximander, an associate of [Thales], says that the limitless contains all the cause of the generation and destruction of the universe. From it, he says, the heavens were separated off and in general all the worlds, limitless in number. He asserted that destruction and, much earlier, generation occur inasmuch as, from limitless ages past, all things are renewed.

He says that the earth is cylindrical in shape and is a third as deep as it is broad.

He says that at the generation of this world something generative of hot and cold separated off from the eternal, and from it a ball of flame grew round the air about the earth, like bark on a tree. When the ball burst and was enclosed in various circles, the sun and the moon and the stars came into being.

Further, he says that originally men were born from animals of a different kind, because the other animals can soon look after themselves while men alone require a long period of nursing; that is why if they had been like this originally they would not have survived.

([Plutarch], *Miscellanies* fragment 179.2 Sandbach, in Eusebius, *Preparation for the Gospel* I viii 2)

Anaximander's most striking thoughts concern biology, astronomy and 'the limitless'. In biology, the remarks of Hippolytus and pseudo-Plutarch can be eked out by three further texts:

Anaximander says that the first animals were born in moisture, surrounded by prickly barks. As they grew older they emerged on to drier parts, the bark burst, and for a short time they lived a different kind of life.　　([Plutarch], *Opinions of the Philosophers on Nature* 908D)

Anaximander of Miletus says he thinks that from water and earth, when they were heated, there arose fish, or animals very like fish, that humans grew in them, and that the embryos were retained inside up to puberty, whereupon the fish-like animals burst and men and women emerged already able to look after themselves.

(Censorinus, *On the Day of Birth* iv 7)

The descendants of Hellen of old sacrifice [fish] to Ancestral Poseidon, believing that men came from the moist substance – as do the Syrians. That is why they revere fish, as being of the same kind and nurture as themselves. Here their philosophy is more equitable than that of Anaximander. For he asserts, not that fish and men were born in the same surroundings, but that at first men came into being inside fish and were nourished there – like sharks – not emerging and taking to the land until they became able to fend for themselves. So just as fire consumes the matter from which it was kindled, its own mother and father (as the poet who inserted the marriage of Ceyx into Hesiod's poems said), so Anaximander, having asserted that fish are at once fathers and mothers of men, condemns them to be eaten.

(Plutarch, *Table Talk* 730DE)

The astronomical theory described by Hippolytus can be given a little more colour:

Anaximander holds that there is a circle twenty-eight times as great as the earth. It is like the wheel of a cart, with a hollow rim full of fire, which at a certain point reveals the fire through a mouthpiece, as through the tube of a bellows. This is the sun.

([Plutarch], *Opinions of the Philosophers on Nature* 889F)

At the hub of the celestial wheel is the stationary earth:

Some say that [the earth] rests where it is because of similarity (so, among the ancients, Anaximander). For there is no reason why what is situated in the middle and is similarly related to the edges should move upwards rather than downwards or sideways. But it cannot move in opposite directions at the same time. So it necessarily rests where it is. (Aristotle, *On the Heavens* 295b11–16)

As for the limitless or infinite principle or element of all things, a few words from Anaximander's book are preserved, the earliest surviving words of Western philosophy. It is uncertain – and a matter of vigorous scholarly controversy – exactly how extensive the citation is.

Of those who hold that [the element] is one, moving, and limitless, Anaximander, son of Praxiades, a Milesian, who was successor and pupil of Thales, said that the limitless is principle and element of the things which exist. (He was the first to introduce this word 'principle'.) He says that it is neither water nor any other of the so-called elements but some different limitless nature, from which all the heavens and the worlds in them come into being. And the things from which existing things come into being are also the things into which they are destroyed, in accordance with what must be. For **they give justice and reparation to one another for their injustice in accordance with the ordering of time** [B 1] (he speaks of them in this way in somewhat poetical words). It is clear that he observed the change of the four elements into one another and resolved not to make any one of them the underlying stuff but rather something else apart from them. He accounts for coming into being not by alteration of the element but by the separating off of the opposites by an eternal motion. (Simplicius, *Commentary on the* Physics 24.13–25)

Simplicius explains why Anaximander's 'element' was different from the four traditional elemental stuffs (earth, air, fire, water). He does not explain why it was limitless or infinite. A passage in Aristotle's Physics *alludes to Anaximander and lists some reasons for a belief in infinitude: it is possible that one or more of these reasons originally came from Anaximander.*

It is with reason that they all make [the limitless] a principle; for it can neither exist to no purpose nor have any power except that of a principle. For everything is either a principle or derived from a principle. But the limitless has no principle – for then it would have a limit. Again, it is ungenerated and indestructible and so is a principle. For what has come into being must have an end, and there is an ending to every destruction. Hence, as I say, it has no principle but itself is thought to be a principle for everything else and to encompass everything and to steer everything – as is said by those who do not set up any other cause (for example mind, or love) apart from the limitless.

And it is also the divine; for it is immortal and indestructible, as Anaximander and most of the natural scientists say. [B 3]

Belief in the existence of something limitless comes mainly from five considerations: from time (since this is limitless), from the division of magnitudes (mathematicians use the limitless); again, because only in this way will generation and destruction not give out – only if there is something limitless from which what comes into being is subtracted; again, because what is limited is always limited by something, so that there cannot be an [ultimate] limit if one thing must always be limited by another. Especially and most importantly, there is something which raises a puzzle for everyone alike: because they do not give out in thought, numbers seem to be limitless, and so do mathematical magnitudes and the region outside the heavens. But if the region

outside is limitless, then body and worlds also seem to be limitless –
for why should they be here rather than there in empty space? Hence
if mass is anywhere, it is everywhere. At the same time, if empty space
and place are limitless, body too must be limitless – for with eternal
things there is no difference between being possible and being actual.

(Aristotle, *Physics* 203b4–30)

4

Anaximenes

Anaximenes was a younger contemporary and pupil of Anaximander, and like him a Milesian. His work followed the same general pattern as that of Anaximander. It is said that

he wrote in a simple and economical Ionian style
(Diogenes Laertius, *Lives of the Philosophers* II 3)

– in contrast to Anaximander's 'somewhat poetical words'.
The fullest account of his views is given by Hippolytus:

Anaximenes too was a Milesian. He was the son of Eurystratus. He said that the principle is limitless air, from which what is coming into being and what has come into being and what will exist and gods and divinities come into being, while from these things, its offspring, comes everything else. The form of the air is this: when it is most uniform it is invisible, but it is made apparent by the hot and the cold and the moist and the moving. It is always in motion; for what changes would not change were it not in motion. As it is condensed and rarefied it appears different: when it is diffused into a more rarefied condition it becomes fire; wind, again, is air moderately condensed; cloud is produced from air by compression; when it is yet more condensed it is water, and then earth; and when it is as dense as possible it is stones. Thus the most important factors in coming into being are opposites – hot and cold.

The earth is flat and rides on air; in the same way the sun and the moon and the other heavenly bodies, which are all fiery, ride the air because of their flatness. The heavenly bodies have come into being from earth, because mist rises from the earth and is rarefied and produces fire, and the heavenly bodies are composed of this fire when it is aloft. There are also some earthy substances in the region of the heavenly bodies which orbit with them. He says that the heavenly bodies move not under the earth, as others have supposed, but round the earth – as a felt cap turns round on our heads. And the sun is hidden not because it goes under the earth but because it is screened by the higher parts of the earth and because of its increased distance from us. The heavenly bodies do not heat us because of their great distance.

Winds are generated when air has been condensed and is driven along. As it collects together and is further thickened, clouds are generated; and in the same way it changes into water. Hail occurs when the water falling from the clouds solidifies, and snow when these same things solidify in a more watery form. Lightning occurs when the clouds are parted by the force of winds; for when they part a bright and fiery flash occurs. Rainbows are produced when the sun's rays fall on compacted air; earthquakes when the earth is considerably altered by heating and cooling.

These are the views of Anaximenes. He flourished in the first year of the fifty-eighth Olympiad [548/7 BC].

(Hippolytus, *Refutation of All Heresies* I vii 1–8)

The notion that the stars 'ride' on air, and the curious reference to felt caps may go back to Anaximenes himself. He seems to have liked such similes: he also imagined that

the sun is flat like a leaf

([Plutarch], *Opinions of the Philosophers on Nature* 890D)

and that the stars are

fixed into the crystalline like nails.

([Plutarch], *Opinions of the Philosophers on Nature* 889A)

Hippolytus' account of the earth's flatness can be supplemented by a passage in Aristotle:

Anaximenes and Anaxagoras and Democritus say that the flatness [of the earth] causes it to rest where it is. For it does not cut the air beneath but covers it like a lid. Flat bodies are observed to do this – for they are not easily moved against the wind because of their resistance. Because of its flatness the earth does the same thing in relation to the air underneath it; and the air, not having enough room to move away, stays motionless in a mass below, like the water in a clepsydra. (Aristotle, *On the Heavens* 294b13–21)

Three texts have been supposed to contain a few of Anaximenes' own words.

Or should we, as old Anaximenes thought, treat the hot and the cold not as substances but rather as common properties of matter which supervene upon changes? For he says that matter which is contracted and condensed is cold, while matter which is rare and **slack** (that is the word he uses) is hot. [13 B 1] Hence it is not unreasonably said that men release both hot and cold from their mouths; for the breath is cooled when it is compressed and condensed by the lips, but when it is expelled from the open mouth it becomes hot by reason of its rareness. (Plutarch, *The Primary Cold* 947F)

Anaximenes the Milesian asserted that air is the principle of the things which exist; for everything comes into being from air and is resolved again into it. For example, **our souls**, he says, **being air, hold us together, and breath and air encompass the whole world** ('air' and 'breath' are used synonymously). [B 2]
([Plutarch], *Opinions of the Philosophers on Nature* 876AB)

Anaximenes opines that there is a single, moving, limitless principle of all existing things, namely air. For he says this:
Air is close to the incorporeal; and because we come into being by an outflowing of air, it is necessary for it to be both limitless and rich because it never gives out. [B 3]
([Olympiodorus], *On the Divine and Sacred Art of the Philosopher's Stone* 25)

In the first passage, only one word can be ascribed to Anaximenes; the second citation is of dubious authenticity and uncertain sense; and the fragment quoted by pseudo-Olympiodorus is usually regarded as spurious.

5

Pythagoras

We hear more about Pythagoras than about any other Presocratic philosopher. For the school of thought to which he gave his name lasted for a millennium, and several works by later Pythagoreans have survived. Yet in many ways Pythagoras is the most obscure and perplexing of all the early thinkers.

Pythagoras himself did not set down his notions in writing, nor did his early followers. (This is the orthodox modern view; but there was disagreement among the ancients on the point.) In the fifth century the school split in two, each group claiming to be the genuine heirs of the Master. A century later, the histories of Pythagoreanism and of Platonism became closely connected, and accounts of Pythagorean philosophy were soon contaminated with Platonic material. Later still, various Pythagorean documents were produced and circulated, projecting onto Pythagoras himself the philosophical ideas of more recent ages. It is difficult to penetrate the fog and discern the original Pythagoras.

Legends rapidly collected about his name. The few threads of historical truth indicate that he was born on the island of Samos in about 570 BC; that some thirty years later he left the island, which was then ruled by the cultivated autocrat Polycrates, and emigrated to Croton in south Italy; that he became a figure of consequence in the political life of Croton; that he aroused hostility among the citizens, and was obliged to leave town; that he then settled in the nearby city of Metapontum, where he died.

This chapter sets out the most important of the early texts which refer to Pythagoras, and reports the few doctrines which can be ascribed to him with any confidence. A later chapter will deal generally with fifth-century Pythagoreanism; and the Pythagoreans Hippasus and Philolaus will have a chapter apiece.

Pythagoras is mentioned by Xenophanes, Heraclitus, Ion and (perhaps) Empedocles:

As to [Pythagoras'] having become different people at different times, Xenophanes refers to it in an elegy which begins with the line:

Now I come to another theme and I will show the path . . .

What he says about him goes like this:

**And once when he passed a puppy which was being
   whipped
they say he took pity on it and made this remark:
'Stop, do not beat it; for it is the soul of a dear friend –
I recognized it when I heard its voice.'** [21 B 7]

(Diogenes Laertius, *Lives of the Philosophers* VIII 36)

[Heraclitus] was uncommonly arrogant and contemptuous, as indeed is clear from his treatise, in which he says:

Much learning does not teach thought – or it would have taught Hesiod and Pythagoras, and again Xenophanes and Hecataeus.

[22 B 40]   (Diogenes Laertius, *Lives of the Philosophers* IX 1)

Some say, mistakenly, that Pythagoras did not leave a single written work behind him. At any rate, Heraclitus the natural scientist pretty well shouts it out when he says:

Pythagoras, son of Mnesarchus, practised inquiry more than any other man, and selecting from these writings he made a wisdom of his own – much learning, mere fraudulence. [22 B 129]

(Diogenes Laertius, *Lives of the Philosophers* VIII 6)

Ion of Chios in his *Triads* says that Pythagoras composed some things and attributed them to Orpheus. [36 B 2]

(Diogenes Laertius, *Lives of the Philosophers* VIII 8)

Ion of Chios says about [Pherecydes of Syrus]:

Thus he, excelling in courage and also in honour,

even after death possesses in his soul a pleasant life –
if indeed Pythagoras is truly wise, who about all
men learned and had knowledge. [36 B 4]

(Diogenes Laertius, *Lives of the Philosophers* I 120)

Empedocles refers to this when he says of [Pythagoras]:

Among them was a man of immense knowledge
who had obtained the greatest wealth of mind,
a master especially of every kind of wise deed.
For when he reached out with all his mind
he easily saw each and every thing
in ten or twenty human generations. [31 B 129]

(Porphyry, *Life of Pythagoras* 30)

Pythagoras is also referred to by the fifth-century historian Herodotus:

As I learn from the Greeks who live on the Hellespont and the Black
Sea, this Salmoxis was a man and lived as a slave in Samos – he was a
slave to Pythagoras, the son of Mnesarchus. Then he gained his
freedom and accumulated a large sum of money, and having done
so returned to his own country. But since the Thracians led mis-
erable lives and were rather stupid, Salmoxis, who was acquainted
with the Ionian way of life and with manners more civilized than
those of the Thracians (he had, after all, associated with Greeks –
and with Pythagoras who was by no means the feeblest of the Greek
sages), prepared a banqueting-hall. There he entertained and feasted
the leading citizens, assuring them that neither he nor his fellow-
drinkers nor any of their descendants would die but would come to
a country where they would live for ever in possession of all good
things.

Now in the place where he did what I have recounted and said
these things he built an underground chamber. When the chamber
was completed he vanished from among the Thracians, descending
into the underground chamber and staying there for three years. They
missed him and mourned for him as though he were dead. But in the

fourth year he appeared to the Thracians – and in this way what Salmoxis had said appeared plausible to them. That is what they say he did. As for the man and his underground chamber, I neither disbelieve the story nor place too much credit in it – and I think that Salmoxis lived many years earlier than Pythagoras.

(Herodotus, *Histories* IV 95–96)

Plato mentions Pythagoras once:

Well, then, if Homer did no public service, is he said to have become during his lifetime an educational leader in private, with pupils who loved him for his company and who handed down a Homeric way of life to their successors – like Pythagoras, who was himself particularly loved on this account and whose successors even now talk of a Pythagorean way of life and are thought to stand out from other men?

(Plato, *Republic* 600AB)

Isocrates, a contemporary of Plato, has the following account:

A man who was not pressed for time might tell many remarkable stories about the piety of [the Egyptians] which I am not the only man nor the first to have observed. On the contrary, many people, both our contemporaries and in the past, have done so, among them Pythagoras of Samos, who went to Egypt and studied with the Egyptians. He was the first to bring philosophy to Greece, and in particular he was concerned, more conspicuously than anyone else, with matters to do with sacrifices and temple purifications, thinking that even if this would gain him no advantage from the gods it would at least bring him high repute among men. And that is what happened. For he so surpassed others in renown that all the young men desired to be his pupils, while the older men were more pleased to see their children associating with him than looking after their own affairs. Nor can we distrust their judgement; for even now those who claim to be his pupils receive for their silence more admiration than those who have the greatest reputation for speaking.

(Isocrates, *Busiris* 28–29)

Some of the legends about Pythagoras were collected by Aristotle in his lost work On the Pythagoreans. *Here is a representative sample:*

Pythagoras, the son of Mnesarchus, first studied mathematics and numbers but later also indulged in the miracle-mongering of Pherecydes. When a cargo ship was entering harbour at Metapontum and the onlookers were praying that it would dock safely because of its cargo, he stood up and said: 'You will see that this ship is carrying a corpse.' Again, in Caulonia, as Aristotle says, <he foretold the appearance of the white she-bear; and Aristotle> in his writings about him tells many stories including the one about the poisonous snake in Tuscany, which bit him and which he bit back and killed. And he foretold to the Pythagoreans the coming strife – which is why he left for Metapontum without being observed by anybody. And while he was crossing the river Casas in company with others he heard a superhumanly loud voice saying 'Good morning, Pythagoras' – and those who were there were terrified. And once he appeared both in Croton and in Metapontum on the same day and at the same hour. Once, when he was sitting in the theatre, he stood up, so Aristotle says, and revealed to the audience his thigh, which was made of gold. Several other bizarre stories are told of him; but since I do not want to be a mere transcriber, enough of Pythagoras.

(Aristotle, *On the Pythagoreans*, fragment 191 Rose, 3rd edn, in Apollonius, *Marvellous Stories* 6)

A large body of teachings came to be ascribed to Pythagoras. They divide roughly into two categories, the mathematico-metaphysical and the moral – as the poet Callimachus put it:

the Phrygian Euphorbus
was the first to draw triangles and polygons
and <to bisect> the circle –
and to teach abstention from breathing things.

(Callimachus, *Iambi* fragment 191.59–62 Pfeiffer)

Modern scholars are sceptical of these ascriptions, and their scepticism is nothing new. The best ancient commentary on Pythagoras' doctrines is to be found in the following passage:

After that, [Pythagoras'] reputation greatly increased: he found many associates in the city of Croton itself (not only men but also women, one of whom, Theano, achieved some fame), and many, both kings and noblemen, from the nearby non-Greek territory. What he said to his associates no one can say with any certainty; for they preserved no ordinary silence. But it became very well known to everyone that he said, first, that the soul is immortal; then, that it changes into other kinds of animals; further, that at fixed intervals whatever has happened happens again, there being nothing absolutely new; and that all living things should be considered as belonging to the same kind. Pythagoras seems to have been the first to introduce these doctrines into Greece.

(Porphyry, *Life of Pythagoras* 19)

The theory of metempsychosis, or the transmigration of the soul, is implicitly ascribed to Pythagoras by Xenophanes in the verses on the whipped whelp. Herodotus also mentions it:

The Egyptians were the first to propound the theory that men's souls are immortal and that when the body dies they enter another animal which is then being born; when they have gone round all the creatures of land, sea and air, they once more enter the body of a man which is then being born. This cycle takes three thousand years. Some of the Greeks – some earlier, some later – put forward this theory as though it were their own: I know their names but I will not write them down. (Herodotus, *Histories* II 123.2–3)

The names Herodotus coyly refrains from transcribing will have included that of Pythagoras. Two later passages may be quoted.

Heraclides of Pontus reports that [Pythagoras] tells the following story of himself. He had once been Aethalides and was considered to be the son of Hermes. Hermes invited him to choose whatever he wanted, except immortality; so he asked that, alive and dead, he should remember what happened to him. Thus in his life he remembered everything, and when he died he retained the same memories.

Some time later he became Euphorbus and was wounded by Menelaus. Euphorbus used to say that he had once been Aethalides and had acquired the gift from Hermes and learned of the circulation of his soul – how it had circulated, into what plants and animals it had passed, what his soul had experienced in Hades, and what other souls undergo.

When Euphorbus died, his soul passed into Hermotimus, who, wanting to give a proof of the fact, went to Branchidae, entered the temple of Apollo and pointed to the shield which Menelaus had dedicated (he said that he had dedicated the shield to Apollo when he sailed back from Troy); it had by then decayed and all that was left was the ivory boss.

When Hermotimus died, he became Pyrrhus, the Delian fisherman; and again he remembered everything – how he had been first Aethalides, then Euphorbus, then Hermotimus, then Pyrrhus. When Pyrrhus died, he became Pythagoras and remembered everything I have related.

(Diogenes Laertius, *Lives of the Philosophers* VIII 4–5)

Pythagoras believed in metempsychosis and thought that eating meat was an abominable thing, saying that the souls of all animals enter different animals after their death. He said that he remembered being, in Trojan times, Euphorbus, Panthus' son, and having been killed by Menelaus. They say that once when he was visiting Argos he saw a shield from the spoils of Troy nailed up, and burst into tears. When the Argives asked him the reason for his emotion, he said that he himself had carried that shield at Troy when he was Euphorbus. They did not believe him and judged him to be mad, but he said he would provide a true sign that it was indeed the case: on the inside of the shield there had been inscribed in archaic lettering EUPHORBUS. Because of the incredible nature of his claim, they all urged that the shield be taken down – and the inscription was found on it.

(Diodorus, *Universal History* X vi 1–3)

The idea of eternal recurrence had a wide currency in later Greek thought. It is ascribed to the Pythagoreans in a passage from Simplicius:

The Pythagoreans used to say that numerically the same things occur again and again. It is worth reading a passage from the third book of Eudemus' *Physics* in which he paraphrases their views:

> One might wonder whether or not the same time recurs, as some say it does. Now we call things 'the same' in different ways: things the same in kind plainly recur – for example summer and winter and the other seasons and periods; again, motions recur the same in kind – for the sun completes the solstices and the equinoxes and its other trajectories. But if we are to believe the Pythagoreans and hold that things the same in number recur – that you will be sitting here and I shall talk to you, holding this stick, and so on for everything else – then it is plausible that the same time too recurs. [Eudemus, *Physics*, fragment 88 Wehrli]

(Simplicius, *Commentary on the* Physics 732.23–33)

6

Alcmaeon

Alcmaeon came from Croton in South Italy, a city where Pythagoras had settled and which was famous for its doctors: he was a pupil of Pythagoras, and he was a medical man – the first of a distinguished line of Greek philosopher-physicians. He is said to have been a younger contemporary of Pythagoras, and he was probably active in the early part of the fifth century BC.

The short notice on Alcmaeon by Diogenes Laertius may be quoted in full:

Alcmaeon of Croton: he too heard Pythagoras. Most of what he says concerns medicine; nevertheless he sometimes engages in natural science too – when he says:

Most human things come in pairs.

He is thought to have been the first to write a work of natural science (as Favorinus says in his *Encyclopaedia*). He held that the moon and everything above it possess an eternal nature.

He was the son of Peirithous, as he himself says at the beginning of his treatise:

Alcmaeon of Croton, son of Peirithous, said this to Brontinus and Leo and Bathyllus: About matters invisible the gods possess clear knowledge, but as far as humans may judge etc. [24 B 1]

He said that the soul is immortal and that it moves continuously like the sun.   (Diogenes Laertius, *Lives of the Philosophers* VIII 83)

Brontinus, Leo and Bathyllus are elsewhere said to have been Pyth-agoreans, Brontinus being a relation by marriage of Pythagoras himself.

Diogenes' first 'quotation' is lifted from Aristotle:

Alcmaeon held similar views to [the Pythagoreans]. For he says that most human things come in pairs, speaking not, like them, of a determinate list of oppositions but rather of any oppositions whatever – such as black and white, sweet and bitter, good and bad, big and small.   (Aristotle, *Metaphysics* 986a29–34)

These oppositions had a medical application:

Alcmaeon says that health is conserved by egalitarianism among the powers – wet and dry, hot and cold, bitter and sweet, and the rest – and that monarchy among them produces disease; for the monarchy of either member of a pair is destructive. And disease comes about *by* an excess of heat or cold, *from* a surfeit or deficiency of nourishment, and *in* the blood or the marrow or the brain. Health is the proportionate blending of the qualities. [B 4]
                    ([Plutarch], *Opinions of the Philosophers on Nature* 911A)

Alcmaeon's ideas about the immortality of the soul, mentioned in Diogenes, are reported at slightly greater length by Aristotle:

Alcmaeon seems to have held a similar view about the soul. For he says that it is immortal because it is like the immortals – and that it is like them insofar as it is always in motion. For the divinities too are always in continuous motion – the moon, the sun, the stars and the whole heaven.   (Aristotle, *On the Soul* 405a29–b1)

At the same time, he held that men, unlike their souls, perish:

Alcmaeon says that men die because they cannot attach the beginning to the end – a clever saying if you take it to have been meant loosely and do not try to make it precise. [B 2]
                                    ([Aristotle], *Problems* 916a33–37)

Theophrastus' essay on the senses contains a summary of Alcmaeon's views on perception:

Of those who do not explain perception by similarity, Alcmaeon first determines the difference between men and animals: he says that men differ from the other animals because they alone understand, whereas the others perceive but do not understand. [B 1a] (He supposes that thinking and perceiving are distinct, not – like Empedocles – the same thing.)

Then he discusses each of the senses. He says that we hear with our ears because there is an empty space inside them which echoes: the cavity sounds and the air echoes in return. We smell with our noses at the same time as we breathe in, drawing the breath towards the brain. We discriminate flavours with our tongues; for, being warm and soft, they dissolve things with their heat, and they accept and transmit them because they are loose-textured and delicate. The eyes see by way of the water surrounding them. It is clear that they contain fire; for when they are struck it flashes out. They see by the gleaming and transparent part, when it reflects – and the purer it is, the better they see.

All the senses are somehow connected to the brain. That is why they are incapacitated if it is moved or displaced; for it obstructs the passages through which the senses work.

As for touch, he said neither how nor by what means it works.

So much for Alcmaeon's views.

(Theophrastus, *On the Senses* 25–26)

In this connection the following report deserves mention (although scholars have doubted its veracity):

We must give an account of the nature of the eye. On this subject many people, among them Alcmaeon of Croton (who busied himself with natural science and who was the first to undertake dissections), . . . published much of value.

(Calcidius, *Commentary on the* Timaeus ccxlvi 279)

Finally, there is an isolated moral maxim:

Alcmaeon of Croton says that it is easier to be on your guard against an enemy than against a friend. [B 5]

(Clement, Miscellanies VI ii 16.2)

7

Xenophanes

*Xenophanes was a man of many parts. He came from Colophon in Ionia.
A peripatetic poet, he travelled about Greece reciting his own and other
men's verses. He wrote on traditional poetical subjects – drink, love, war,
games – and also on historical themes. A number of his verses are
philosophical in content. The Greeks regarded him as a philosopher, the
teacher of Parmenides. If modern scholars have sometimes doubted that
he was a systematic thinker, the surviving fragments warrant his inclusion
among the philosophers.*

According to Diogenes Laertius,

he wrote in verse, both elegiac and iambic, against Hesiod and Homer,
censuring them for their remarks about the gods. He also recited his
own poems. He is said to have disagreed with Thales and with
Pythagoras, and to have attacked Epimenides. He lived to an advanced
age, as he himself says:

> **Already seven and sixty years have been
> tossing my thought about the land of Greece;
> and from my birth there were twenty five to add to
> them –
> if I know how to speak truly about these things.** [21 B 8]
>> (Diogenes Laertius, *Lives of the Philosophers* IX 18–19)

*Xenophanes, ninety-three when he wrote these lines, is said to have lived
to be over a hundred, and the rest of our evidence suggests that his life
spanned the century from 580 to 480 BC.*

*This chapter translates only – and all – the extant fragments which
have a more or less philosophical content. (The fragment on Pythagoras*

has already been cited in Chapter 5; and a non-philosophical text was quoted in the Introduction.) These texts divide roughly into three groups: on knowledge, on the gods, on nature.

In the later tradition, Xenophanes acquired a reputation for scepticism. It rested primarily on the first of the following three fragments.

According to some, Xenophanes takes this [sceptical] position; for he says that everything is inapprehensible when he writes:

> **And the clear truth no man has seen nor will anyone**
> **know concerning the gods and about all the things of which**
> **I speak;**
> **for even if he should actually manage to say what is the**
> **case,**
> **nevertheless he himself does not know it; but belief is found**
> **over all.** [B 34]
>> (Sextus Empiricus, *Against the Mathematicians* VII 49)

Ammonius, having declaimed, as is his custom, the words of Xenophanes:

> **Let these things be believed as similar to the truth,** [B 35]

invited us to assert and say what we believed.

>> (Plutarch, *Table Talk* 746B)

No comparatives ending in *-ôn* have a penultimate upsilon; hence Xenophanes' *glussôn* ['sweeter'] is remarkable:

> **If god had not made yellow honey, they would say**
> **that figs are far sweeter.** [B 38]
>> (Herodian, *On Singularities of Language* II 41 [*Grammatici Graeci* III ii, 946.22–24])

But Xenophanes also spoke in a modestly optimistic way about the progress of human knowledge:

Xenophanes:

> **Not at first did the gods reveal all things to mortals,**

but in time, by inquiring, they make better discoveries.
[B 18]

(Stobaeus, *Anthology* I viii 2)

In verbs ending in -*si* the penultimate syllable is naturally long ...
But the poets often make it short, as in Xenophanes:
Since at first everyone has learned according to Homer ...
[B 10]
and again:
As many things as they have shown to mortals to see ...
[B 36]
(Herodian, *On Double Quantities* 296 [*Grammatici Graeci* III ii,
16.17–22])

*Among the theological fragments there are several which are sharply
critical of traditional religious notions:*

[The myths of the theologians and poets] are full of every impiety;
hence Xenophanes, criticizing Homer and Hesiod, says:
**Homer and Hesiod attributed to the gods everything
which among men is shameful and blameworthy –
theft and adultery and mutual deception.** [B 11]
(Sextus Empiricus, *Against the Mathematicians* IX 192–193)

Homer and Hesiod, according to Xenophanes of Colophon,
**recounted many lawless deeds of the gods –
theft and adultery and mutual deception.** [B 12]
For Cronus, under whom they say was the golden age, castrated his
father and ate his children ...
(Sextus Empiricus, *Against the Mathematicians* I 289)

Xenophanes of Colophon, teaching that god is one and incorporeal,
rightly says:
**There is one god, greatest among gods and men,
similar to mortals neither in shape nor in thought.** [B 23]
And again:

42

> **But mortals think that gods are born,**
> **and have clothes and speech and shape like their own.**
> [B 14]

And again:

> **But if cows and horses or lions had hands**
> **and drew with their hands and made the things men**
> **make,**
> **then horses would draw the forms of gods like horses,**
> **cows like cows,**
> **and each would make their bodies**
> **similar in shape to their own.** [B 15]
>
> (Clement, *Miscellanies* V xiv 109.1–3)

The Greeks suppose that just as the gods have human shapes so they have human feelings; and just as each race depicts their shapes as similar to their own, as Xenophanes says (the Ethiopians making them dark and snub-nosed, the Thracians red-haired and blue-eyed [B 16]), so too they imagine that they are similar to themselves in their souls. (Clement, *Miscellanies* VII iv 22.1)

Further fragments reveal a positive side to Xenophanes' thought about the gods, and certain reports suggest that his views were elaborated with some sophistication and detail.

If the divine exists, it is a living thing; if it is a living thing, it sees – for **he sees as a whole, he thinks as a whole, he hears as a whole.** [B 24] If it sees, it sees both white things and black.

(Sextus Empiricus, *Against the Mathematicians* IX 144)

(The line cited by Sextus is ascribed to Xenophanes on the basis of Diogenes Laertius, Lives of the Philosophers IX 19.)

Theophrastus says that Xenophanes of Colophon, the teacher of Parmenides, supposed that there is one principle, or that what exists is one and all, and neither limited nor limitless, neither moving nor motionless. He agrees that an account of his views belongs to a different inquiry from the study of nature; for Xenophanes said that this 'one and all' is god.

He shows that god is one from the fact that he is most powerful of all things; for if there were more than one, he says, they would all have to possess equal power, but what is most powerful and best of all things is god. He showed that god is ungenerated from the fact that what comes into being must do so either from what is similar or from what is dissimilar; but similar things, he says, cannot be affected by one another (for it is no more fitting that what is similar should generate what is similar to it than that it should be generated by it), and if it comes into being from what is dissimilar, then what exists will come from what does not exist. In this way he showed god to be ungenerated and eternal. He is neither limitless nor limited because what is limitless, having no beginning, no middle and no end, does not exist, while what is limited is a plurality of things limiting one another. He does away with motion and rest in a similar fashion: it is what does not exist which is motionless (for nothing else would pass into it nor it into anything else), while it is a plurality of things which move (for one thing changes into another). Hence when he says that god reposes in the same state and does not change –

Always he reposes in the same state, moving not at all,
  nor is it fitting for him to come and go now here now there
  [B 26]

– he means that god reposes not in virtue of rest as opposed to motion but in virtue of a repose which is above both motion and rest.

According to Nicolaus of Damascus in his work *On Gods*, he says that the principle is limitless and motionless. According to Alexander he says that it is limited and spherical (but it is clear from what I have said that he shows it to be neither limitless nor limited) – limited and spherical because he says that it is similar in all directions. And he says that it thinks of all things, when he writes:

But far from toil he governs everything by thought. [B 25]
    (Simplicius, *Commentary on the* Physics 22.26–23.20)

The fragments dealing with natural science are sparse:

Porphyry says that Xenophanes believes the dry and the moist – I
mean earth and water – to be principles, and he quotes a text which
indicates this:

> **Earth and water are all things which grow and come into
> being.** [B 29]
>> (Philoponus, *Commentary on the* Physics 125.27–30)

Xenophanes, according to some, holds that [everything has come into
being] from earth:

> **For all things are from earth and in earth all things end.**
> [B 27]

The poet Homer holds that everything has come into being from two
things, earth and water, . . . and according to some Xenophanes of
Colophon agrees with him. For he says:

> **For we all come into being from earth and water.** [B 33]
>> (Sextus Empiricus, *Against the Mathematicians* X 313–314)

Xenophanes in *On Nature*:

> **Sea is source of water and source of wind;**
> **for there would be no wind without the great ocean,**
> **nor streams of rivers nor rain-water in the air;**
> **but the great ocean produces clouds and winds**
> **and rivers** [B 30]

– like Homer: 'From which all rivers . . .'
>> (Geneva scholia on Homer, *Iliad* XXI 195)

Xenophanes thinks that the earth is not aloft but reaches downwards
limitlessly; for he says:

> **This upper limit of the earth is seen at our feet,**
> **neighbouring the ether; but below, it reaches on limitlessly.**
> [B 28]
>> (Achilles, *Introduction to Aratus* 4)

[Homer] calls the sun Hyperion ['that which goes above'] ... We should understand it to be Hyperion inasmuch as it always passes above the earth – as I think Xenophanes of Colophon also says:

And the sun, passing above and warming the earth ...
[B 31]

(Heraclitus, *Homeric Questions* 44.5)

Xenophanes says:

And in certain caves [*speatessi*] the water drips down. [B 37]
But the form *speas* does not occur.

(Herodian, *On Singularities of Language* II 30 [*Grammatici
Graeci* III ii, 936.18–20])

Remember that Xenophanes describes the rainbow in his hexameters thus:

What they call Rainbow, that too is a cloud,
purple and scarlet and green to see. [B 32]

(Eustathius, *Commentary on the* Iliad XI 24)

Finally, here is the brief account of Xenophanes' thought given by Hippolytus:

Xenophanes of Colophon, son of Orthomenes. He lived until the reign of Cyrus. He was the first to say that everything is inapprehensible, putting it thus:

for even if he should actually manage to say what was the
case,
nevertheless he himself does not know it; but belief is found
over all. [B 34.3–4]

He says that nothing comes into being or is destroyed or changes, and that the universe is one and changeless. He also says that god is eternal and unique and homogeneous in every way and limited and spherical and capable of perception in all his parts.

The sun comes into existence each day from small sparks which collect together. The earth is limitless and surrounded neither by air nor by the heavens. There are suns and moons without limit. Everything is made from earth.

He said that the sea is salty because many compounds flow together in it. (Metrodorus holds that it is salty because it is filtered through the earth.) Xenophanes thinks that the earth mixes with the sea and in time is dissolved by the moisture, offering as proof the fact that shells are found in the middle of the land and on mountains; and he says that in the quarries in Syracuse there was found an impression of a fish, on Paros the impression of a goby deep in the rock, and on Malta traces of all sea-creatures. He says that these were formed long ago when everything was turned into mud – the impressions dried in the mud. All men are destroyed when the earth is carried down into the sea and turns into mud; then they begin to be born again. And this is how all the worlds begin.

(Hippolytus, *Refutation of All Heresies* I xiv 1–6)

8

Heraclitus

Heraclitus came from Ephesus in Asia Minor; he belonged to an eminent family; he flourished in about 500 BC. His thought and his writings were notorious for their difficulty: he was nicknamed 'The Obscure' and 'The Riddler'.

They say that Euripides gave [Socrates] a copy of Heraclitus' book and asked him what he thought of it. He replied: 'What I understand is splendid; and so too, I'm sure, is what I don't understand – but it would take a Delian diver to get to the bottom of it.'

(Diogenes Laertius, *Lives of the Philosophers* II 22)

This attitude of puzzled admiration has been shared by later students of Heraclitus.

It is hard to know how best to present the surviving fragments of Heraclitus' work. The problems of identifying them, of establishing the Greek text, and of translating the Greek into English, are greater for Heraclitus than for any other Presocratic author. (The Riddler delights in puns and word-play – most of which are lost in translation.) But there is a further problem: how to arrange the texts? Any arrangement insinuates some general interpretation of Heraclitus' thought, and every interpretation of Heraclitus' thought is controversial. Some scholars have preferred an arbitrary ordering of the texts. But this is no solution at all – for it suggests that Heraclitus was not a systematic thinker, a suggestion which has more scholarly opponents than advocates.

The following arrangement begins, uncontroversially, with the opening words of Heraclitus' book. Then come two long and complementary accounts of Heraclitus' thought, which have a number of important fragments embedded in them.

First, then, the opening passage of Heraclitus' book. It is referred to by Aristotle:

It is difficult to punctuate Heraclitus' writings because it is unclear whether something goes with what follows or with what precedes it – for example, at the very beginning of his treatise. He says:
Of this account which holds forever men prove uncomprehending [22 B 1]
– it is unclear what 'forever' goes with.

(Aristotle, *Rhetoric* 1407b14–18)

More of this text is preserved by Hippolytus (and quoted below) and yet more by Sextus Empiricus:

At the beginning of his writings on nature, and pointing somehow to what surrounds us, [Heraclitus] says:
Of this account which holds forever men prove uncomprehending, both before hearing it and when first they have heard it. For although all things come about in accordance with this account, they are like tiros as they try words and deeds of the sort which I expound as I divide each thing according to nature and say how it is. Other men fail to notice what they do when they are awake, just as they forget what they do when asleep. [B 1]
Having thus explicitly established that everything we do or think depends upon participation in the divine account, a little later he adds:
For that reason one must follow what is comprehensive (i.e. what is common – for the comprehensive account is common). **But although the account is comprehensive, most men live as though they had a private comprehension of their own.** [B 2]

(Sextus Empiricus, *Against the Mathematicians* VII 132–133)

The first of the two extended accounts of Heraclitus' thought comes from a chapter in Hippolytus' Refutation of All Heresies, in which he argues that Heraclitus is the source of the heretical views of the Christian Noetus. (The word 'account' in B 1, B 2 and B 50 translates the Greek term logos. *The term occurs in the Greek Bible, where it is customarily translated as 'the Word (of God)'. Hippolytus associates Heraclitus' use of* logos *with this Christian use.)*

Heraclitus says that the universe is divisible and indivisible, generated and ungenerated, mortal and immortal, Word and Eternity, Father and Son, God and Justice.

Listening not to me but to the account, it is wise to agree that all things are one [B 50],

Heraclitus says. He rebukes everyone for not knowing this and not agreeing with it, thus:

They do not comprehend how, in differing, it agrees with itself – a back-turning harmony, like that of a bow and a lyre. [B 51]

That the universe is the Word, always and for all eternity, he says in this way:

Of this account which holds forever men prove uncomprehending, both before hearing it and when first they have heard it. For although all things come about in accordance with this account, they are like tiros as they try words and deeds of the sort which I expound as I divide each thing according to nature and say how it is. [B 1]

That the universe is a child and an eternal king of all things for all eternity he states as follows:

Eternity is a child at play, playing draughts: the kingdom is a child's. [B 52]

That the Father of everything which has come about is generated and ungenerated, creation and creator, we read in these words:

War is father of all, king of all: some it has shown as gods, some as men; some it has made slaves, some free. [B 53]

That <. . .> **harmony, like that of a bow and a lyre.** [Cf. B 51]

That [God] is unapparent, invisible, unknown to men, he says in these words:

Unapparent harmony is better than apparent [B 54]

– he praises and admires the unknown and unseen aspect of His power above the known. But that He is visible to men and not undiscoverable he says in these words:

Those things which are learned by sight and hearing, he says, **I honour more** [B 55] – i.e. the visible more than the invisible.

<The same thought> is readily grasped from the following remarks:

Men have been deceived, he says, **with regard to their knowledge of what is apparent in the same way as Homer was – and he was the wisest of all the Greeks. For some children who were killing lice deceived him by saying: 'What we saw and caught we leave behind, what we neither saw nor caught we take with us.'** [B 56]

Thus Heraclitus gives equal rank and honour to the apparent and the unapparent, as though the apparent and the unapparent were admittedly one. For, he says,

Unapparent connection is better than apparent [B 54]; and:

Those things which are learned by sight and hearing (i.e. by the sense-organs) **I honour more** [B 55] – he does not honour the unapparent more.

Hence Heraclitus says that darkness and light, evil and good, are not different but one and the same. For example, he rebukes Hesiod for not knowing day and night – for day and night, he says, are one, expressing it thus:

A teacher of most is Hesiod: they are sure he knows most who did not recognize day and dusk – for they are one. [B 57]

And so are good and bad. For example, doctors, Heraclitus says, †who cut and cauterize and wretchedly torment the sick in every way are praised – they deserve no fee from the sick, for they have the same effect as diseases†. [B 58] And straight and twisted, he says, are the same:

The path of the carding-comb, he says, **is straight and crooked.** [B 59]

The turning of the instrument called the screw-press in a fuller's shop is straight and crooked, for it goes upwards and in a circle at the same time – he says it is one and the same. And up and down are one and the same:

The path up and down is one and the same. [B 60]

And he says that the polluted and the pure are one and the same, and that the drinkable and the undrinkable are one and the same:

The sea, he says, is most pure and most polluted water: for fish, drinkable and life-preserving; for men, undrinkable and death-dealing. [B 61]

And he explicitly says that the immortal is mortal and the mortal immortal in the following remarks:

Immortals are mortals, mortals immortals: living their death, dying their life. [B 62]

He also speaks of a resurrection of this visible flesh in which we are born, and he knows that God is the cause of this resurrection – he says:

There they are said to rise up and to become wakeful guardians of the living and the dead. [B 63]

And he says that a judgement of the world and of everything in it comes about through fire; for **fire**, he says, **will come and judge and convict all things.** [B 66]

He says that this fire is intelligent and the cause of the management of the universe, expressing it thus:

The thunderbolt steers (i.e. directs) **all things** [B 64]

– by the thunderbolt he means the eternal fire, and he calls it need and satiety [B 65] (the formation of the world, according to him, being need and the conflagration satiety).

In the following passage he has set down the sum of his own thought – and at the same time of that of the sect of Noetus, whom I have briefly shown to be a disciple not of Christ but of Heraclitus. For he says that the created world is itself the creator and maker of itself:

God is day and dusk, winter and summer, war and peace, satiety and famine (all the contraries – that is his meaning); **but he changes †like olive oil which†, when it is mixed with perfumes, gets its name from the scent of each.** [B 67]

It is clear to everyone that the mindless followers of Noetus and the champions of his sect, in subscribing to the opinions of Noetus, evidently confess the same beliefs as Heraclitus, even if you deny they were taught by him.

(Hippolytus, *Refutation of All Heresies* IX ix 1–x 9)

Diogenes Laertius' Life also offers a summary account, with supporting quotations and paraphrases, of Heraclitus' thought:

Heraclitus, son of Bloson (or, as some say, of Heracon), an Ephesian. He flourished in the sixty-ninth Olympiad [504/501 BC]. He was uncommonly arrogant and contemptuous, as indeed is clear from his treatise, in which he says:

Much learning does not teach thought – or it would have taught Hesiod and Pythagoras, and again Xenophanes and Hecataeus. [B 40]

For he says that **wisdom is one thing: to grasp the knowledge of how all things are steered through all.** [B 41]

And he said that Homer deserved to be expelled from the games and flogged – and Archilochus too. [B 42] He also said:

You should quench violence more quickly than a fire. [B 43]

And:

The people should fight for the law as for the city wall. [B 44]

He also assails the Ephesians for expelling his friend Hermodorus. He says:

The Ephesians deserve to die to a man, every one of them: they should leave the city to the young. For they expelled Hermodorus, the best man among them, saying: 'Let no one of us be best: if there is such a man, let him be elsewhere and with others.' [B 121]

When they asked him to write laws for them, he refused on the grounds that the city had already been mastered by a wicked constitution. He retired into the temple of Artemis and played dice with the children. When the Ephesians stood round him, he said: 'Why are you staring, you wretches? Isn't it better to do this than to play politics with you?'

In the end he became a misanthrope, leaving the city and living in the mountains where he lived off herbs and plants. Because of this he contracted dropsy and returned to the town. He asked the doctors in his riddling fashion if they could change a rainstorm into a drought. When they failed to understand him, he buried himself in a byre, hoping that the dropsy would be vaporized by the heat of the dung. But he met with no success even by this means and died at the age of sixty . . .

He was remarkable from an early age: as a young man, he used to say that he knew nothing, and when he had become adult that he had learned everything. He was no one's pupil, but said that he had inquired into himself [cf. B 101] and learned everything from himself. Sotion reports that some say that he was a pupil of Xenophanes, and that Aristo, in his book *On Heraclitus*, says that he was actually cured of the dropsy and died of another disease. Hippobotus too says this.

The book of his which is in circulation is, as far as its general theme is concerned, about nature; but it is divided into three sections – one on the universe, one political, one theological. He deposited it in the temple of Artemis, having, as some say, deliberately written somewhat unclearly, in order that the powerful should have access to it and it should not be despised for being hackneyed. Timon describes him as follows:

> Among them Heraclitus the mocker, the reviler of the mob,
> the riddler, rose up.

Theophrastus says that because of his impulsive temperament he left some things half-finished and wrote others in different ways at different times. As a sign of his arrogance Antisthenes says in his *Successions* that he resigned from the kingship in favour of his brother. His treatise gained such a reputation that it actually gave rise to a sect, the so-called Heracliteans.

His views, in general terms, were the following. All things are constituted from fire and resolve into fire. All things come about in accordance with fate, and the things which exist are harmonized by the transformation of opposites. All things are full of souls and spirits. He spoke also about all the events which occur in the world, and he said that the sun is the size it appears. [Cf. B 3] He also said:

You will not find the limits of the soul although you travel all the path – so deep is its account. [B 45]

He said that conceit is an epilepsy, and that sight is fallacious. [B 46] Sometimes in his treatise he expresses himself brilliantly and clearly, so that even the most stupid easily understand him and gain an enlargement of soul; and the brevity and weight of his style are incomparable.

In detail, his doctrines are these. Fire is an element, and all things are an exchange for fire [cf. B 90], coming about by rarefaction and condensation. (But he expresses nothing clearly.) All things come about through opposition, and everything flows like a river. [Cf. B 12]

The universe is limited in extent, and there is one world. [Cf. B 30] It is generated from fire and it is consumed in fire again, alternating in fixed periods throughout the whole of eternity. And this happens by fate.

Of the opposites, that which leads to generation is called war and strife [cf. B 80], and that which leads to conflagration is called agreement and peace. Change is a path up and down [cf. B 60], and the world is generated in accordance with it. For fire as it is condensed becomes moist, and as it coheres becomes water; water as it solidifies turns into earth – this is the path downwards. Then again earth dissolves, and water comes into being from it, and everything else from water (he refers pretty well everything to the exhalation given off by the sea) – this is the path upwards.

Exhalations are given off by the earth and by the sea, some of them bright and pure, others dark. Fire is increased by the bright exhalations, moisture by the others. He does not indicate what the surroundings are like. But there are bowls in it, their hollow side turned towards us. The bright exhalations gather in them and produce flames, and these are the heavenly bodies. The flame of the sun is the brightest and hottest. For the other heavenly bodies are further away from the earth and for that reason give less light and heat, while the moon, though it is nearer the earth, does not travel through a pure region. The sun, however, lies in a translucent and uncontaminated region, and it preserves a proportionate distance from us; that is why it gives more heat and light. The sun and the moon are eclipsed when the bowls turn upwards. The moon's monthly changes of shape come about as its bowl gradually turns. Day and night, the months and the seasons of the year and the years, and rains and winds and the like, come about in virtue of the different exhalations. For the bright exhalation, when it bursts into flame in the circle of the sun, makes day, and the opposite exhalation, when it has gained power, produces night. As the heat from the brightness increases it makes summer, and as the moisture from the darkness mounts up it produces winter.

He explains the other phenomena in conformity with all this; but he does not say anything about what the earth is like, nor even about the bowls. Those were his views.

The story about Socrates and what he said when he read the treatise (having been shown it by Euripides, according to Aristo) I have recounted in the *Life* of Socrates. Seleucus the grammarian, however, says that someone called Croton relates in his *Diver* that someone called Crates first brought the book to Greece and that it was he who said that it would take a Delian diver not to get drowned in it. Some entitle it *Muses*, others *On Nature*; Diodotus calls it

A sure steerage to the goal of life;

others *Judgement, Manners, Turnings, One World for All* . . .

Demetrius in his *Homonyms* says that he despised even the Athenians, though he had the highest reputation [among them], and that though he was scorned by the Ephesians he preferred what was his own. Demetrius of Phaleron mentions him in his *Apology of Socrates*. Very many people have offered interpretations of his treatise: Antisthenes, Heraclides of Pontus, Cleanthes, Sphaerus the Stoic, and also Pausanias (who was called the Heraclitean), Nicomedes, Dionysius – and of the grammarians, Diodotus, who says that the treatise is not about nature but about politics and that the remarks on nature are there by way of illustrations. Hieronymus says that Scythinus the iambic poet attempted to put his account into verse.

(Diogenes Laertius, *Lives of the Philosophers* IX 1–3, 5–12, 15)

The rest of this chapter assembles the remaining Heraclitean frag-ments, together with a number of paraphrastic texts. After two excerpts from Stobaeus, the texts are grouped thematically. It must be confessed that the assignment of a passage to one or another group is often hazardous, or even arbitrary. Moreover, when two fragments are quoted together in an ancient source I have kept them together even if they deal with different issues. All this is far from satisfactory – but it is less unsatisfactory than any other arrangement.

Next, then, two short sequences of quotations from the Anthology *of John Stobaeus.*

Heraclitus:

Of those whose accounts I have heard, no one comes so far as to recognize that the wise is set apart from all things. [B 108]

It is better to hide folly than to make it public. [B 109] = [B 95]

It is not good for men to get what they want. [B 110]

Disease makes health pleasant and good, hunger satiety, weariness rest. [B 111]

To be self-controlled is the greatest excellence. And wisdom is speaking the truth and acting with knowledge in accordance with nature. [B 112]

Thinking is common to all. [B 113]

Speaking with comprehension one should rely on what is comprehensive of all, as a city on its law – and with yet greater reliance. For all human laws are nourished by the one divine; for it is as powerful as it wishes, and it suffices for all, and it prevails. [B 114]

Socrates:

Soul has a self-increasing account. [B 115]

(Stobaeus, *Anthology* III i 174–180)

Heraclitus:

All men can know themselves and control themselves. [B 116]

A man when he is drunk is led by a beardless boy, stumbling, not knowing where he goes, his soul moist. [B 117]

A dry soul is wisest and best. [B 118]

(Stobaeus, *Anthology* III v 6–8)

(Despite Stobaeus' heading, B 115 is generally ascribed to Heraclitus rather than to Socrates. On the other hand, the authenticity of B 109, B 112, B 113 and B 116 has frequently been doubted.)

The first thematic group of texts documents Heraclitus' attitude to ordinary mortals and to other thinkers (compare B 1, B 2, B 40, B 56, B 57, B 108). Only Bias, in the last of the extracts, escapes censure.

Most do not understand the things they meet with – not even when they have learned them do they know them; but they seem to themselves to do so [B 17], according to the excellent Heraclitus. Do you not think that he too blames unbelievers?

(Clement, *Miscellanies* II ii 8.1–2)

Heraclitus caustically remarks that some people are without faith, **not knowing how to hear nor even to speak** [B 19] – he was aided here, no doubt, by Solomon: 'If thou desire to hear, thou shalt receive; and if thou incline thine ear, thou shalt be wise' [Ecclesiasticus 6:33].

(Clement, *Miscellanies* II v 24.5)

The excellent Heraclitus rightly excoriates the mob as unintelligent and irrational. For **what thought or sense**, he says, **do they have? They follow the popular singers and they take the crowd as their teacher, not knowing that most men are bad and few good.** [B 104] Thus Heraclitus – which is why [Timon] called him 'the reviler of the mob'. (Proclus, *Commentary on the* First Alcibiades 256.1–6)

The Ionian Muses [*i.e. Heraclitus*] say explicitly that most men, fancying themselves wise, follow the popular singers and obey the laws, not knowing that most men are bad and few good. [Cf. B 104] But the best pursue reputation. For **the best**, he says, **choose one thing in return for all: ever-flowing fame from mortals; but most men satisfy themselves like beasts** [B 29], measuring happiness by the belly and the genitals and the most shameful parts in us.

(Clement, *Miscellanies* V ix 59.4–5)

The contemptuous and the brash get little benefit from what they hear, while those who are credulous and guileless are rather harmed – they do not give the lie to Heraclitus, who said:
A foolish man is put in a flutter by every word. [B 87]
(Plutarch, *On Listening to Lectures* 40F–41A)

Iamblichus, *On the Soul*: How much better, then, is Heraclitus, who deemed human opinions to be children's toys. [B 70]
(Stobaeus, *Anthology* II i 16)

The *Introduction* to rhetoric, all the theorems of which are directed to this end [sc. deception], is, in Heraclitus' words, the leader of liars. [B 81]
(Philodemus, *Rhetoric*, Herculaneum Papyrus 1004, col. LXII 3–9)

Some say, mistakenly, that Pythagoras did not leave a single written work behind him. At any rate, Heraclitus the natural scientist pretty well shouts it out when he says:

Pythagoras, son of Mnesarchus, practised inquiry more than any other man, and selecting from these writings he made a wisdom of his own – much learning, mere fraudulence. [B 129]

(Diogenes Laertius, *Lives of the Philosophers* VIII 6)

Bias is also mentioned by Hipponax, as I said before, and the fastidious Heraclitus gave particular praise to him when he wrote:

In Priene lived Bias, son of Teutames, who is of more account than the others. [B 39]   (Diogenes Laertius, *Lives of the Philosophers* I 88)

The second group assembles some texts which bear upon issues of natural science.

Heraclitus of Ephesus is very clearly of this opinion [that everything will change into fire]. He holds that there is a world which is eternal and a world which is perishing, and he recognizes that the created world is the former in a certain state. Now that he recognized that the individual world which consists of the totality of substance is eternal, is evident when he says:

The world, the same for all, neither any god nor any man made; but it was always and is and will be, fire ever-living, kindling in measures and being extinguished in measures. [B 30]

And that he believed it to be generated and destructible is indicated by the following:

Turnings off fire: first, sea; of sea, half is earth, half lightning-flash. [B 31a]

He says in effect that, by reason and god which rule everything, fire is turned by way of air into moisture, the seed, as it were, of creation, which he calls sea; and from this, again, come earth and heaven and what they contain. He shows clearly in the following words that they are restored again and become fire:

Sea is dissolved and measured in the same proportion as before it became earth. [B 31b]

And the same holds for the other elements.

(Clement, *Miscellanies* V xiv 104.1–5)

Just as [the principle] alternately makes the world from itself and again itself from the world, and **all things**, Heraclitus says, **are an exchange for fire and fire for all things, as goods for gold and gold for goods** [B 90], so the conjunction of the number five with itself produces nothing incomplete or alien.

(Plutarch, *On the E at Delphi* 388DE)

They would think it unreasonable if, while the whole heaven and each of its parts all have order and reason in their shapes and powers and periods, there is nothing of the sort among the principles of things but the most beautiful world, as Heraclitus says, is like rubbish scattered at random. [B 124]

(Theophrastus, *Metaphysics* 7a10–15)

Time . . . is an orderly motion, with measures and limits and periods. Of these the sun is overseer and guardian, defining and arbitrating and revealing and illuminating the changes and the seasons which bring all things, according to Heraclitus. [B 100]

(Plutarch, *Platonic Questions* 1007DE)

Heraclitus: [the Great Year] lasts 10,800 years.

(anonymous *Commentary on the* Republic, Oxyrhynchus Papyrus 1808, col. 1 4)

Each of the planets revolves in a single sphere, as though on an island, and guards its order. For **the sun will not overstep its measures**, Heraclitus says, **otherwise the Furies, ministers of justice, will find it out.** [B 94]   (Plutarch, *On Exile* 604A)

In the same way, Heraclitus, transforming what is common, destroys what is peculiar. He is <. . .> when he says that the sun in its own nature is the breadth of a human foot [B 3], not overstepping its limits; for if it <. . .> the Furies, ministers of justice, will find it out. [Cf. B 94]

(anonymous *Orphic Commentary*, Derveni Papyrus, col. IV 5–9)

[The sea] makes for collaboration and friendship. Heraclitus indeed says that if the sun did not exist it would be dusk [B 99]; but we may say that if the sea did not exist man would be the most wild and destitute of animals.

([Plutarch], *Is Fire or Water the More Useful?* 957A)

If it is nourished in the same way [as flames are], as they say, then it is clear that the sun is not only, as Heraclitus says, new each day [B 6], but always and continuously new.

(Aristotle, *Meteorology* 355a12–15)

Heraclitus:

When the months come together [the moon] **does not appear for three consecutive days: eve, new-moon, second. Sometimes it changes in fewer days, sometimes in more.**

(anonymous *Commentary on the* Odyssey, Oxyrhynchus Papyrus 3710, col. IV 43–47)

I have discussed elsewhere whether one should suppose that certain days are unlucky, or whether Heraclitus was right to criticize Hesiod, who makes some good and others bad, for not recognizing that the nature of every day is the same. [B 106]

(Plutarch, *Camillus* xix, 137F–138A)

Heraclitus is better and more Homeric (and like Homer he calls the Arctic Circle the bear):

Limits of morning and evening are the bear and, opposite the bear, the boundary of bright Zeus [B 120] – for the Arctic Circle, not the bear, is the boundary of the sun's rising and setting.

(Strabo, *Geography* I i 6)

Some think that the smoky exhalation is smell, since it is composed of earth and air. That is why Heraclitus said that if all the things which exist were to become smoke the nose would distinguish them. [B 7]

(Aristotle, *On the Senses and their Objects* 443a21–24)

The third group of extracts bears upon human nature – and in particular upon death (compare B 45, B 63, B 66, B 115, B 117, B 118).

Heraclitus well compares the soul to a spider and the body to a spider's web. Just as a spider, he says, standing in the middle of its web, is aware as soon as a fly has broken one of its threads and runs there quickly as though grieving over the cutting of the thread, so a man's soul, when some part of his body is hurt, hurries quickly there as if unable to bear the hurt to the body to which it is firmly and appropriately joined. [B 67a]

(Hisdosus, *Commentary on the* Timaeus 17v)

Heraclitus said that a man's character is his fate. [B 119]

(Stobaeus, *Anthology* IV xl 23)

Does not Heraclitus, like Pythagoras and Socrates in the *Gorgias*, call birth death when he says:
Death is what we see asleep, sleep what we see awake? [B 21]

(Clement, *Miscellanies* III iii 21.1)

We all work together to one end, some knowingly and consciously, others unknowingly – so Heraclitus, I think, says that even those asleep are workers and fellow-workers in the events of the world. [B 75]   (Marcus Aurelius, *Meditations* VI 42.1)

Heraclitus says that for those awake there is a single common world, but that asleep each enters a private world [B 89] – but the superstitious have no common world, nor a private one either.

(Plutarch, *On Superstition* 166C)

Is it remarkable that the cuttable should be cut, the meltable melt, the burnable burn and the destructible be destroyed? And when is death not present in our very selves? As Heraclitus says,

†the same thing, there are present† living and dead, the awake and the sleeping, young and old; for the latter change and are the former, and again the former change and are the latter. [B 88]

([Plutarch], *Consolation to Apollonius* 106DE)

What is said of sleep should be understood also of death. For each state – the one more, the other less – shows the absence of the soul, as we can also learn from Heraclitus:

†A man in the dusk looks for a light, his sight being quenched: living, he looks on the dead while sleeping; awake, he looks on the sleeping.† [B 26]   (Clement, *Miscellanies* IV xxii 141.1–2)

Orpheus wrote:

    Water is death for souls . . .

    But from water comes earth, from earth again water,

    and thence soul, springing through all the ether.

Heraclitus, basing his remarks on these lines, writes as follows:

For souls it is death to become water, for water death to become earth; but from earth water comes into being, from water soul. [B 36]   (Clement, *Miscellanies* VI ii 17.1–2)

They think that souls live in the water, which is breathed on by god, as Numenius says. . . . Hence (they say) Heraclitus says that for souls it is pleasure, not death, to become moist [B 77], and that for them the fall into birth is pleasure; and elsewhere he says that we live their death and they live our death. [Cf. B 62]

(Porphyry, *The Cave of the Nymphs* 10)

Heraclitus is clearly berating birth when he says:

Being born, they wish to live and to meet their doom (or rather, to rest) and they leave behind children, born for their doom [B 20]; and Empedocles plainly agrees with him.

(Clement, *Miscellanies* III iii 14.1)

Flavours need salt to stir perception – otherwise they strike the taste as heavy and nauseous; for **corpses should be thrown out more readily than dung** [B 96], according to Heraclitus, and meat is corpse or part of a corpse.   (Plutarch, *Table Talk* 668F–669A)

Heraclitus seems to agree with [Socrates in the *Phaedo*] when, speaking of men, he says:
There await men when they die things they neither expect nor even believe. [B 27]   (Clement, *Miscellanies* IV xxii 144.3)

Such rites are suitable to night and fire and to the noble – or rather, foolish – people of the Erechtheids, and also to the rest of the Greeks, for whom await when they die things they do not expect. [Cf. B 27] For whom does Heraclitus prophesy? For night-prowlers, magicians, bacchants, revellers, initiates – for them he threatens what comes after death, for them he prophesies fire. For the mysteries practised among men are impious initiations. [B 14]
                              (Clement, *Protreptic* II 22.1–2)

Good souls . . . must spend a fixed time in the gentlest region of the air, which they call the meadows of Hades . . . They are nourished by any sort of exhalation, and Heraclitus was right in saying that souls smell things in Hades. [B 98]
                              Plutarch, *On the Face in the Moon* 943C, E)

Fourthly, there are some items which may be reckoned as belonging to moral and political philosophy (compare B 43, B 44, B 114, B 121).

For 'the law is not made for a righteous man', the Scriptures say [I Timothy 1:9]. Thus Heraclitus rightly says:
They would not know the name of justice if these things did not exist [B 23], and Socrates says that law would not have come into being for the sake of good men.   (Clement, *Miscellanies* IV iii 10.1)

Worse men have conquered better, but to set up in your soul a victory monument over anger – with which Heraclitus says it is hard to fight, for whatever it wants, it buys with soul [B 85] – that is a mark of great and victorious strength. (Plutarch, *The Control of Anger* 457D)

Next, Heraclitus says:
Gods and men honour those slain in battle. [B 24]
(Clement, *Miscellanies* IV iv 16. 1)

For **a greater doom wins a greater share** [B 25], according to Heraclitus. (Clement, *Miscellanies* IV vii 49.3)

Envy, the greatest of political ills, scarcely attacks old age; for dogs bark at those they do not know, according to Heraclitus [B 97], and envy attacks the beginner as it were at the door of office and does not give him entrance.

(Plutarch, *Should Old Men Take Part in Politics?* 787C)

This work is not for dilettantes but for those who are sufficiently diligent and serious. There are very few such men today; but, as Heraclitus says, one man for me is ten thousand [B 49] and I would rather write for that one than for ten thousand who are worth one man or no one at all. (Galen, *On the Diagnosis of Pulses* VIII 773)

Always remember Heraclitus' view that the death of earth is to become water, and the death of water to become air, and of air fire, and the reverse. [Cf. B 76] Remember too the man who forgets where the road leads [B 71]; and that they differ from that with which they most constantly associate – the account which governs everything; and that what they meet with every day seems foreign to them [B 72]; and that we should not act and speak like sleepers [B 73] (for then too we think we act and speak), nor like children of our parents [B 74] (i.e., in plain prose, in the way in which we have been brought up).

(Marcus Aurelius, *Meditations* IV 46.1–6)

The fifth group collects fragments of a theological and a religious significance.

I know that Plato, too, supports Heraclitus who writes:

One alone is the wise, unwilling and willing to be called by the name of Zeus. [B 32]

And again:

It is law also to follow the counsel of one. [B 33]

And if you want to adduce the saying 'He that hath ears to hear, let him hear' [Luke 14:35], you will find it expressed somewhat as follows by the Ephesian:

The uncomprehending, when they hear, are like the deaf. To them applies the saying: though present they are absent. [B 34]

(Clement, Miscellanies V xiv 115.1–3)

[All animals] are born, flourish and die in obedience to the ordinances of god; for every beast is pastured by blows [B 11], as Heraclitus says.

([Aristotle], On the World 401a8-11)

A man may perhaps escape the attention of the visible light, but the intelligible he cannot – for, as Heraclitus says, how could anyone escape the attention of that which never sets? [B 16] Then let us not wrap ourselves in darkness; for the light is within us.

(Clement, The Tutor II x 99.5)

In all respects superior to us, [god] is especially unlike and different from us in his acts; but of divine acts, the majority, according to Heraclitus, **escape our knowledge through lack of trust.** [B 86]

(Plutarch, Coriolanus xxxviii, 232D)

Heraclitus, finding fault with those who sacrifice to the spirits, says:

They vainly purify themselves with blood when they are defiled, as though you stepped in mud and then washed in mud. Any man who saw you doing so would think you were mad. And they pray to these statues as though one were to gossip to the houses, not knowing who the gods and who the heroes are. [B 5]

The same man said to the Egyptians:

If they are gods, why do you mourn them? If you mourn them, no longer think them gods. [B 127]

... Heraclitus, seeing the Greeks giving honour to the spirits, said: **They pray to statues of demons who do not hear them as though they heard them; they do not give as though they had not asked.** [B 128] (anonymous *Theosophy* 68–69, 74)

As a mystical reminder of that affair, phalluses are set up to Dionysus in the cities. For **if they did not make a procession for Dionysus and sing a paean to the penis, they would act most shamelessly,** Heraclitus says, **and Hades is the same as Dionysus for whom they rave and ritualize** [B 15] – not, I think, from drunkenness of the body so much as from a disgraceful inculcation of licentiousness.

(Clement, *Protreptic* II 34.5)

Hence Heraclitus reasonably called [phallic ceremonies] remedies, since they will cure our troubles and drain our souls of the misfortunes of birth. [B 68] (Iamblichus, *On the Mysteries* I xi)

Do you not see with what grace Sappho's verses charm and seduce the hearer? But the Sibyl, with raving mouth, according to Heraclitus, speaking without mirth or adornment or perfume [B 92], traverses with her voice a thousand years with the help of the god.

(Plutarch, *Why the Pythia No Longer Prophesies in Verse* 397AB)

I think that you know Heraclitus' remark that the king whose is the oracle at Delphi neither speaks nor conceals but indicates [B 93] – attend to these wise words and suppose that here the Pythia gets her voice from the god as the moon gets its light from the sun.

(Plutarch, *Why the Pythia No Longer Prophesies in Verse* 404 E)

The sixth group of passages (with which compare B 54 and B 55) concerns Heraclitus' view of the scope and nature of human knowledge.

Nevertheless, [Celsus] wanted to show that this too was a fiction we [Christians] had taken from the Greek sages who said that human wisdom is one thing, divine wisdom another. And he quotes remarks of Heraclitus, in one of which he says:

For human ways have no insights, divine ways have [B 78];
and in another:
Men are called infantile by spirits as children are by men. [B 79]
(Origen, *Against Celsus* VI xii)

Perhaps it is not pleasing to God that such harmony should ever be
found among men. For nature, according to Heraclitus, likes to hide
itself [B 123] – and still more so the creator of nature, whom we
especially revere and admire because knowledge of him is not readily
gained.   (Themistius, *Speeches* V 69B)

According to [the Pyrrhonists], Xenophanes and Zeno of Elea and
Democritus were sceptics . . . Also Heraclitus:
Let us not conjecture at random about the most important things.
[B 47]   (Diogenes Laertius, *Lives of the Philosophers* IX 73)

Let these notes . . ., as their name says, be miscellaneous, passing
continually from one item to another . . . For **those who search for
gold**, says Heraclitus, **dig over much earth and find a little.** [B 22]
(Clement, *Miscellanies* IV ii 4.2)

Hence the apostle exhorts us that 'our faith should not stand in the
wisdom of men' who promise to persuade us, 'but in the power of God'
[I Corinthians 2:5], which alone can save us without proofs and by
mere faith. For **the most esteemed know and guard what they believe**
[B 28a], and moreover **justice will convict the fashioners and witnesses of falsehoods** [B 28b], as the Ephesian says. For he too learned
from non-Greek philosophy about the purification through fire of
those who have lived evil lives.   (Clement, *Miscellanies* V i 9.2–4)

Thus the prophet's remark, 'If ye will not believe, surely ye shall not
understand' [Isaiah 7:9], is proved abundantly true. And Heraclitus
of Ephesus was paraphrasing it when he observed:
**If you do not expect the unexpected you will not discover it; for it
is hard to track down and difficult to approach.** [B 18]
(Clement, *Miscellanies* II iv 17.4)

It has been divinely shown that knowledge and ignorance are the boundaries of happiness and unhappiness. For **philosophical men must be versed in very many things** [B 35], according to Heraclitus, and it is in truth necessary to 'wander many ways in the search to be good'.   (Clement, *Miscellanies* V xiv 140.5–6)

Heraclitus says, as though he had achieved something great and noble, **I inquired into myself** [B 101], and of the rules at Delphi 'Know thyself' was thought the most divine.

(Plutarch, *Against Colotes* 1118C)

[Heraclitus] rejects perception when he says, in these words: **Bad witnesses for men are the eyes and ears of those who have foreign souls** [B 107] – i.e. it is the mark of a foreign soul to trust in non-rational perceptions.

(Sextus Empiricus, *Against the Mathematicians* VII 126)

We have two natural instruments, as it were, by which we learn everything and conduct our business, namely hearing and sight; and sight, according to Heraclitus, is not a little truer – for eyes are more accurate witnesses than ears. [B 101a]

(Polybius, *Histories* XII xxvii 1)

The final group of texts can be given the vague label 'metaphysics': first, the relatively sparse references to the 'theory of flux'; then the more numerous items which bear upon the nature of contraries or opposites and their puzzling unity (compare B 50, B 51, B 59, B 60, B 61, B 62, B 67, B 111).

Heraclitus says somewhere that everything moves and nothing rests; and, comparing what exists to a river, he says that you would not step twice into the same river.   (Plato, *Cratylus* 402A)

On the subject of the soul, Cleanthes sets out the doctrines of Zeno [the Stoic] and compares them to those of the other natural scientists. He says that Zeno, like Heraclitus, says that the soul is an exhalation capable of perception. For, wanting to show that souls as they are exhaled always become new, he likened them to rivers, saying:

In the same rivers ever different waters flow – and souls are exhaled from what is moist. [B 12]

So Zeno, like Heraclitus, says that the soul is an exhalation; but he says that it is capable of perception for the following reasons . . .

> (Arius Didymus, *Epitomes* fragment 39 Diels, in Eusebius,
> *Preparation for the Gospel* XV xx 2)

Heraclitus the Obscure gives a theological account of the natural world as being unclear and capable of being guessed at by way of symbols. He says:

Gods are mortal, men immortal, living their death, dying their life. [Cf. B 62]

And again:

We step and do not step into the same rivers, we are and we are not. [B 49a]

Everything he says about nature is riddling and allegorical.

> (Heraclitus, *Homeric Questions* 24.3–5)

Old Heraclitus of Ephesus was called clever because of the obscurity of his remarks:

Cold things become hot, hot cold, wet dry, parched moist. [B 126]

> (Tzetzes, *Commentary on the* Iliad, p.126 Hermann)

All mortal nature, lying between generation and destruction, offers only a dark and unstable show and appearance of itself . . . Reason can grasp nothing which is at rest or which is really real; for it is not possible to step twice into the same river, according to Heraclitus, nor to touch mortal substance twice in [the same] condition: by the swiftness and speed of its change, it scatters and collects again – or rather, it is not again and later but simultaneously that it comes together and departs, approaches and retires. [B 91]

> (Plutarch, *On the E at Delphi* 392AB)

Things which have this movement by nature are preserved and stay together because of it – if indeed, as Heraclitus says, the barley-drink separates if it is not moving. [B 125]   (Theophrastus, *On Vertigo* 9)

I wonder . . . how my soul has come to be in my body, being as it appears in itself although it is in a body. For Heraclitus, who urges us to inquire into this, posits necessary exchanges between contraries [cf. B 90], and talks of **a path up and down** [cf. B 60], and **changing, it rests** [B 84a], and **it is weariness to labour at the same tasks and to be ruled** [B 84b] – he leaves us to conjecture and omits to make his argument clear to us, no doubt because we should inquire for ourselves as he himself inquired and found. [Cf. B 101]

(Plotinus, *Enneads* IV viii 1.8–17)

[Celsus] says that the ancients refer riddlingly to a war among the gods, as when Heraclitus says:
You should know that war is comprehensive, that justice is strife, that all things come about in accordance with strife and with what must be. [B 80]   (Origen, *Against Celsus* VI xlii)

They say it is indecent if the sight of warfare pleases the gods. But it is not indecent; for noble deeds please. Again, wars and battles seem terrible to us, but to God not even they are terrible. For all things complete the harmony of the universe. So Heraclitus says that to God all things are fair and just but men have supposed some things to be unjust and others just. [B 102]

(Scholia **b** and **T** on Homer, *Iliad* IV 4)

Surely nature yearns for contraries and effects harmony from them and not from similars . . . That was also said by Heraclitus the Obscure:
Combinations – wholes and not wholes, concurring differing, concordant discordant, from all things one and from one all things.
[B 10]
In this way the structure of the universe – I mean, of the heavens and the earth and the whole world – was arranged by one harmony through the blending of the most contrary principles.

([Aristotle], *On the World* 396b7–8, 20–25)

On these matters [the love of like for like] some seek a deeper and more scientific account. Euripides says that the earth when dried up longs for rain, and the majestic heaven when filled with rain longs to fall to the earth. Heraclitus says that what is adverse concurs, that the noblest harmony comes from things which differ [B 8], and that everything comes about in accordance with strife. [Cf. B 80]

(Aristotle, *Nicomachean Ethics* 1155b2–6)

It seems that the ancients used the word *bios* ambiguously to mean 'bow' and 'life'. For example, Heraclitus the Obscure:

Thus the word for the bow is *bios*, its deed is death. [B 48]

(*Etymologicum Magnum*, s.v. *bios*)

But the circumference of a circle as a whole no longer <has a direction>; for whatever point on it you think of is both a beginning and an end – for beginning and end on the circumference of a circle are the same, according to Heraclitus. [B 103]

(Porphyry, *Notes on Homer*, on *Iliad* XIV 200)

Socrates: Very well. I see that when he asks that question we must answer thus: 'My dear man, Don't you realize the truth of Heraclitus' remark that the most beautiful ape is ugly compared to another kind [B 82], and that the most beautiful of pots is ugly compared to a woman, as Hippias the Wise says?' Isn't that so, Hippias?
Hippias: Yes, Socrates, an excellent answer.
Socrates: Now next I'm sure he'll say: 'Well, Socrates, if someone compares a woman to a god, won't the same thing happen as when pots were compared to women? Won't the most beautiful woman appear ugly? Doesn't Heraclitus – whom you adduce – say the same thing, that in relation to god the wisest of men will seem an ape in wisdom and beauty and everything else? [B 83]

(Plato, *Hippias Major* 289AB)

It seems that each animal has its own pleasure ... The pleasures of horses, dogs and men are different – so Heraclitus says that donkeys would prefer rubbish to gold [B 9] (for food is more pleasing to donkeys than gold).   (Aristotle, *Nicomachean Ethics* 1176a3, 5–8)

Dry dust and ash ... should be put down [in the poultry-run] so that the birds can sprinkle themselves with it; for this is how they wash their feathers and wings, if we are to believe Heraclitus of Ephesus who says that pigs wash in mud and farmyard birds in dust or ashes. [B 37]   (Columella, *On Agriculture* VIII iv 4)

[Vetch] is the cow's favourite pasture, and cows eat it with pleasure. Hence Heraclitus said that if happiness resided in bodily pleasures, we should call cows happy when they find some vetch to eat. [B 4]
     (Albert the Great, *On Plants* V iii 14)

PART II

PART II

9

Parmenides

Parmenides, son of Pyres, came from Elea, a Greek foundation in southern Italy. It is reported that

he organized his own country by the best laws, so that each year the citizens still get the officials to swear that they will abide by Parmenides' laws.

(Plutarch, *Against Colotes* 1126AB)

A passage in Plato (which will be quoted in the chapter on Zeno) suggests that Parmenides was born in about 515 BC; but the Greek chroniclers put his birth at 540.

According to Diogenes Laertius,

he was a pupil of Xenophanes but did not follow him. He was also associated (as Sotion said) with Ameinias, son of Diochaites, the Pythagorean, a poor man but of good character. It was rather Ameinias that he followed: when Ameinias died he set up a shrine for him (he himself came from a famous and wealthy family); and he was led to calm by Ameinias and not by Xenophanes.

(Diogenes Laertius, *Lives of the Philosophers* IX 21)

The story about Ameinias has led scholars to look (in vain) for Pythagorean elements in Parmenides' thought.

Parmenides produced one short work written in ungainly hexameter verse. A substantial proportion of the poem survives. It opened with a fanciful prologue, after which the main body of the work divided into two parts: the first part, the 'Way of Truth', purported to offer a correct account of the nature of reality; the second part, the 'Way of Opinion', professed a false account and followed the traditional Ionian pattern of works On Nature.

The prologue and most of the 'Way of Truth' survive; there are fragments of the 'Way of Opinion'.

Parmenides' poem is a bizarre production. The second half of it is confessedly 'deceitful'; but then why write it? The first half is not intended to be deceitful, but the views it advocates are paradoxical in the extreme. Moreover, Parmenides is not a friendly writer: his meaning is never plain at first glance, and several lines of his poem are obscure to the point of unintelligibility. None the less, Parmenides had, through the medium of Plato, an unrivalled influence on the course of Western philosophy.

The prologue is presented by Sextus Empiricus. (The passage continues with some lines which will be quoted a little later; and Sextus adds an allegorical interpretation of Parmenides' verses which I shall not transcribe.)

Parmenides, [Xenophanes'] associate, condemned the sort of reason associated with belief – I mean reason which has weak opinions – but supposed that the sort of reason associated with knowledge, or infallible reason, was a criterion of truth (for he also gave up trust in the senses). Thus at the beginning of *On Nature* he writes in this way:

> The mares that carry me as far as my heart may reach
> conveyed me: they had come and set me on the celebrated
>   road
> of the goddess which carries a man of knowledge †ever
>   straight ahead†.
> There was I being carried; for there the wise mares were
>   carrying me,
> straining at the chariot, and young girls were leading the
>   way.
> The axle in the axle-box shrilled in its socket,
> blazing – for it was driven on by two whirling
> wheels on either side – while they hastened to convey me,
> the girls, daughters of the sun, who had left the house of
>   Night

for the light and pushed back with their hands the veils
    from their heads.
Here are the gates of the paths of Night and Day,
and a lintel and a stone threshold enclose them.
They themselves, high in the air, are filled by great doors,
and punitive Justice holds the keys which fit them.
Her the girls appeased with soft words,
subtly persuading her to push back for them the bolted bar
swiftly from the gates. They flew back
and made a yawning gap between the doors,
swinging in turn in their sockets the bronze pivots,
fitted with pegs and pins. And through them
the girls held the chariot and mares straight on the
    highway.
And the goddess graciously received me and took
my right hand in hers; and she spoke thus and addressed
    me:
'Young man, companion to the immortal charioteers,
who come to my house with the mares who carry you,
welcome. For no evil fate sent you to travel
this road (for indeed it is far from the tread of men)
but Right and Justice. You must learn all things,
both the unwavering heart of persuasive truth
and the opinions of mortals in which there is no true
    warranty.' [28 B 1.1–30]
        (Sextus Empiricus, *Against the Mathematicians* VII 111)

*Simplicius adds two further lines which appear to have completed the
prologue:*

Parmenides says:

        You must learn all things,
both the unwavering heart of well-rounded truth
and the opinions of mortals in which there is no true
    warranty.

> But nevertheless you will learn these things too – how what
> they believe
> would really have to be, forever traversing everything.
> [B 1.28–32]
> (Simplicius, *Commentary on* On the Heavens 557.24–558.2)

*The beginning of the 'Way of Truth' – or at any rate, the earliest of
its surviving lines – is preserved by Proclus:*

Plato explicitly distinguishes different types of reason and knowledge,
corresponding to the different objects of knowledge. Parmenides too,
though his poetry makes him obscure, nevertheless points in this
direction when he says:

> ... both the unwavering heart of well-lit truth
> and the opinions of mortals in which there is no true
> warranty [B 1.29–30];

and again:

> But come, I will tell you – preserve the account when you
> hear it –
> the only roads of enquiry there are to think of:
> one, that it is and that it cannot not be,
> is the path of persuasion (for truth accompanies it);
> another, that it is not and that it must not be –
> this I say to you is a trail of utter ignorance. [B 2.1–6]

And:

> For you could not recognize that which is not (for that is
> not to be done),
> nor could you mention it; ... [B 2.7–8]
> (Proclus, *Commentary on the* Timaeus I 345.11–27)

*The half-line at the end of B 2 can be completed, both metrically and
philosophically, by a half-line preserved elsewhere:*

Parmenides had already touched on this doctrine inasmuch as he
identified being and thought and did not locate being in sensible
objects. He said:

. . . for the same things can be thought of and can be. [B 3]
(Plotinus, *Enneads* V i 8.14–18)

The next surviving lines of the poem can be patched together from two separate passages in Simplicius. One of them, which assembles a few short quotations from Parmenides, includes these sentences:

That there is one and the same account of everything, the account of what is, Parmenides states in the following words:
What can be said and be thought of must be; for it can be, and nothing cannot. [B 6.1–2]
Now if whatever anyone says or thinks is being, then there will be one account of everything, the account of what is.
(Simplicius, *Commentary on the* Physics 86.25–30)

The second passage begins by quoting B 2.3–8, and continues thus:

That contradictories are not true together [Parmenides] states in the verses in which he finds fault with those who identify opposites. For having said:
for it can be,
and nothing cannot. This I bid you ponder.
For from this first road of inquiry <I bar> you [B 6.1–3],
<he adds:>
and then from the road along which mortals who know
nothing
wander, two-headed; for impotence in their
breasts guides their erring thought. And they are carried along
both deaf and blind, bewildered, undiscerning crowds,
by whom to be and not to be are deemed the same
and not the same; and the path of all turns back on itself.
[B 6.4–9]
(Simplicius, *Commentary on the* Physics 117.2–13)

Next, a continuous passage of some sixty-six verses emerges from three different texts. The first two lines are quoted by Plato:

When we were boys, my boy, the great Parmenides would testify against [the view that what is not is] from beginning to end, constantly saying both in prose and in verse that:

Never will this prevail, he says: **that what is not is –
bar your thought from this road of inquiry.** [B 7.1–2]

(Plato, *Sophist* 237A)

The quotation is continued by Sextus (though Sextus himself cites the lines as though they were continuous with B 1.30):

**Bar your thought from this road of inquiry,
and do not let habit, full of experience, force you along this
road,
directing unobservant eye and echoing ear
and tongue; but judge by reason the battle-hardened proof
which I have spoken. One story, one road, now
is left.** [B 7.2–8.2]

(Sextus Empiricus, *Against the Mathematicians* VII 111)

The quotation in Sextus is in turn continued by Simplicius:

And not to seem niggardly, let me append to this commentary Parmenides' verses (they are not many) on the one being, both to justify what I have said about the matter and because of the rarity of Parmenides' treatise. After he has done away with what is not, he writes:

**One story, one road, now
is left: that it is. And on this there are signs
aplenty that, being, it is ungenerated and indestructible,
whole, of one kind and unwavering, and complete.
Nor was it ever, nor will it be, since now it is, all together,
one, continuous. For what generation will you seek for it?
How, whence, did it grow? That it came from what is not I
shall not allow
you to say or think – for it is not sayable or thinkable
that it is not. And what need would have impelled it,**

82

later or earlier, to spring up – if it began from nothing?
Thus it must either altogether be or not be.
Nor from what is will the strength of warranty ever permit it
to come to be anything apart from itself. For that reason
Justice has not relaxed her fetters and set it free to come
    into being or to perish,
but she holds it. Decision in these matters lies in this:
it is or it is not. But it has been decided, as is necessary,
to leave the one road unthought and unnamed (for it is not
    a true
road), and to take the other as being and being genuine.
How might what is then perish? How might it have come
    into being?
For if it came into being it is not, nor if it is ever going to
    be.
Thus generation is quenched and perishing unheard of.
    Nor is it divided, since it all alike is –
neither more here (which would bar it from cohering)
nor less; but it is all full of what is.
Hence it is all continuous; for what is approaches what is.
    And unmoving in the limits of great chains
it is beginningless and ceaseless, since generation and
    destruction
have been banished far away, and true warranty has pushed
    them back.
The same and remaining in the same state, it lies by itself,
and thus remains there fixedly. For powerful necessity
holds it enchained in a limit which bars it on all sides,
because it is right that what is be not incomplete.
For it is not lacking – if it were it would lack everything.
    Thinking and a thought that it is are the same thing.
For without what is, in which it has been expressed,
you will not find thinking. For nothing else either is or will
    be
apart from what is, since fate has fettered it
to be whole and unmoving. Hence all things are a name

which mortals have stored up, trusting them to be true –
coming into being and perishing, being and not being,
and changing place and altering bright colour.
  And since there is a last limit, it is completed
on all sides, like the bulk of a well-rounded ball,
equal in every way from the middle. For it must not be at all
    greater
or smaller here or there.
For neither is there anything which is not, which might stop
    it from reaching
its like, nor anything which is in such a way that it might be
more here or less there than what is, since it all is, inviolate.
Therefore, equal to itself on all sides, it lies uniformly in its
    limits.
  Here I cease for you the warranted account and thought
about the truth. Henceforward learn mortal opinions,
listening to the deceitful arrangement of my words.
  [B 8.1–52]

These, then, are Parmenides' verses about the One. After them he discusses the objects of opinion, postulating for them different principles.   (Simplicius, *Commentary on the* Physics 144.25–146.27)

Another short fragment has been thought to come from the 'Way of Truth', though it is hard to see where the lines should be inserted.

Parmenides too, in his poem, riddles about Hope in these words:
  Look at things which, though absent, are yet present firmly
    to thought;
  for you will not cut off what is from holding to what is,
  neither scattering everywhere in every way about the world
  nor coming together. [B 4]
For one who hopes, like one with faith, sees in thought the objects of thought and the things to come.   (Clement, *Miscellanies* V iii 15.5)

There is also a stray verse, the middle of the three quoted in the following extract:

Parmenides, as I have said before, recognized being itself – I mean, that which transcends everything and is the highest of all beings, and in which being was primarily manifested; but he was not unaware of the plurality of intelligible objects. For it is he who says:

For what is approaches what is [B 8.25],

and again:

it is indifferent to me
whence I begin, for there again shall I return [B 5],

and elsewhere:

equal from the middle [B 8.43]

– in all these passages he shows that he takes there to be a plurality of intelligible objects.

(Proclus, *Commentary on the* Parmenides 708.7–22)

Now for the 'Way of Opinion', the first lines of which are preserved by Simplicius:

Having completed his account of the intelligible realm, Parmenides continues thus . . . :

Here I cease for you the warranted account and thought
about the truth. Henceforward learn mortal opinions,
listening to the deceitful arrangement of my words.
For they determined in their minds to name two forms,
one of which they should not – and that is where they have
      erred.
And they distinguished them as opposite in kind and set up
      signs
for them separately from one another: here the ethereal fire
      of flame,
gentle, very light, in every direction the same as itself
and not the same as the other; and that too, by itself,
opposite – unknowing night, dense in kind and heavy.
All this plausible arrangement I recount to you
so that no mortal may ever outstrip you in knowledge.
      [B 8.50–61]

Now he calls this account a matter of opinion and deceitful not because it is simply false but because it has fallen from the intelligible world of truth into the perceptible realm of appearance and seeming. A little later, having discussed the two elements, he continues by mentioning the productive cause:

> **The narrower [bands] were filled with unmixed fire,**
> **the next with night (but they emit a portion of flame),**
> **and in the middle of them, a goddess who governs all**
> **things.** [B 12.1–3]

He says that she is actually the cause of the gods –

> **first of all the gods she devised Love** [B 13]

etc. He says that she sends souls sometimes from light to darkness and sometimes in the other direction.

I am compelled to write at length on this point because people now are largely ignorant of the ancient writings.

(Simplicius, *Commentary on the* Physics 38.29–39.21)

Simplicius quotes the beginning of the 'Way of Opinion' in another passage:

In his remarks about opinion [Parmenides] makes hot and cold into principles, and he calls them fire and earth, and light and night or darkness. After his remarks about truth he says: ... ([B 8.53–59]). And again a little later:

> **And since all things have been named light and night**
> **and their powers assigned to these things and to those,**
> **everything is full alike of light and invisible night,**
> **both equal, since nothing falls to neither.** [B 9]

If nothing falls to neither, it is clear that they are both principles and that they are contraries.

(Simplicius, *Commentary on the* Physics 179.31–180.13)

Elsewhere Simplicius cites B 8.53–59 a third time; and he adds:

In the middle of the verses a short passage in prose is inserted which purports to come from Parmenides himself. It goes like this:

To this are assigned the rare and the hot and brightness and the soft and the light; and to the dense are given the names of cold and gloom and hard and heavy; for these have been separated off, each group in its own way.
Thus he clearly assumes two opposing elements.

(Simplicius, *Commentary on the* Physics 31.3–7)

(No doubt Simplicius is right to suggest scepticism about the authenticity of the prose fragment.)
   Two further verses can be added to B 12:

Parmenides clearly speaks of a productive cause not only for bodies in the realm of becoming but also for incorporeal items:
   The next with night (but they emit a portion of flame),
   and in the middle of them, a goddess who governs all
      things.
   For everywhere she rules over hateful birth and union,
   sending female to unite with male and again conversely
   male with female. [B 12]

(Simplicius, *Commentary on the* Physics 31.10–17)

The 'bands' of B 12 are described in more detail in a late report:

Parmenides says that there are bands encircling one another, one made of the rare, one of the dense, and others between them mixed from light and darkness. What surrounds them all, like a wall, is solid, and beneath it is a fiery band; so too is what is in the middle of them all, around which again is a fiery band. Of the mixed bands the middlemost is cause of all motion and coming into being for all of them: this he calls the governing goddess and the keyholder, and Justice and Necessity. Air is a secretion of the earth, vaporized by its more violent compression. The sun and the circle of the Milky Way are the breath of fire. The moon is a mixture of both – air and fire. The ether surrounds them, above everything; under it is arranged the fiery part we call the sky, and under that the regions around the earth.   (Stobaeus, *Anthology* I xxii 1a)

There are further fragments of an astronomical nature:

[Parmenides and Melissus] clearly refer to the generation of perceptible objects – Melissus when he says that the cold becomes hot
etc., and from water earth and stone come about [cf. 30 B 8]; and
Parmenides, at the beginning of his remarks about perceptible objects,
says that he will tell

> **how earth and sun and moon**
> **and ether common to all and the Milky Way and outermost**
> **Olympus**
> **and the hot force of the stars were moved**
> **to come into being.** [B 11]

And he describes the generation of things that come into being and
perish, right down to the parts of animals.

(Simplicius, Commentary on On the Heavens 559.18–27)

Once he has attained to the true teaching [of Christ], let who will
listen to the promises of Parmenides of Elea:

> **You will know the nature of the ether and all the signs in**
> **the ether**
> **and the bright sun's pure**
> **torch and its destructive deeds and whence they came into**
> **being,**
> **and you will learn the revolving deeds of the round-eyed moon**
> **and its nature, and you will know too the sky which**
> **encloses them –**
> **whence it sprang and how necessity led and fettered it**
> **to hold the limits of the stars.** [B 10]

(Clement, Miscellanies V xiv 138.1)

Someone who denies that red-hot iron is fire or that the moon is a
sun – thinking it rather, with Parmenides,

> **night-shining, wandering about the earth, another's light**
> [B 14]

– does not abolish the use of iron or the nature of the moon.

(Plutarch, Against Colotes 1116A)

As a star or a light or a divine and celestial body, [the moon], I fear, is shapeless and indecent and disgraces her noble name – if indeed of the things in the heavens, numerous as they are, she alone goes about in need of another's light, as Parmenides says,

always gazing at the rays of the sun. [B 15]

(Plutarch, *On the Face in the Moon* 929AB)

Parmenides in his poem called the earth **water-rooted.** [B 15a]

(Scholia to St Basil, *Sermons on the Six Days of Creation* I 8)

Two brief reports are worth adding:

[Parmenides] was the first to declare that the earth is spherical and lies in the middle [of the universe].

(Diogenes Laertius, *Lives of the Philosophers* IX 21)

Parmenides places the Morning Star first in order in the ether (he thinks that it is the same as the Evening Star). After it comes the sun, beneath which are the stars in the fiery region which he calls the sky.

(Stobaeus, *Anthology* I xxiv 2e)

Next, two fragments on biology, the second of which survives only in a Latin translation.

Others of the older generation have also said that the male is conceived in the right-hand part of the womb. Parmenides put it like this:

In the right-hand parts boys, in the left girls. [B 17]

(Galen, *Commentary on Hippocrates'* Epidemics Book 6
XVIIA 1002)

In the books he wrote *On Nature* Parmenides says that as the result of conception men are sometimes born soft or smooth. Since he wrote in Greek verse, I too shall put the point in verses – I have composed some Latin verses, as close to his as I could, so as to avoid a mixture of languages:

> When a woman and a man together mix the seeds of Love,
> then a formative power from the different blood in the
>   veins,
> if it preserves proportion, fashions well-built bodies.
> But if when the seed is mixed, the powers conflict
> and do not produce one power in the mixed body, then
>   cruelly
> will they trouble the nascent sex with a twin seed. [B 18]
>
> (Caelius Aurelianus, *Chronic Diseases* IV ix 134–135)

Theophrastus gives an account of Parmenides' ideas about thought.

Parmenides determined nothing at all [about perception] – only that
there are two elements and that knowledge depends on the dominant
one. For if the hot or the cold dominates, thought becomes different
– better and purer when it depends on the hot, though this too
requires a certain proportionality:

> For as on each occasion, he says, is the blending of the
>   wandering limbs,
> so stands thought for men; for it is the same
> thing which thinks – the nature of the limbs –
> for each and every man; for what exceeds is thought. [B 16]

For he speaks of perceiving and thinking as the same thing – that is
why memory and forgetfulness derive from these things through their
blending. But he said nothing further about what happens if they are
equal in the mixture – whether or not it will be possible to think, and
what the disposition will be. That he makes perception too occur by
opposites in their own right is clear from the passage where he says
that corpses do not perceive light or heat or sound because of the
deficiency of fire, but that they do perceive their opposites – cold and
silence and so on. And in general, everything which exists has some
knowledge. (Theophrastus, *On the Senses* 3–4)

*Finally, Simplicius preserves three lines from the end of Parmenides'
poem:*

Having described the world of perception, he adds:

Thus, according to opinion, these things sprang up and now are,

and then, hereafter, having been nourished they will cease to be:

and on them men have set names, a mark for each. [B 19]

(Simplicius, *Commentary on* On the Heavens 558.8–11)

10

Melissus

In 441 BC Athens declared war on Samos and despatched a fleet to the island. During the protracted operations, Pericles, the Athenian commander, led some of his ships away on an expedition:

When he had sailed off, Melissus, son of Ithagenes, a philosopher who was then in command at Samos, despising the small number of their ships or the inexperience of their commanders, persuaded his fellow-citizens to attack the Athenians. In the battle that followed, the Samians were victorious. They captured many men and destroyed many ships, thereby gaining control of the sea and acquiring war-supplies of which they had previously been short. Aristotle says that Pericles himself had earlier been defeated by Melissus in a sea-battle.

(Plutarch, *Pericles* xxvi 166CD)

The Samians were beaten in the end; but Melissus had made his mark on history.

The year of the battle gives us the only known date in Melissus' life. In philosophy, he was a follower of Parmenides. Indeed, his book is a version in clear prose, revised and modified, of Parmenides' 'Way of Truth'. Substantial fragments have survived, all of them preserved by Simplicius. In addition, there are two paraphrases of his argument, one in the essay On Melissus, Xenophanes and Gorgias, falsely ascribed to Aristotle, and the other in Simplicius' commentary on Aristotle's Physics. Here is the latter.

Melissus uses the axioms of the natural philosophers and begins his treatise on generation and destruction as follows:

If it is nothing, what could be said about it as though it were something? If it is something, either it came into being or it has always existed. But if it came into being, it did so either from the existent or from the non-existent. But it is not possible for anything to come into being either from the non-existent (not even some other nothing, let alone something actually existent) or from the existent (for in that case it would have existed all along and would not have come into being). What exists, therefore, has not come into being. Therefore it has always existed. Nor will what exists be destroyed. For what exists can change neither into the non-existent (the natural scientists agree on this) nor into the existent (for in that case it would remain and not be destroyed). Therefore what exists neither has come into being nor will be destroyed. Therefore it always has existed and will exist.

Since what comes into existence has a beginning, what does not come into existence has no beginning. But what exists has not come into being. Therefore it has no beginning. Again, what is destroyed has an end, and if something is indestructible it has no end. Therefore what exists, being indestructible, has no end. But what has neither beginning nor end is in fact limitless. Therefore what exists is limitless.

If it is limitless, it is one. For if there are two they cannot be limitless but will have limits against one another. But what exists is limitless. Therefore there is not a plurality of existents. Therefore what exists is one.

If it is one, it is also changeless. For what is one is always similar to itself, and what is similar will neither perish nor become larger nor change its arrangement nor suffer pain nor suffer anguish. For if it undergoes any of these things it will not be one. For anything which undergoes any change of whatever sort moves from one state into a different one. But nothing is different from what exists. Therefore it will not change.

Again, nothing is empty of what exists. For what is empty is nothing; and hence, being nothing, it will not exist. Hence what exists does not move – for it has no way to retreat if nothing is empty. Nor can it contract into itself. For in that case it would be both rarer and denser than itself, and that is impossible. For what is rare cannot be as full as what is dense; rather, what is rare is thereby emptier than what is dense – but what is empty does not exist. One should judge whether what exists is full or not by seeing whether or not it accommodates anything else: if it does not accommodate anything, it is full; if it does accommodate, it is not full. Now if it is not empty it is necessarily full; and if so, then it cannot move – not because it is not possible to move through what is full, as we say in the case of bodies, but because the whole of what exists can move neither into the existent (for there exists nothing apart from it) nor into the non-existent (for the non-existent does not exist).

(Simplicius, Commentary on the Physics 103.13–104.15)

The paraphrase largely fixes the order in which the fragments should be set out.

Melissus showed the ungenerability of what exists, using the common axiom [that nothing comes into being from nothing]. He writes as follows:

Whatever existed always existed and always will exist. For if it came into being, then necessarily before coming into being it was nothing. Now if it was nothing it will in no way have come to be anything from being nothing. [30 B 1]

(Simplicius, Commentary on the Physics 162.23–26)

Melissus puts the point as follows:

Now since it did not come into being but exists, it always existed and always will exist, and it has no beginning and no end but is limitless. For if it came into being it will have a beginning (for it will at some time have begun coming into being) and an end (for it will at some time have ceased coming into being). And if it neither began nor ended and always existed and always will exist, then it has no beginning and no end. For what does not exist wholly cannot exist always. [B 2]

... Just as he asserts that what has at some time come into being is limited in its being, so he says that what always exists is limitless in its being. He makes this clear when he says:

But just as it exists always, so in magnitude too it must always be limitless. [B 3]

By magnitude he does not mean extension; for he himself shows that what exists is indivisible:

If what exists has been divided, he says, **it is moving; but if it is moving it will not exist.** [B 10]

Rather, by magnitude he means degree of reality. For he shows that he means what exists to be incorporeal when he says:

Now if it exists, it must be one; but being one it must fail to possess a body. [Cf. B 9]

And he co-ordinates limitlessness with eternity, in respect of being, when he says:

Nothing which has a beginning and an end is either eternal or limitless [B 4], so that what does not have them is limitless.

From limitlessness he inferred that it is one, by way of the proposition that if it were not one it would be limited against something else [B 5]. Eudemus criticizes this on the grounds that it is unspecified. He writes:

> If you were to concede that what exists is limitless, why will it be one? Not because a plurality of things will be limited against one another; for time past is thought to be limitless even though it is limited against time present. Perhaps a plurality of things will not be limitless in all directions; but it will be evident that they can be so in one direction. So it must be specified in which way a plurality will not be limitless. [Eudemus, *Physics* fragment 41 Wehrli]

(Simplicius, *Commentary on the* Physics 109.19–110.11)

And if Melissus entitled his work *On Nature or on What Exists*, it is clear that he thought nature to be what exists, and natural objects, i.e. perceptible objects, to be the things which exist. Perhaps that is why Aristotle said that, in declaring what exists to be one, he supposed that there was nothing else apart from perceptible substances. For given that what is perceptible seems plainly to exist, then if what exists is one there will not exist anything else apart from this. Melissus says: **For if it is <limitless> it will be one. For if there are two, they**

cannot be limitless, but will have limits against one another. [B 6]
(Simplicius, *Commentary on* On the Heavens 557.10–17)

Since Melissus wrote in an archaic style but not unclearly, let us set down his archaic words themselves so that those who read them may judge more accurately which are the more appropriate interpretations. So, drawing the conclusions I have already mentioned and introducing his treatment of change, Melissus says:

In this way, then, it is eternal and limitless and one and altogether similar to itself. And it will neither perish nor become larger nor change its arrangement nor suffer pain nor suffer anguish. For if it undergoes any of these things it will no longer be one.

For if it alters, necessarily what exists will not be similar: rather, what previously existed will perish and what did not exist will come into being. Now if it becomes altered by a single hair in ten thousand years, it will perish wholly in the whole of time.

Nor can it change its arrangement. For the arrangement which previously existed is not destroyed nor will one which did not exist come into being. And since nothing is added or perishes or alters, how could anything which exists change its arrangement? For if it alters in any way it will thereby also change its arrangement.

Nor does it suffer pain. For if it is in pain it will not wholly exist; for a thing in pain cannot exist always, nor does it have equal power with what is healthy. Nor will it be similar if it suffers pain; for it will suffer pain by the loss or the addition of something, and it will no longer be similar. Nor could what is healthy suffer pain; for the health which existed would perish and what did not exist would come into being.

With regard to suffering anguish, the same argument holds as for being in pain.

Nor is it empty in any respect. For what is empty is nothing; and hence, being nothing, it will not exist.

Nor does it move. For it has no way to retreat but is full. For if it were empty it would retreat into the empty part, but since nothing is empty it has no way to retreat. And it will not be dense and rare. For what is rare cannot be as full as what is dense; rather, what is

rare is thereby emptier than what is dense. You should judge what is full and what is not full in this way: if it yields at all or accommodates, it is not full; if it neither yields nor accommodates, it is full. Now necessarily it is full if it is not empty. So if it is full it does not move. [B 7]
That is what Melissus says.

(Simplicius, *Commentary on the* Physics 111.15–112.15)

Their existent One, being indivisible, will not be limited or limitless in the way bodies are. For Parmenides places bodies among the objects of opinion, and Melissus says:
Being one, it must fail to possess a body. But if it has bulk it will have parts and will no longer be one. [Cf. B 9]

(Simplicius, *Commentary on the* Physics 87.4–7)

The final fragment shows that Melissus' book contained a critical as well as a constructive section.

Melissus, inasmuch as he wrote in prose, gave a clearer account [than Parmenides] of his views on [perceptible objects] throughout his work – and especially in the following passage. Having said about what exists that it is one and ungenerated and motionless and interrupted by no emptiness but wholly full of itself, he continues:
Now this argument is the greatest sign that there exists just one thing; but there are also the following signs. If there exist more things than one, they will have to be such as I say the one thing is. For if there exist earth and water and air and iron and gold and living things and dead and black and white and the other things which men say are true – if these things exist and we see and hear correctly, then each of them must be such as it seemed to us at first: they cannot change or become altered, but each must always be just what it is. Now we are saying that we see and hear and understand correctly. But what is hot seems to us to become cold, and what is cold hot, and what is hard soft, and what is soft hard, and living things seem to die and to come into being from what is not alive, and all these things seem to alter, and what was and what

is now do not seem to be similar; rather, iron, which is hard, is rubbed away by contact with the fingers, and so are gold and stones and everything else which seems to be strong; and earth and stones seem to come into being from water. [[So that it results that we neither see nor know the things that exist.]]*

Now these things do not agree with one another. For we said that there are many things with forms and strength, but they all seem to us to alter and to change from what they were each time they were seen. So it is clear that we do not see correctly, and that those many things do not correctly seem to exist. For they would not change if they were true; rather, each would be as it seemed to be; for nothing is stronger than what is true. And if they change, what exists will have perished and what does not exist will have come into being. In this way, then, if there exist many things, they must be such as the one thing is. [B 8]

Melissus thus clearly explains why they [*i.e. Parmenides and Melissus*] say that perceptible objects do not exist but seem to exist.

(Simplicius, *Commentary on* On the Heavens 558.17–559.13)

---

*The sentence enclosed in double brackets is clearly out of place: it should probably be deleted.

11

Zeno

Zeno, like Parmenides, came from Elea. Virtually nothing is known about his life. Plato tells of an encounter between Zeno and Socrates: the story, though a fiction, is worth repeating since what it says about the nature and the scope of Zeno's work may well be true.

According to Antiphon, Pythodorus said that Zeno and Parmenides once came [to Athens] for the festival of the Great Panathenaea. Parmenides was already a very old man, white-haired but of distinguished appearance – he was about sixty-five. Zeno was then nearly forty, tall and pleasant to look at – he was said to have been Parmenides' lover. They were staying with Pythodorus, outside the city wall in the Ceramicus. Socrates had gone there, and many others with him, eager to hear Zeno's writings – for this was the first time they had brought them to Athens. Socrates was then very young.

Zeno himself read to them while Parmenides happened to be out. There was only very little of the argument still left to be read, Pythodorus said, when he himself came in and with him Parmenides and Aristotle (who became one of the thirty tyrants); so they heard just a little of the writings – although Pythodorus himself had actually heard Zeno before.

When Socrates had heard him out, he asked Zeno to read again the first hypothesis of the first argument. When it had been read he said: 'Zeno, what do you mean? Are you saying that if more things than one exist, then they must be both similar and dissimilar, which is impossible – for dissimilar things cannot be similar or similar things dissimilar? Is that it?'

'Yes,' said Zeno.

'So if it is impossible for dissimilar things to be similar and similar things dissimilar, it cannot be that more things than one exist. For if several things did exist, they would have impossible properties. Is this the point of your arguments – to contest, against everything people say, that there do not exist more things than one? And do you take each of your arguments to be evidence for this conclusion, so that you suppose yourself to provide as many pieces of evidence as you have composed arguments to show that there do not exist more things than one? Is that what you mean, or have I misunderstood you?'

'No,' said Zeno, 'you have grasped perfectly the overall point of the book.'

'I see, Parmenides,' said Socrates, 'that Zeno here wants to be associated with you not only by his love for you but also by his treatise. For he has in a way written the same thing as you, although by changing it he is trying to mislead us into thinking that he is saying something different. You say in your poems that the universe is one, and you produce evidence for the view with great skill. He says that there do not exist more things than one, and he too produces many impressive pieces of evidence. One of you says that one thing exists, the other that there do not exist more things than one, and each of you expresses himself in such a way that you seem not to be saying the same things at all even though you are saying pretty well the same things – something which seems to be above the heads of the rest of us.'

'Yes, Socrates,' said Zeno; 'but you haven't altogether seen the truth about my book. Like a Spartan hound, you are good at chasing and tracking down what I have said. But, first, you haven't seen that my book isn't really so very conceited – I did not write with the intention you describe only to hide the fact from people, as though that were a great achievement. You have mentioned an accidental feature of the book: in truth it is a sort of defence of Parmenides' argument against those who try to ridicule it on the grounds that if there exists only one thing then the argument leads to many ridiculous and contradictory conclusions. My book attacks those who say that more things than one exist, giving them as good as they gave and more, and aiming to show that their hypothesis – that more things than one exist – leads to even more ridiculous results, if you examine it properly, than the hypothesis that only one thing exists. It was with that sort of ambition that I wrote it when I was young. After it was written someone stole it, so that I could not even consider whether it should be brought out into the light or not.'   (Plato, *Parmenides* 127A–128D)

Zeno's treatise, according to this story, consisted of a series of arguments each designed to show that the common-sense 'hypothesis' that there exist more things than one leads to absurdity. Later sources say that there were forty arguments in all. There are substantial fragments of two of the arguments; Aristotle provides a critical paraphrase of four more; and we possess accounts of a further two. These arguments apart, nothing is known of Zeno's philosophy – if indeed there was anything else to know.

The fragments are preserved in Simplicius' Commentary on the Physics. Simplicius is discussing a passage where Aristotle refers to two arguments, the argument that 'everything is one' and the argument 'from dichotomy'. The passage was understood in different ways by Aristotle's commentators, and Simplicius' citations of Zeno occur in his survey of their dispute.

Alexander says that the second argument, from dichotomy, comes from Zeno and that Zeno says that if what exists has size and is divided, then it will be many and no longer one, thus proving that the One does not exist . . . Alexander seems to have taken his opinion that Zeno does away with the One from Eudemus' writings. For in his *Physics* Eudemus says:

Then does this not exist although some one thing does exist? That was the puzzle. They report that Zeno said that he would be able to talk about what exists if only someone would explain to him how on earth anything could be *one* thing. He was puzzled, it seems, because each perceptible item is called many things both by way of predication and by being divisible into parts, whereas points are nothing at all (for he thought that what neither increases when added nor decreases when subtracted was not an existent thing). [Eudemus, *Physics* fragment 37a Wehrli]

Now it is indeed likely that, by way of intellectual exercise, Zeno
argued on both sides of the case (that is why he is called 'two-tongued')
and that he actually published arguments of this sort to raise puzzles
about the One. But in his treatise, which contains many arguments,
he shows in each case that anyone who says that more things than
one exist falls into inconsistencies.

There is one argument in which he shows that if more things than
one exist they are both large and small – so large as to be limitless in
size, so small as to have no size at all. Here he shows that what has no
size, no mass, and no bulk, does not even exist. For, he says,

**if it were added to another existent, it would not make it larger.
For if it is of no size but is added, there cannot be any increase at
all in size. Thus what is added will therefore be nothing. And if
when it is subtracted the other thing is no smaller – and will not
increase when it is added again – then clearly what was added and
subtracted was nothing.** [29 B 2]

Zeno says this not to do away with the One but in order to show that
each of the plurality of things possesses a size – a size which is actually
limitless by virtue of the fact that, because of limitless divisibility,
there is always something in front of whatever is taken. This he shows,
having first shown that they possess no size at all from the fact that
each member of the plurality is the same as itself and one. (Themistius
says that Zeno's argument establishes that what exists is one from the
fact that it is continuous and indivisible; 'for if it were divided,' he
says, 'it would not strictly speaking be one because of the limitless
divisibility of bodies.' But Zeno seems rather to say that there will not
exist more things than one.)

Porphyry holds that the argument from dichotomy comes from
Parmenides, who attempted to show by it that what exists is one. He
writes as follows:

Parmenides had another argument, the one based on dichotomy, which purports to show that what exists is one thing only
and, moreover, partless and indivisible. For if it is divisible, he
says, suppose it to have been cut in two – and then each of its
parts in two. Since this goes on for ever, it is clear, he says, that
either some final magnitudes will remain which are minimal

and atomic and limitless in number, so that the whole thing
will be constituted from minimal items limitless in number; or
else it will disappear and be dissolved into nothing, and so be
constituted from nothing. But these consequences are absurd.
Therefore it will not be divided but will remain one. Again,
since it is everywhere alike, if it is divisible it will be divisible
everywhere alike, and not divisible in one place and not in
another. Then suppose it to have been divided everywhere. It is
clear, again, that nothing will remain but that it will disappear;
and if it is constituted at all, it will again be constituted from
nothing. For if anything remains, it will not yet have been
divided everywhere. Thus from these considerations too it is
evident, he says, that what exists will be indivisible and partless
and one. [Porphyry, *Commentary on the* Physics, fragment 135
Smith] . . .

It is correct, as Porphyry says, that the argument from dichotomy is
pertinently mentioned inasmuch as it introduces the indivisible One
by way of the absurdity consequent upon division; but it is worth
asking whether the argument comes from Parmenides rather than
from Zeno, as Alexander thinks. For nothing of the sort is stated in
the Parmenidean writings, and most scholars ascribe the puzzle of the
dichotomy to Zeno – indeed it is mentioned as Zeno's in [Aristotle's]
work *On Motion* [*i.e.* Physics 6].

And why say more when it is actually found in Zeno's own treatise?
For, showing that if more things than one exist the same things are
limited and limitless, Zeno writes in the following words:

**If more things than one exist, it is necessary for them to be as many
as they are, and neither more nor fewer. But if they are as many as
they are, they will be limited. If more things than one exist, the
things which exist are limitless. For there are always others between
the things which exist, and again others between them. And in this
way the things which exist are limitless.** [B 3]

And in this way he showed limitlessness in number from the dichotomy. As for limitlessness in size, he showed that earlier in the same
argument. For having first shown that if what exists had no size it
would not even exist, he continues:

But if it exists, it is necessary for each thing to have some bulk and size, and for one part of it to be at a distance from the other. And the same argument applies to the protruding part. For that too will have a size, and a part of it will protrude. Now it is all one to say this once and to say it for ever. For it will have no last part of such a sort that there is no longer one part in front of another. In this way, if there exist more things than one, it is necessary for them to be both small and large – so small as not to have a size, so large as to be limitless. [B 1]

Perhaps, then, the argument from dichotomy comes from Zeno, as Alexander holds, but he is not doing away with the One but rather with a plurality of things (by showing that those who hypothesize a plurality are committed to inconsistencies), thus confirming Parmenides' argument that what exists is one.

> (Simplicius, *Commentary on the* Physics 138.3–6,
> 138.29–140.6, 140.18–141.11)

Aristotle discusses four of Zeno's arguments in the Physics. *The account is concise (and the text is in places uncertain).*

Zeno argues fallaciously. For if, he says, everything is always at rest when it is in a space equal to itself, and if what is travelling is always in such a space at any instant, then the travelling arrow is motionless. This is false; for time is not composed of indivisible instants – nor is any other size.

Zeno's arguments about motion which embarrass those who try to resolve them are four in number.

The first maintains that nothing moves because what is travelling must reach the halfway point before it reaches the end. We have discussed this earlier.

The second is the so-called Achilles. This maintains that the slowest thing will never be caught when running by the fastest. For the pursuer must first reach the point from which the pursued set out, so that the slower must always be ahead of it. This is the same argument as the dichotomy, but it differs in that the additional sizes are not divided in half. Now it follows from the argument that the slower is not caught; but it depends on the same assumption as the dichotomy (in both arguments it follows that you do not reach the end if the size is divided in a certain way – but here there is the additional point that not even the fastest runner in literary tradition will reach his goal when he pursues the slowest); hence the solution must also be the same. And it is false to claim that the one ahead is not caught: he is not caught while he is ahead, but none the less he is caught (provided you grant that they can cover a limited distance).

Those, then, are two of the arguments. The third is the one we have just stated, to the effect that the travelling arrow stands still. It depends on the assumption that time is composed of instants; for if that is not granted the inference will not go through.

The fourth is the argument about the bodies moving in the stadium from opposite directions, an equal number past an equal number; the one group starts from the end of the stadium, the other from the middle; and they move at equal speed. He thinks it follows that half the time is equal to its double. The fallacy consists in claiming that objects of equal size, moving at equal speeds – the one past a moving object and the other past a stationary object – travel for an equal length of time. But this is false.

For example, let the stationary equal bodies be AA; let BB be those beginning from the middle, equal in number and in size to them; and let CC be those beginning from the end, equal in number and in size to them and equal in speed to the Bs. It follows that, as they move past one another, the first B and the first C are at the end at the same time. And it follows that the C has travelled past all of them but the B past half of them. Hence the time is half – for each of the two is alongside each for an equal time. At the same time it follows that the first B has travelled past all the Cs; for the first C and the first B will be at opposite ends at the same time (the C being, as he says, alongside each of the Bs for a time equal to that for which it is alongside each of the As) – because both are alongside the As for an equal time. That is the argument, and it depends on the falsity we have mentioned.

(Aristotle, *Physics* 239b5–240a18)

At 239b13–14, Aristotle refers back to his earlier discussion of the first of Zeno's arguments:

Zeno's argument falsely assumes that it is impossible to traverse limitlessly many things, or to touch a limitless number of things individually, in a limited time. For both lengths and times – and in general all *continua* – are said to be limitless in two ways: either by division or in respect of their extremities. Now it is not possible to touch a quantitatively limitless number of things in a limited time, but it is possible so to touch things limitless by division. For time itself is limitless in this way. Hence it follows that what is limitless is traversed in a limitless and not in a limited time, and that the limitless things are touched at limitlessly and not at limitedly many instants.

(Aristotle, *Physics* 233a21–31)

Two further Zenonian arguments are referred to by Aristotle and explained in more detail by Simplicius:

It is clear that nothing can be in itself as its primary place. Zeno's puzzle – that if places exist then they will be in something – is not difficult to resolve. For nothing prevents the primary place of a thing from being in something else – not as in a place, but rather as health is in hot things (as a state of them) or heat in a body (as a quality of it). (Aristotle, *Physics* 210b21–27)

Zeno's argument seemed to do away with the existence of place. It was propounded as follows: If places exist, they will be in something; for everything which exists is in something. But what is in something is in a place. Therefore places will be in places – and so *ad infinitum*. Therefore places do not exist. [B 5] . . .

Eudemus relates Zeno's opinion as follows:

Zeno's puzzle seems to lead to the same conclusion. For he claims that everything which exists is somewhere. But if places are among the things which exist, where will they be? Surely in another place – and that in another, and so on . . . Against Zeno we shall say that things are said to be somewhere in several

ways. If he claims that whatever exists is in a place, then what he claims is not correct; for you would not say that health or courage or a thousand other things were in a place. But if 'somewhere' is taken in another way, then places may be somewhere – for the limit of a body is somewhere on the body, namely at its extremity. [Eudemus, *Physics* fragment 78 Wehrli]
(Simplicius, *Commentary on the* Physics 562.3–6, 563.17–28)

Zeno's argument – that any part of a millet-seed makes a sound – is not true; for nothing prevents it from having no effect at all, in any length of time, on the air which the whole bushel set in motion by its fall. (Aristotle, *Physics* 250a19–22)

Having said that if the whole force moved the whole weight a certain distance in a certain time, it does not thereby follow that half the force will in the same time move the whole weight half – or any fraction – of the distance (nor will every fraction of the force which moved the whole weight be capable of moving the whole weight for a given time and over a given distance), [Aristotle] thus resolves the argument which Zeno of Elea put to Protagoras the sophist. 'Tell me, Protagoras,' he said, 'does one millet-seed – or the ten-thousandth part of a seed – make a sound when it falls?' Protagoras said that it did not. 'But,' he said, 'does a bushel of millet-seed make a sound when it falls or not?' When he replied that a bushel does make a sound, Zeno said: 'Well then, isn't there a ratio between the bushel of millet-seed and the single seed – or the ten-thousandth part of a single seed?' Protagoras agreed. 'Well then,' said Zeno, 'will the same ratios not hold between the sounds? For as are the sounders so are the sounds. And that being the case, if the bushel of millet-seed makes a sound, the single seed – and the ten-thousandth part of a seed – will also make a sound.' That was Zeno's argument.
(Simplicius, *Commentary on the* Physics 1108.14–28)

Finally, Diogenes Laertius offers a short fragment, the authenticity of which most scholars doubt:

According to [the Pyrrhonists], Xenophanes and Zeno of Elea and Democritus are sceptics ... Zeno does away with motion by saying: **What is moving moves neither in the place in which it is nor in the place in which it is not.** [B 4]

(Diogenes Laertius, *Lives of the Philosophers* IX 72)

PART III

12

Empedocles

Empedocles came from Acragas in Sicily. His family was rich and distinguished – his grandfather won a victory in the horse-racing at the Olympic Games of 496 BC. As for his dates, the figures given by our sources do not tally; but the period from about 495 to about 435 BC may be roughly right for his life-span.

He wrote several works, all of them in verse, of which the most important were later entitled On Nature *and* Purifications. *The opening of* Purifications *is preserved:*

That he was from Acragas in Sicily he himself says at the beginning of the *Purifications*:

> **Friends who live in the great town by the tawny Acragas
> on the heights of the citadel . . .** [31 B 112.1–2]
>
> (Diogenes Laertius, *Lives of the Philosophers* VIII 54)

Later, Diogenes Laertius gives a longer extract:

Heraclides says that the woman who did not breathe was in such a state that her body remained without breath and without a pulse for thirty days. That is why Heraclides calls [Empedocles] both a doctor and a seer, relying also on the following lines:

> **Friends who live in the great town by the tawny Acragas
> on the heights of the citadel, caring for good deeds,
> greetings: I, an immortal god, no longer mortal,
> travel, honoured by all, as is fitting,
> wreathed with ribbons and fresh garlands.
> †Whenever† I enter a thriving town**

I am revered by men and women. They follow me
in their thousands, asking where lies the path to gain:
some want prophecies, others for diseases
of every sort demand to hear a healing word. [B 112.1–2,
    4–11]

(Diogenes Laertius, *Lives of the Philosophers* VIII 61)

*A stray line is generally inserted into this passage, and two further texts
may be associated with it:*

Empedocles says of [the Acragantines]:
**Compassionate harbours for strangers, inexperienced in
evil.** [B 112.3]

(Diodorus, *Universal History* XIII lxxxiii 1–2)

[Grammarians] are blind in these matters – and also with regard to
the poems written about them – as when Empedocles says:
**Greetings: I, an immortal god, no longer mortal,
travel, honoured by all** [B 112.4–5];
and again:
**But why do I attack them as though I were achieving
something great
If I prove superior to much-perishing mortal men?** [B 113]
Grammarians and laymen will suppose that the philosopher said this
from boastfulness and contempt for other men – something which is
alien even to one moderately versed in philosophy, let alone to a man
of his stature.

(Sextus Empiricus, *Against the Mathematicians* I 302–303)

And it occurs to me to praise highly the Acragantine poet who hymns
trust in these words:
**My friends, I know that there is truth in the stories
which I shall tell; but hard indeed
for men and unwelcome is the impulse of trust on their
minds.** [B 114]

(Clement, *Miscellanies* V i 9.1)

It may be that the first line of the other poem, On Nature, *has also been saved:*

Pausanias, according to Aristippus and Satyrus, was [Empedocles'] lover, to whom he addressed *On Nature* thus:

Pausanias, son of wise Anchitus, listen . . . [B 1]

    (Diogenes Laertius, *Lives of the Philosophers* VIII 60)

The lines contained in the next extract perhaps come from near the beginning of On Nature – *although most scholars have associated them rather with* Purifications, *and Plutarch's phrase 'at the beginning of his philosophy' is irritatingly indeterminate:*

Empedocles at the beginning of his philosophy says by way of preface that

> **There is an oracle of necessity, an ancient decree of the gods, that whenever anyone errs and defiles in fear his dear**
> > **limbs –**
>
> **one of the spirits who have been allotted long-lasting life –**
> **he shall wander thrice ten thousand seasons far from the**
> > **blessed ones.**
>
> **Such is the road I now follow, an exile from the gods and a**
> > **wanderer.** [B 115.1, 3, 5–6, 13]

He proves from his own case that not just he himself but all of us are immigrants here and strangers and exiles. For it is not blood, my friends, nor blended breath (he says) which provides the substance and principle of our souls: from these the body has been fashioned, earth-born and mortal; but the soul has come here from elsewhere – and he calls birth by the gentlest of terms, a journey abroad.

And what is most true, the soul flees and wanders, driven by divine decrees and laws . . . When it is tied to the body, it cannot recall or remember

> **from what honour and from what breadth of bliss** [B 119]

it has come, having exchanged not Sardis for Athens, nor Corinth for Lemnos or Scyros, but the heavens and the moon for earth and an earthly life.   (Plutarch, *On Exile* 607CE)

The lines quoted by Plutarch are usually amalgamated with those in the following passage from Hippolytus, the amalgam becoming the single fragment, B 115.

About his own birth Empedocles speaks as follows:

Among them am I too now, an exile from the gods and a wanderer [cf. B 115.13]

– that is, he means by God the One and the unity in which he existed before he was torn away by Strife and found himself among the plurality of things here in the dispensation of Strife. For, he says,

<trusting in mad> Strife . . . [B 115.14]

– by Strife, mad and disturbed and unstable, Empedocles means the creator of this world. For this is the sentence and the necessity imposed on souls whom Strife tears away from the One and creates and produces. He says:

whoever having erred swears a false oath –
one of the spirits who have been allotted long-lasting life
  [B 115.4–5]

– he call souls 'long-lasting spirits' because they are immortal and live long lives –

he shall wander thrice ten thousand seasons far from the blessed ones [B 115.6]

– he calls blessed those who are gathered together by Love from the many into the unity of the intelligible world. These, then, he says must wander and

become in time all kinds of mortals,
changing the hard paths of life. [B 115.7–8]

The hard paths of the souls, he says, are their changes and transformations into bodies. He says:

changing the hard paths of life [B 115.8],

inasmuch as souls change from body to body, transformed and punished by Strife and not allowed to remain in unity. Rather, souls undergo every punishment at the hands of Strife as they change from body to body:

> **The ethereal power,** he says, **pursues souls to the sea,**
> **the sea spits them up onto the threshold of the earth, the**
> **earth into the light**
> **of the bright sun, and the sun hurls them into the whirls of**
> **the ether:**
> **the one receives them from the other: all hate them.**
> [B 115.9–12]

This is the punishment which the creator visits on them, like a smith transforming iron and taking it from the fire to plunge it in water. For the ether is fire, whence the creator hurls the souls into the sea, and the earth is dry land; so he means: 'from water to land, from land to air'. He says:

> **... the earth into the light**
> **of the bright sun, and the sun hurls them into the whirls of**
> **the ether:**
> **the one receives them from the other: all hate them.**
> [B 115.10–12]

Thus souls are hated and tortured and punished in this world, according to Empedocles, and then gathered together by Love, who is good and who takes pity on their lamentation and on the disorderly and vile arrangements of mad Strife; she is eager to lead them gradually from the world and to make them appropriate to the One, labouring to ensure that everything, led by her, comes to unity.

Such being the dispensation of fatal Strife in this divided world, Empedocles urges his followers to abstain from all living things; for he says that the bodies of the animals we eat are the dwelling-places of punished souls. And he teaches those who hear his words to keep themselves from intercourse with women so that they may not become fellow-workers and fellow-labourers in the enterprises which Strife creates, as it continuously dissolves and pulls apart the work of Love. This, Empedocles says, is the greatest law for the ordering of the universe. He says:

> **There is an oracle of necessity, an ancient decree of the**
> **gods,**
> **eternal, sealed with broad oaths** [B 115.1–2]

– by necessity he means the change from One to many by Strife and from many to One by Love; and by the gods, as I said, he means the four mortal gods (fire, water, earth, air) and the two immortals, who are ungenerated and eternally at war with one another: Strife and Love.   (Hippolytus, *Refutation of All Heresies* VII xxix 14–23)

Numerous fragments of Empedocles' works survive, some of them quite lengthy; but the sources rarely ascribe them to one poem rather than to another and rarely indicate the order in which they appeared within their original context. It is relatively easy to put together a cento of passages which, certainly or with probability, derive from the two Books of On Nature *and which together outline Empedocles' general conception of the nature and the history of the universe. These texts are here preceded by some fragments which may plausibly be imagined to have formed part of an introduction to Empedocles' cosmic exposition. After them, the remaining fragments are grouped thematically. Many of the passages in groups (6), (8), (9) and (10) have traditionally been assigned to the* Purifications; *but the state of our evidence makes any such attribution perilous.*

Pausanias, to whom On Nature *was addressed, was promised remarkable powers, and urged to guard his knowledge carefully:*

According to Satyrus, [Gorgias] says that he himself was present when Empedocles did magical deeds, and in his poems Empedocles himself professes his magic – and much else besides – where he says:

> What drugs there are for ills and what help against old age
> you will learn, since for you alone shall I accomplish all
>   this.
> And you will stop the power of the tireless winds which
>   sweep over the earth
> and destroy the crops with their blowings,
> and again, if you wish, you will bring on compensating
>   breezes.
> And after black rain you will produce a seasonable
>   drought
> for men, and after the summer drought you will produce
> tree-nourishing streams †which live in the ether†.

And you will lead from Hades the power of dead men.
[B 111]
(Diogenes Laertius, *Lives of the Philosophers* VIII 59)

Happy,
then, it seems, according to Empedocles,
is he who has gained the wealth of divine thoughts,
wretched he whose belief about the gods is dark. [B 132]
(Clement, *Miscellanies* V xiv 140.5)

[Empedocles] advises Pausanias, in Pythagorean fashion, to **hide** his doctrines **within a silent mind** [B 5]; and in general, those men think that silence is divine. (Plutarch, *Table Talk* 728E)

Such, according to Empedocles' philosophy, is the generation and destruction of our world and its composition from good and evil. He says that there is also a third intelligible power which can be conceived of on the basis of these things. He says:
For if you press them into your throbbing mind
and watch over them in kindly fashion with pure attention,
these will indeed all remain with you throughout your life,
and you will gain many others from them; for they
themselves will grow
each into your character as is the nature of each.
But should you reach out for things of a different kind
which among men
are numberless and wretched and which blunt their
thoughts,
they will leave you at once as time revolves,
desiring to come to their own dear kind;
for know that they all have intelligence and a share of
thought. [B 110]
(Hippolytus, *Refutation of All Heresies* VII xxix 25–26)

Superior understanding depends on a proper appreciation of the sources of human knowledge:

As for the view that the judging of truth does not lie with the senses,
[Empedocles] writes as follows:

> For narrow are the devices dispersed over the limbs,
> and many things wretched strike in and blunt the thought.
> Having seen in their lives a small part of life,
> swift to die, carried up like smoke, they fly away,
> persuaded only of what each has met with
> as they are driven in every direction. Who then claims to
>   find the whole?
> These things are not in this way to be seen by men nor to be
>   heard
> nor to be grasped in thought. [B 2. 1–8]

As for the view that truth is not completely unattainable but can be
grasped to the extent that human reason reaches, he makes this clear
when he continues the lines just quoted:

> So you, since you have come here,
> will learn: no more has mortal wit aroused. [B 2.8–9]

In the following lines he attacks those who pretend to know more,
and establishes that what is grasped through each of the senses is
trustworthy provided that reason is in charge of them (even though
he had earlier run down the reliability of the senses). For he says:

> But, you gods, turn the madness of these men from my
>   tongue,
> and from holy mouths channel a pure spring.
> And you, Muse of long memory, white-armed maiden,
> I beseech: what it is right for creatures of a day to hear,
> send to me, driving the well-reined chariot of piety.
> She will not compel you to accept the flowers of glory and
>   honour
> from mortals on condition that you say more than is holy
> with temerity. And then indeed do you sit on the summit of
>   wisdom.
> But come, observe with every device in the way in which
>   each thing is clear:
> neither hold sight in more trust than hearing,
> nor resounding hearing above the clarities of the tongue,

> nor let any of the other limbs by which there is a passage
>   for thinking
> be deprived of trust, but think in the way in which each
>   thing is clear. [B 3]

Such are Empedocles' views.
>   (Sextus Empiricus, *Against the Mathematicians* VII 123–125)

For the divine, as the poet from Acragas says,
> cannot be brought close in our eyes
> or grasped by our hands, by which the greatest
> highway of persuasion leads to the mind of men. [B 133]
>   (Clement, *Miscellanies* V xii 81.2)

For most people require proof as a pledge of the truth, not being
satisfied with the bare security which comes from trust:
> The bad who have power do not care to trust;
> but as the assurances from our Muse enjoin,
> learn, once you have divided the argument in your breast.
>   [B 4]

For evil men, Empedocles says, customarily want to have power over
the truth by distrusting.   (Clement, *Miscellanies* V iii 18.3–4)

*With the references to the Muse in B 3 and B 4, compare the following
text:*

The just account which strives on the side of Love is called the Muse
by Empedocles, and he invokes her to strive on his side in these lines:
> If ever for the sake of some creature of a day, immortal
>   Muse,
> <it pleased you> that my cares should pass through your
>   mind,
> now again, as I pray, stand by me, Calliope,
> as I reveal a good account about the blessed gods. [B 131]
>   (Hippolytus, *Refutation of All Heresies* VII xxxi 4)

On Nature *described a complex, cyclical history of the universe.*

Everything is compounded from four elements or 'roots', earth and air and fire and water. There are also two elemental powers, Love and Strife. The elements periodically unite into a divine and homogeneous Sphere. The Sphere then dissolves; various mixtures and unions take place, in the course of which our familiar world is formed; and eventually the elements separate entirely from one another in four concentric spheres. This state of affairs too is dissolved: various mixtures and unions take place, and eventually all is fused into a homogeneous Sphere. Such is the Cosmic Cycle. It rolls on like the Tour de France, repeatedly, without beginning and without end.

Empedocles' poem contained repetitions and reprises. This is clear in the surviving fragments, and Empedocles himself avows it:

But, lest I shall be thought to play the Empedocles and,
> **attaching one heading to another,**
> not †complete† **a single path in my tales** [B 24],
let me bring my introductory remarks to their appropriate end.
(Plutarch, On the Decline of Oracles 418C)

'Twice and thrice for the noble': a proverb, meaning that one should speak often about what is noble. The verse from which the proverb comes is by Empedocles. He says:
> **For it is noble to say twice what should be said.** [B 25]
(Scholia on Plato, Gorgias 498E)

Two long extracts from Simplicius' Commentary on the Physics provide some account of the general structure of Empedocles' cosmic history. Into the first extract there may be interpolated the longest piece of the Strasbourg Papyrus.

In the first book of his *Physics*, Empedocles describes the One and the limited many, and the periodic return, and generation and destruction by association and dissociation, in the following way:
> **I shall tell a twofold tale. Now they grew to be one alone**
> **from many, and now they grew apart again to be many**
> **from one.**

Double is the generation of mortal things, double their
    passing away:
the one is born and destroyed by the congregation of
    everything,
the other is nurtured and flies apart as they grow apart
    again.
And these never cease their continual change,
now coming together by Love all into one,
now again all being carried apart by the hatred of Strife.
<Thus insofar as they have learned to become one from
    many>
and again become many as the one grows apart,
to that extent they come into being and have no lasting life;
but insofar as they never cease their continual interchange,
to that extent they exist forever, unmoving in a circle.
    But come, hear my stories; for learning enlarges the
      mind.
As I said before when I revealed the limits of my stories,
I shall tell a twofold tale. For now they grew to be one alone
from many, and now they grew apart again to be many
    from one –
fire and water and earth and the boundless height of air,
and cursed Strife apart from them, balanced in every way,
and Love among them, equal in length and breadth.
Her you must regard in thought: do not sit staring with
    your eyes.
She is deemed to be innate also in mortal bodies,
and by her they think friendly thoughts and perform deeds
    of peace,
calling her Joy by name and Aphrodite,
whom no one has seen as she whirls †among them† –
no mortal man. But listen to the course of my argument,
    which does not deceive:
these are all equal and of the same age,
but they hold different offices and each has its own
    character;

and they have power in turn as time revolves.
And in addition to them nothing supervenes or ceases to be.
For if they were continually being destroyed they would no
    longer exist.
And what might increase the universe? and whence might it
    come?
And whither might it disappear, since nothing is empty of
    these things?
But these themselves exist, and running through one
    another
they become different at different times – and are ever and
    always alike. [B 17]

Here he says that that which comes from many – from the four
elements – is one, and he shows that it exists now under the domi-
nation of Love and now under that of Strife. For that neither of these
completely passes away is shown by the fact that they are all equal
and of the same age and that nothing supervenes or ceases to be. The
many from which the One derives are plural – for Love is not the
One, since Strife too brings them into unity.

Having mentioned several other things, he goes on . . .

          (Simplicius, *Commentary on the* Physics 157.25–159.10)

*The Strasbourg Papyrus of Empedocles consists of fifty-two scraps. The
scraps can be pieced together into larger units, and many of the gaps in
these units can be plausibly filled. Four of the units will be translated
here (the others contain no more than letters or half-words). Bold type
marks words all or part of which can be read on the papyrus; roman
type, between angled brackets, translates the supplements cautiously
suggested by the editors of the papyrus. The first and longest unit begins
with B 17.31–35. Its final line is labelled '300' in the papyrus, and was
presumably the 300th line of Book I of* On Nature.

    <For if they were continually being destroyed, they would>
      no longer exist;
    <And what might increase the universe? and> **whence might
      it come?**

<And whither might it disappear, since> **nothing is empty**
 <of these things?>
<But these themselves exist:> **running** <through one
 another>
<they become different at different times – and are ever and>
 always alike.
<But under Love,> **we come together to make one world,**
<and in Hatred it grew apart again,> **to be many from one,**
<from which is everything which was and which is> **and will
 be hereafter –**
<trees sprang up, and men> **and women,**
and beasts, and birds, <and fish> **which feed in the water,**
and even gods, long-lived, <highest> **in honour.**
And then they never <cease> **their continual hurry**
in frequent whirls <. . .>
unceasingly, never <. . .>
many prior ages <. . .>
<before> **passing from them** <. . .>
<and they never cease from> **their continual hurry in every
 way.**
For neither the sun <. . .>
<. . .> **here, heavy with** <. . .>
nor any of the others <. . .>
But, changing, they <hurry> **in a circle** <in every way.>
For then, untrodden, the earth runs, and the sun,
<and the sphere,> **as large as even now men may** <judge it to
 be.>
In the same way, all these things <ran> **through one
 another,**
and they came each to different places as they wandered,
 <. . .
. . .;> **and we came to the middle places,** <to be> **one thing**
 <alone>.
<But when> **Strife** <reaches> **the uttermost depths**
of the whirl, and Love <finds herself> **in the middle eddy,**
then all these things come together <to be> **one** <alone>.

<Make sure> that <this story reaches> further than your
    ears alone
<and> as you hear me <look at> the clear signs which are
    all around.
I shall show you to your eyes where <they find> a larger
    body:
first, a congregation and an unfolding of <what is born>
and all things which even now are left of this <generation>
– among the savage <kinds> of mountain-wandering beasts,
among the double offspring of men, <among>
the produce of root-bearing <fields> and <the grapes>
    clinging to the vine.
From these stories preserve in your mind unerring proofs;
for you will see a congregation and an unfolding <of what is
    born.>
    (Empedocles, *On Nature* I 262–300 [Strasbourg Papyrus **a**])

(Lines 269–272 of this passage are quoted by Aristotle, Metaphysics
1000a29–32 – cf. B 21.9–12.)
Now back to the first of the two long extracts from Simplicius:

Having mentioned several other things, he goes on to characterize
each of them, calling fire Sun, air Brightness and Heaven, and water
Rain and Sea. This is what he says:
    But come, consider these witnesses to my former songs,
    if anything I said before was defective in form:
    the sun, bright to see and everywhere hot,
    the divine bodies flooded †in heat† and shining light,
    rain everywhere, dark and shivering,
    and from earth flow forth things firm and solid.
    In Anger they have different forms and are all apart,
    but in Love they come together and are desired by one
        another.
    For from these comes everything which was and which is
        and will be –
    trees sprang up, and men and women

and beasts and birds and fish which feed in the water,
and even gods, long-lived, highest in honour.
For these themselves exist, and running through one
    another
they become different; †for so does blending change them.†
    [B 21]

He set down a clear illustration of how different things come from
the same things:

Just as painters, when they decorate offerings –
men well taught by wit in their art –
take the many-coloured pigments in their hands,
and, harmoniously mixing them, some more some less,
make from them shapes resembling all things,
creating trees and men and women
and beasts and birds and fish which feed in the water,
and even gods, long-lived, highest in honour:
so let not error persuade your mind that there is anywhere
    else
a source for the countless mortal things we see.
But know this clearly, having heard the story from a god.
    [B 23]

That he considers these many things, and not only Strife but also
Love, to be in the generated world, is clear when he says that trees
and men and women and beasts have come into being from them.
That they change into one another, he shows when he says:

They have power in turn as the circle revolves,
and they decline into one another and increase in their
    allotted turn. [B 26.1–2]

He shows that even what comes into being and is destroyed possesses
eternity by way of succession when he says:

But insofar as they never cease their continual change,
to that extent they exist forever, unmoving in a circle.
    [B 17.12–13]

He also hints at a double world – one intelligible and the other
perceptible, one divine and the other mortal, one containing things
as paradigms and the other as copies. He showed this when he said

that not only generated and perishable things are composed of these but so too are the gods (unless this should be explained in terms of Empedoclean usage). In the following verses too you might think he is hinting at a double world:

> **For they are all at peace with their own parts –**
> **Sun and Earth and Heaven and Sea –**
> **which have been separated from them and grown in mortal**
> **   things.**
> **In the same way, those which are more ready to blend,**
> **made similar by Aphrodite, love one another.**
> **Most hostile are the things which most differ from one**
> **   another**
> **in birth and blending and moulded shape,**
> **quite unaccustomed to come together and deeply dismal**
> **†at their strife-birth because they were born in anger.†**
> **[B 22]**

He shows that they are harmonized even in mortal things, but in intelligible things they are more united and,

> **made similar by Aphrodite, love one another.** [B 22.5]

And even if this happens everywhere, nevertheless intelligible things are made similar by Love, whereas perceptible things are overpowered by Strife and torn further apart and in the blending of their birth they subsist in shapes which are moulded and copied, strife-born and unaccustomed to union with one another.

He too supposed that generation takes place in virtue of an association and dissociation, as is shown by the first passage I set down:

> **Now they grew to be one alone**
> **from many, and now they grew apart again to be many**
> **   from one.** [B 17.1–2]

See also his remark to the effect that generation and destruction are nothing else

> **but only mixing and interchange of what is mixed** [B 8.3]

and

> **a congregation and an unfolding of what is born.** [*On*
> *Nature* I 300]

>   (Simplicius, *Commentary on the* Physics 159.10–161.20)

Most think that according to Empedocles Love alone made the intelligible world and Strife alone the perceptible world. But in fact he gives both of them their appropriate functions everywhere, as we can see from what he says in the *Physics*, where he asserts that Aphrodite or Love is a cause of the creative composition of this world too. He calls fire Hephaestus and Sun and Flame, water Rain, air Ether. He says this in many places, for example the following verses:

> **Earth, roughly equal to them, happened to come together**
> **with**
> **Hephaestus and Rain and shining Ether,**
> **anchored in the perfect harbours of Aphrodite,**
> **either a little more or less †where they were more†.**
> **And from them came blood and different forms of flesh.**
> [B 98]

Before these verses he refers in others to the activity of both [Love and Strife] in the same areas, as follows:

> **When Strife reaches the lowest depths**
> **of the whirl, and Love comes to be in the middle eddy,**
> **then all these things come together to be one alone,**
> **not suddenly, but coming together unwillingly, each from a**
> **different place.**
> **As they mingled, innumerable types of mortal things**
> **poured forth.**
> **But as they blended with one another, many stood**
> **unmixed –**
> **those which Strife, aloft, still holds; for not perfectly**
> **does it all stand out from them at the furthest limits of the**
> **circle,**
> **but parts of it remain in the members, and parts have**
> **stepped out.**
> **And as far as it ever ran out ahead, so far ever pursued**
> **the gentle, immortal onrush of perfect Love.**
> **And at once became mortal those things which formerly**
> **learned to be immortal,**
> **and mixed those which formerly were unmixed,**
> **interchanging their paths.**

As they mingled, innumerable types of mortal things
    poured forth,
fitted with every sort of shape, a wonder to see. [B 35.3–17]
Here he clearly says both that mortal things have been harmonized
by Love and that Strife does not yet all stand outside the areas where
Love predominates.

Again, in the verses where he states the characteristics of each of
the four elements and of Strife and Love, he clearly affirms the mixture
of both – of Strife and of Love – in all of them. Thus:

The sun, bright to see and everywhere hot,
the divine bodies, flooded †in heat† and shining light,
rain everywhere, dark and shivering,
and from earth flow forth things firm and solid.
In Anger they have different forms and are all apart,
but in Love they come together and are desired by one
    another.
For from these comes everything which was and which is
    and will be –
trees sprang up, and men and women
and beasts and birds and fish which feed in the water,
and even gods, long-lived, highest in honour. [B 21.3–12]
A little further on he says:
They have power in turn as the circle revolves,
and they decline into one another and increase in their
    allotted turn.
For these themselves exist, and running through one
    another
they become men and the other kinds of beasts,
now by Love coming together into one world,
now again each being carried apart by the hatred of
    Strife,
until having grown together as one, they are completely
    subdued.
Thus insofar as they have learned to become one from
    many
and again become many as the one grows apart,

**to that extent they come into being and have no lasting life;
but insofar as they never cease their continual change,
to that extent they exist forever, unmoving in a circle.** [B 26]
Thus both the one-from-many (which comes about because of Love)
and the many-from-one (which occurs when Strife predominates)
are seen by him in this sublunary world in which mortal things are
found, it being clear that at different times and for different periods
now Strife and now Love predominates.

(Simplicius, *Commentary on the* Physics 31.31–34.8)

The remaining fragments are grouped thematically.

(1) PARMENIDEAN ECHOES

*Certain lines in the passages just cited indicate that Empedocles was
aware of the Parmenidean objections to generation and change, and
that he hoped to have evaded them. Some further fragments have a
Parmenidean background.*

Then Colotes, as though he were talking to an unlettered king, fastens
next on Empedocles, as one who breathes the same doctrine:

**Another thing I will tell you: there is no birth for any
mortal thing, nor any cursed end in death;
only mixing and interchange of what is mixed,
those things are – but men name them birth.** [B 8]

(Plutarch, *Against Colotes* 1111F)

[Empedocles] was so far from upsetting what exists and fighting
against the appearances that he did not even banish the expressions
from ordinary language: rather, removing the harmful factual error
which they produced, he gave the words their customary use, in these
lines:

**When †they come into the air mixed† in the form of a man
or of a kind of wild beast or plant
or bird, then †they call this† coming into being;**

129

**and when they have separated off, this they call wretched
fate.**

**†They do not call things as they should† – but I myself also
subscribe to the convention. [B 9]**

Colotes himself cites these lines but does not notice that Empedocles
did not do away with men and beasts and plants and birds, which he
says are produced as the elements mix; and having pointed out their
mistake to those who call this association and dissociation **birth** and
wretched fate and **vengeful death** [B 10], he did not do away with
the use of the customary expressions for them.

Now I do not think that Empedocles is here upsetting our mode of
expression; rather, as I said earlier, he is in substantial disagreement
over generation from the non-existent, which some call birth. He
shows this most clearly in the following verses:

Fools – they have no far-ranging ideas:

**they suppose that what did not exist before comes into
being**

or that something may die and perish entirely. [B 11]

These are verses of one who shouts aloud to all who have ears that he
is not doing away with coming into being but only with coming into
being from what does not exist, nor with destruction but only with
complete destruction, i.e. destruction into what does not exist. If you
wish something gentler than that savagely simple denunciation, the
following passage might lead you to accuse him of excessive kindness.
Empedocles says:

No man wise in these things would suppose in his mind

that while men live – what they call life –

for so long do they exist and experience ill and good,

**but that before they were compacted as humans and after
they are dissolved they are nothing. [B 15]**

Those are the words not of one who denies that those who have been
born and are living exist, but rather of one who thinks that both those
who have not yet been born and those who have already died exist.

(Plutarch, *Against Colotes* 1113AD)

Again, even if it is quite impossible both for what does not exist to come into being and for what exists to perish, why should not some things nevertheless be generated and others eternal, as Empedocles says? For he too, having admitted all this – namely that

> **from what does not exist nothing can come into being,**
> **and for what exists to be destroyed is impossible and**
>   **unaccomplishable –**
> **for †there will it† always be, wherever anyone may press it**
> [B 12]

– nevertheless he says that some existent things are eternal (fire, water, earth, air) while the others come into being and have come into being from them.

> ([Aristotle], *On Melissus, Xenophanes, Gorgias* 975a36–b6)

Similarly, Empedocles says that all existent things are always continuously moving as they associate, and nothing is <empty> – he says:

> **No part of the universe is empty: whence, then, might**
>   **anything come?** [B 13]

And when they have been associated together into a single form, so as to be one, he says that nothing **is empty, nor yet overfull.** [B 14] For what prevents them from being carried into one another's places and from moving round simultaneously, one into the place of another, the other into that of another, and something else always changing into that of the first?

> ([Aristotle], *On Melissus, Xenophanes, Gorgias* 976b23–30)

(2) THE 'ROOTS', LOVE AND STRIFE

Parmenides is right to reject generation and destruction: the items which really exist – the four elements or 'roots' and the twin powers of Love and Strife – are eternal. The roots are described more than once:

Empedocles [derives everything] from four items:

> **Hear first the four roots of all things:**
> **bright Zeus and life-bringing Hera and Aidoneus,**

and Nestis, who waters the human stream with her tears.
[B 6]
(Sextus Empiricus, *Against the Mathematicians* X 315)

It is better to think of the ether as containing and binding everything, as Empedocles says:

Come and I will tell you †. . .†
from which all the things we now see came to be:
earth and the billowy sea and the damp air,
Titan, and the ether, binding everything in a circle. [B 38]
(Clement, *Miscellanies* V viii 48.3)

There will be no such thing as growth according to Empedocles – except by way of addition; for fire increases by fire

and earth increases her own shape, ether increases ether.
[B 37]

But these are additions, and what grows is not thought to grow in this way.   (Aristotle, *On Generation and Corruption* 333a35–b3)

Some think that [the word *anopaia*] is used in the sense of 'upward'. They refer to Empedocles, who says of fire:

And swiftly upward [*anopaion*] . . . [B 51]
(Eustathius, *Commentary on the* Odyssey I 321)

Love and Strife are frequently presented as the causal powers in the universe:

The creator and maker of the generation of everything which has come into being is deadly Strife, while the change and departure from the world of what has come into being, and the restoration of the One, is the work of Love. Empedocles says that the two of them are immortal and ungenerated and never had a beginning of generation – he writes as follows:

For they are as they were before and as they will be, nor
**   ever, I think,**
will boundless eternity be emptied of these two. [B 16]

What are these two? – Love and Strife.

(Hippolytus, *Refutation of All Heresies* VII xxix 9–10)

Perhaps even though Strife predominates in this world and Love in the Sphere, yet both are said to be produced by both. There is no reason why we should not set down some of Empedocles' verses which make this clear:

But I shall come back again to the path of songs
which I traced before, channelling from that account
this one: when Strife reaches the lowest depths
of the whirl, and Love comes to be in the middle eddy,
then all these things come together to be one alone,
not suddenly, but coming together unwillingly, each from a
    different place.
As they mingled, innumerable types of mortal things
    poured forth.
But as they blended with one another, many stood
    unmixed –
those which Strife, aloft, still holds; for not perfectly
does it all stand out from them at the furthest limits of the
    circle,
but parts of it remain in the members, and parts have
    stepped out.
And as far as it ever ran out ahead, so far ever pursued
the gentle, immortal onrush of perfect Love.
And at once became mortal those things which formerly
    learned to be immortal,
and mixed those which formerly were unmixed,
    interchanging their paths. [B 35.1–15]

Here it is made clear that in the creation of the world Strife draws back and Love predominates when it **comes to be in the middle eddy** [B 35.4], i.e. of the whirl; hence the whirl exists even when Love predominates. It is clear too that some of the elements remain unmixed by Strife, while those which mix make mortal animals and plants, since what mixes is again dissolved. And speaking about the generation of eyes – of these corporeal eyes – he says:

From which divine Aphrodite compacted tireless eyes . . .
[B 86]

and a little later:

Aphrodite, having fitted them with pegs of affection . . .
[B 87]

And explaining why some see better by day and others by night, he says:

When first they grew together at the hands of Cypris . . .
[B 95]

He is speaking about the things in this world, as you may read in the following verses:

If your trust was at all defective on any of these matters –
how, when water and earth and ether and sun
were blended, the forms and colour of mortal things came
into being,
as many as there are now, harmonized by Aphrodite . . .
[B 71]

And a little later:

So then Cypris, when she had moistened earth in rain,
busily
making forms, gave them to swift fire to harden. [B 73]

And again:

Those which have been compacted dense inside but loose
outside,
chancing upon such a fluidity in the hands of Cypris . . .
[B 75]

I have set down these verses from the first few I hit upon.

(Simplicius, *Commentary on* On the Heavens 528.30–530.1)

There is reason to place in this group (and to connect with B 71) a second piece of the Strasbourg Papyrus:

<. . .> rock-dwelling <. . .>
<There you will see> **earth** <dwelling on top of> **flesh;**
<and the carapace> **of strong-backed <. . .>**
<yes, and> **of stony-skinned sea-snails** <and of tortoises,>

<. . .> **spears of horned stags** <. . .>
<But I should not end> **were I to recount all.**

(Empedocles, On Nature [Strasbourg Papyrus b])

Two of the lines in this snippet are quoted by Plutarch, who adds a third to them:

You see that God, our noble craftsman as Pindar called him, did not everywhere send fire up and earth down, but arranged them as the needs of bodies demanded.

> **So in shellfish, heavy-backed sea-dwellers –**
> **yes, and of stony-skinned sea-snails and of tortoises,**

says Empedocles,

> **there you will see earth dwelling on top of flesh.** [B 76]

(Plutarch, Table Talk 618B)

On a third piece of the Strasbourg Papyrus only a handful of letters can be made out, but the text was almost certainly the following passage:

For Empedocles says that here too [in the sublunary world] Love and Strife predominate in turn over men and fish and beasts and birds. He writes as follows:

> **. . . in the splendid mass of human members:**
> **now by Love we all come together into one,**
> **limbs which have acquired a body when life is thriving at its**
>   **peak;**
> **now again, divided by evil Conflicts,**
> **each wanders apart along the shore of life.**
> **So too is it with plants and fish of the watery halls**
> **and beasts of the mountain lairs and flying gulls.** [B 20]

(Simplicius, Commentary on the Physics 1124.9–18 = Strasbourg
Papyrus c)

Empedocles calls [Aphrodite] **life-giving.** [B 151]

(Plutarch, On Love 756E)

(3) CAUSATION

If Love and Strife are the primary cosmic agents, Empedocles sometimes ascribes causal powers to the elements themselves, he sometimes invokes the force of necessity, and he sometimes appears to allow room in the universe for chance events.

In general, fire separates and divides, water is adhesive and retentive, conserving and fixing things by its moisture. Empedocles alluded to this every time he referred to fire as **cursed Strife** [cf. B 17.19] and to water as **tenacious Love.** [B 19]   (Plutarch, *The Primary Cold* 952B)

[Love] collects and conjoins and conserves, consolidating by conversation and friendliness –
    as when rennet pegs and ties white milk [B 33],
as Empedocles says (for love likes to make such unity and cohesion).
                                    (Plutarch, *On Having Many Friends* 95A)

The moist causes the dry to be bounded, and each is a sort of glue for the other, as Empedocles said in his *Physics*:
    ... having glued barley-meal with water [B 34]
– and for this reason the bounded body is made of both.
                                    (Aristotle, *Meteorology* 381b31–382a3)

Eudemus takes it that the period of motionlessness occurs under the dominance of Love during the Sphere, when everything has been associated:
    there neither the swift limbs of the sun are discerned
        [B 27.1],
but, as he says,
    in this way it is held fast in the dense secrecy of Harmony,
    a rounded Sphere, rejoicing in the surrounding solitude.
        [B 27.3–4]
When Strife has again begun to predominate, then again motion occurs in the Sphere:

For all the limbs of the god shook, one after another. [B 31]
What is the difference between saying 'because that is its nature' and
saying 'by necessity', without adding any explanation? That is what
Empedocles appears to say in the line:

They have power in turn as time revolves [B 17.29],

and again where he makes necessity the cause of what comes into
being:

**There is an oracle of necessity, an ancient decree of the
    gods,
eternal, sealed with broad oaths.** [B 115.1–2]

For he says that each predominates in turn because of necessity and
these oaths. Empedocles says this too of the predominance of Strife:

**But when Strife had been nurtured great in the members
and rose to office as the time was completed
which had been marked for them alternately by the broad
    oath ...** [B 30]

Now [Aristotle] says that to say this without any explanation is simply
to say that 'that is its nature'.

(Simplicius, *Commentary on the* Physics 1183.28–1184.18)

Necessity is unmusical, Persuasion musical – †she loves† the Muses
far more, I should say, than Empedocles' Grace and **hates intolerable
necessity.** [B 116]   (Plutarch, *Table Talk* 745D)

Strife dissociated them; but ether was carried upwards not by Strife
but, as he sometimes says, as if by chance –

**Then it happened to come together, running in this way –
    but often otherwise** [B 53]

– and sometimes he says that fire is naturally carried upwards, while
ether, he says,

sank with long roots into the earth. [B 54]

(Aristotle, *On Generation and Corruption* 334a1–5)

It is equally absurd if they supposed that [chance] does not exist or if
they believed in it but set it aside – especially since they sometimes
make use of it, as when Empedocles says that air does not always

separate off to the highest point, but as chance has it. Thus he says in his cosmogony that

> **then it happened to come together, running in this way –**
> **but often otherwise** [B 53];

And he says that the parts of animals are mostly formed by chance.

(Aristotle, *Physics* 196a20–24)

That [the early natural scientists] had some notion of things happening by chance is shown by the fact that they sometimes use the word – as Empedocles says that fire does not always separate off upwards but as chance has it. Thus he says in his cosmogony that

> **then it happened to be running in this way, but often**
> **otherwise** [B 53],

and elsewhere:

> **... as they all happened to come together.** [B 59.2]

And he says that the parts of animals are mostly formed by chance, as when he says:

> **Earth, roughly equal to them, happened to come**
> **together ...** [B 98. 1];

and again:

> **Gentle flame chanced on a little earth** [B 85];

and elsewhere:

> **Chancing upon such a fluidity in the hands of Cypris.**
> [B 75.2]

You could produce many other examples of this sort from Empedocles' *Physics*, such as:

> **There by the will of chance all things think** [B 103];

and a little later:

> **And insofar as the most rare-textured things happened to**
> **come together as they fell.** [B 104]

But [Empedocles], who seems to use chance only in small matters, does not merit much attention, not having explained what chance is.   (Simplicius, *Commentary on the* Physics 330.31–331.16)

As for the mechanics of causation, Empedocles' 'physics' and his 'chemistry' depend on a theory of effluences and channels:

Consider the matter, then, having with Empedocles recognized that
**there are effluences from all things that have come into
being** [B 89]
– for not only animals and plants and earth and sea, but stones too,
and bronze and iron, continuously give off numerous streams.

(Plutarch, *Scientific Explanations* 916D)

You should not think of such images [in mirrors] in the way in which
Democritus and Epicurus did, nor say with Empedocles that effluences
come from each object mirrored. [B 109a]

(anonymous *Commentary on the* First Alcibiades,
Oxyrhynchus Papyrus 1609)

Empedocles said – as Aristotle stated in *On Generation and Corruption*
– that in all sublunary things (water, oil, etc.) channels and solid parts
are mingled. He called the channels hollow and the solid parts dense.
Where the solid parts and the channels, i.e. the hollow and the dense
parts, are commensurate in such a way as to pass through one another,
he said that mixing and blending take place (for example water and
wine), but where they are incommensurate, he said they do not mix
(for example oil and water); for he says that water
**has an affinity with wine, but with oil
it will not ...** [B 91]
Applying this to all bodies, he attempted to explain the sterility of
mules.

(Michael of Ephesus, *Commentary on the
Generation of Animals* 123.13–21)

A varied diet sends from itself into the mass of the body numerous
qualities and distributes to each part what is appropriate; so that there
occurs what Empedocles described:
**Thus sweet grasped sweet and bitter set upon bitter,
sharp came to sharp, and †hot coupled with hot†.** [B 90]

(Plutarch, *Table Talk* 663A)

Different things are appropriate and fitting to different things, as blue copper and purple or nitre and saffron seem to make a mixed dye –
the gleam of bright saffron is mixed with the linen [B 93],
as Empedocles said.   (Plutarch, *On the Decline of Oracles* 433B)

Again, a joint exists in a way for the sake of locomotion (which is why Empedocles wrote
†**a joint binds two things**† [B 32]),
whereas points are found also in immovable items.
       ([Aristotle], *On Indivisible Lines* 972b29–31)

(4) THE SPHERE

Periodically, all the roots are intermingled to form a divine and homo-geneous Sphere, with Love at its centre and Strife banished to its surface:

About the form which the world has when it is being arranged by Love he says this:
There are no two branches springing from its back,
no feet, no swift legs, no generative organs:
it was a Sphere, equal to itself . . . [B 29]
Such is the most beautiful form of the world which Love makes, One from many.   (Hippolytus, *Refutation of All Heresies* VII xxix 13–14)

That is why the sage of Acragas, having criticized the stories of anthropomorphic gods told by the poets, added – speaking in the first instance about Apollo (with whom his argument was immediately concerned), but also in the same way about every divinity –
For it is not furnished with a human head on its limbs,
there are no two branches springing from its back,
no feet, no swift legs, no hairy genitals:
merely a mind, holy and unutterable,
rushing with rapid thought over the whole world. [B 134]
       (Ammonius, *Commentary on* On Interpretation 249.1–10)

Beware that, in changing and removing everything to its natural place, you do not dissolve the world and introduce Empedocles' Strife – or rather stir up the old Titans and the Giants against nature – and long to see that mythical and fearful chaos and horror, separating everything heavy and everything light:

There neither the bright form of the sun †is seen†

nor the shaggy power of the earth, nor the sea [cf. B 27.1–2],

as Empedocles says.   (Plutarch, *On the Face in the Moon* 926E)

And it, from all directions equal to itself and completely boundless,

a rounded Sphere, rejoicing in the surrounding solitude, ...
  [B 28]

(Stobaeus, *Anthology* I xv 2)

(The last text is cited anonymously by Stobaeus: the ascription to Emped-ocles is a plausible conjecture.)

(5) THE FOUR GENERATIONS

The state of Separation is not described in detail in the surviving frag-ments. But note the stray line (quoted by Stobaeus as though it were continuous with B 6):

When they were coming together, Strife was standing out to the furthest limit. [B 36]

(Stobaeus, *Anthology* I x 11)

Between Separation and Sphere two chief stages of life were distinguished, and two again between Sphere and Separation:

Empedocles says that the first generations of animals are not at all whole but disjointed and with uncombined parts; the second generations, when the parts are combined, are monstrous; the third

are the generations of whole-natured things; the fourth no longer
come to be from homogeneous items but rather from one another.

([Plutarch], *Opinions of the Philosophers on Nature* 908DE)

Several fragments refer to the disjointed and the monstrous generations:

[Aristotle] asks whether there could not then have been a disorderly
motion which produced certain mixtures . . . of the sort which Empedocles says come about in the time of Love
>   **where many neckless heads sprang up.** [B 57.1]

. . . But how could a mixture be signified by a neckless head and by
the other things described by Empedocles when he says:
>   **Naked arms wandered, devoid of shoulders,**
>   **and eyes strayed alone, begging for foreheads** [B 57.2–3],

and many other things which are certainly not examples of mixtures
from which natural objects are compounded? . . . Perhaps Empedocles
does not mean that these things come about under the predominance
of Love (as Alexander thought) but rather at the time when Strife
does not yet
>   **all stand out at the furthest limits of the circle,**
>   **but parts of it remain in the members, and parts have**
>   **stepped out.**
>   **And as far as it** (he means Strife) **ever ran out ahead, so far**
>   **ever pursued**
>   **the gentle, immortal onrush of perfect Love.** [B 35.10–13]

So in this world the limbs, still 'single-membered' from the dissociation of Strife, strayed and desired to mix with one another.
>   **But when,** he says, **god mingled more with god**

– when Love achieved complete predominance over Strife –
>   **these things fell together as they all happened to come**
>   **together,**
>   **and many others in addition to these continuously came**
>   **into being.** [B 59]

Thus Empedocles said that the former phenomena occur under Love,
not in the sense that Love was already predominant but in the sense

that she was about to predominate and was still showing unmixed
and single-membered things.

(Simplicius, Commentary on On the Heavens 586.6–7,
10–12, 29–587.4, 12–26)

Empedocles the natural scientist, who also speaks of the peculiarities
of animals, says that some hybrids were generated, different in the
blending of their forms but connected by the unity of their bodies.
These are his words:

> **Many were born double-headed and double-chested –**
> **man-faced oxen arose, and again**
> **ox-headed men – creatures mixed partly from male**
> **and partly from female nature, fitted with dark limbs.** [B 61]

(Aelian, On Animals XVI 29)

These things, and many others more dramatic, are like the monsters
of Empedocles which the [Epicureans] laugh at – the **lumberers with
countless hands** [B 60] and the **man-faced oxen**. [B 61.2]

(Plutarch, Against Colotes 1123B)

The third generations are described in this passage:

In the second book of his *Physics*, before discussing the articulation
of male and female bodies, Empedocles has these verses:

> **Come now, hear how the shoots of men and piteous women**
> **were raised at night by fire, as it separated,**
> **thus – for my story does not miss the mark, nor is it**
> **ill-informed:**
> **first, whole-natured forms arose from the earth,**
> **having a portion of both water and heat.**
> **Fire sent them up, wishing to come to its like,**
> **and they showed as yet no desirable shape in their**
> **members,**
> **nor any voice, nor †speech† native to man.** [B 62]

(Simplicius, Commentary on the Physics 381.29–382.3)

(6) THE FOURTH GENERATIONS

The fourth generations are the generations of the world which we know and inhabit. Empedocles took a black view of our position in it:

> To fall apart from one another and meet their fate
> most unwillingly, by dismal necessity
> rotting; and for us who now have Love and Good Will,
> the Harpies with the lot of death will <be with us.>
> Alas that the pitiless day <did not destroy> me first,
> <before> with my claws I practised the terrible deeds of eating.
> <But> in vain in that storm did I drench my cheeks;
> for we are approaching, I think, <the whirl> with its many
>   depths,
> <and countless pains> will afflict our hearts against our will
> <. . .> But we shall again embark you on those accounts:
> <. . .> the tireless flame came about
> <. . .> bringing a blending full of woe
> <. . .> capable of reproduction, were born
> <. . .> even now the dawn beholds their remains
> <. . .> I went to the furthermost place.
>
> (Empedocles, *On Nature* [Strasbourg Papyrus **d**])

(Lines 4–5 of this piece are quoted by Porphyry, On Abstinence II 31 – *in the fragment known as B 139.)*

Heraclitus is clearly berating birth when he says:
Being born, they wish to live and to meet their doom (or rather, to rest), **and they leave behind children, born for their doom** [22 B 20], and Empedocles plainly agrees with him when he says:
> I wept and I lamented as I saw the unfamiliar country.
> [B 118]

And again:
> For from living things it made corpses, changing their
>   forms. [B 125]

And again:

> **Alas, wretched race of mortals, unhappy ones,**
> **from what conflicts and what groans did you come into**
>   **being.** [B 124]

> (Clement, *Miscellanies* III iii 14.1–2)

The Pythagoreans, and after them Plato, declared that the world was a cave or cavern. For in Empedocles, the powers which guide souls say:

> **We have come to this roofed cave** [B 120],

and in Plato, in the seventh Book of the *Republic* . . .

> (Porphyry, *The Cave of the Nymphs* 8)

For man descends and leaves the place of happiness, as Empedocles the Pythagorean says:

> **exile from the gods and a wanderer,**
> **trusting in mad Strife** . . . [B 115.13–14]

But he ascends and resumes his old condition if he escapes earthly things and the **pleasureless country** [B 121.1], as the same man says,

> **where are Slaughter and Rage and the tribes of other**
>   **Plagues.** [B 121.2]

Those who fall into this country

> **wander in the darkness on the meadows of Ruin.** [B 121.4]

> (Hierocles, *Commentary on the* Golden Verses XXIV 2)

It is not true, as Menander says, that

> By every man a spirit stands,
> from birth: a guide for his life,
> a good one.

Rather, as Empedocles says, two fates or spirits take over and govern each of us when we are born –

> **there were Earth and far-seeing Sun,**
> **bloody Discord and grave-faced Harmony,**
> **Beauty and Ugliness, Speed and Slowness,**
> **desirable Clearness and black-eyed Obscurity.** [B 122]

> (Plutarch, *On Tranquillity of Mind* 474 BC)

After that comes the generation of the so-called Titans. They must represent the differences among things. For Empedocles enumerates them in scientific terms –

Birth and Death, Sleep and Wakefulness,
Motion and Rest, much-garlanded Greatness
†and Lowliness, Silence and Speech† [B 123],

and many others – he is clearly hinting at the variety of things.

(Cornutus, *Summary of Greek Theology* 17)

We, once the sons of lawlessness, are now by the philanthropy of the Word become sons of God; but as for you, your own poet, Empedocles of Acragas, says:

For that reason, distraught by cruel evils,
you will never relieve your heart from wretched pains.
[B 145]

(Clement, *Protreptic* II 27.3)

The same [grammatical construction] is also found in Empedocles when he says:

Him neither the roofed halls of sceptre-bearing Zeus
nor the roof of Hades receives . . . [B 142]

(Demetrius of Laconia, [title unknown], Herculaneum Papyrus 1012, col. XL 5–10)

(7) OUR WORLD

This group of texts describes various features of the world of the fourth generations:

(a) Sun and Moon

Apollo is called Eleleus because he turns [*elittesthai*] round the earth . . . or because he orbits in a collected mass of fire, as, Empedocles says:

Hence, collected together, he orbits the great heaven. [B 41]

(Macrobius, *Saturnalia* I xvii 46)

You Stoics laugh at Empedocles when he says that the sun, which
is produced about the earth by the reflection of heavenly light,
again
>   **shines back on Olympus with fearless face.** [B 44]
>   (Plutarch, *Why the Pythia No Longer Prophesies in Verse* 400B)

The pegs on sundials are instruments and measures of time, not by
changing along with the shadows but by staying still, imitating the
part of the earth which blocks the sun as it travels beneath it – as
Empedocles says,
>   **Earth makes night by standing in the way of the light.** [B 48]
>   (Plutarch, *Platonic Questions* 1006E)

In the dark air
>   **of deserted, blind-eyed night** [B 49],
as Empedocles puts it . . .   (Plutarch, *Table Talk* 720E)

Empedocles expresses their difference charmingly:
>   **sharp-arrowed sun and gentle moon.** [B 40]
>   (Plutarch, *On the Face in the Moon* 920C)

[The moon] pretty well touches the earth and, orbiting near it,
>   **†turns, like the axle-box† of a chariot**
– as Empedocles puts it –
>   **which †skirts the edge† <of the post>.** [B 46]
>   (Plutarch, *On the Face in the Moon* 925B)

The moon herself is invisible then, and she has often hidden [the sun]
and made it disappear –
>   **she blocked its light,**
as Empedocles says,
>   **†as it travelled† above, and obscured as much of the earth**
>   **as the bright-eyed moon is broad.** [B 42]
>   (Plutarch, *On the Face in the Moon* 929CD)

Just as voices when reflected give an echo fainter than the original utterance, and the blows of ricocheting missiles strike with less violence,

so the sunlight, having struck the broad circle of the moon
[B 43],

flows weakly and dimly to us, its force diminished by the deflection.

(Plutarch, *On the Face in the Moon* 929E)

Some say that the sun is first, the moon second, Saturn third; but according to the general view, the moon is first, since they say that it is actually a fragment from the sun – so Empedocles:

In a circle round the earth she winds, another's light.
[B 45]

(Achilles, *Introduction to Aratus* 16)

Pure [*agês*]: this is taken from the compound *euagês* or *panagês*. Empedocles:

For opposite she observes the pure circle of the king. [B 47]
(anonymous *Useful Expressions, Anecdota Graeca* I 337.13–15
Bekker)

(b) The Earth

Some say that downwards the earth is limitless (for example Xenophanes of Colophon), so that they need not take the trouble to look for an explanation [of why the earth is at rest]. That is why Empedocles criticized them, saying:

If the depths of the earth are boundless and the ether immense,
as the tongues of many mouths have vainly said
and poured forth, seeing little of the whole ... [B 39]
(Aristotle, *On the Heavens* 294a21–28)

There are streams of fire under the earth, as Empedocles somewhere says:

Many fires burn beneath the ground. [B 52]
(Proclus, *Commentary on the* Timaeus II 8.26–28)

Empedocles:

Salt was compacted, forced by the beatings of the sun.
[B 56]

(Hephaestion, *Handbook* I iii 4)

Poseidon is commanded by Iris who calls him either to the sea or to the gods, as Empedocles or someone else says:

Iris brings wind or much rain from the sea. [B 50]

(Tzetzes, *Allegories in the* Iliad XV 86)

It is equally absurd for anyone to think, like Empedocles, that when he says that sea is earth's sweat [B 55], he has said something illuminating. (Aristotle, *Meteorology* 357a25–26)

(c) Plants and animals

If the air continuously favoured [the trees], then perhaps not even what the poets say would seem unreasonable – as Empedocles says that, evergreen and ever-fruiting [B 77], they flourish

throughout the year with abundant fruit, thanks to the air.
[B 78]

(He supposes that a certain blending of the air – the spring blending – is common to all seasons.)

(Theophrastus, *Causes of Plants* I xiii 2)

[Plants] reproduce from themselves, and the so-called seeds which they produce are not semen but embryos – Empedocles puts this well when he says:

Thus tall trees lay eggs: first, olives ... [B 79]

For an egg is an embryo. (Aristotle, *Generation of Animals* 731a1–6)

Empedocles says:

Hence pomegranates are late-fruiting and apples
    exceptionally sweet [*huperphloa*]. [B 80]

... In what sense the sage called apples *huperphloa* is a puzzle, especially as the man is not one to embellish the facts, for the sake of fine writing, with showy epithets (as with gorgeous colours) but rather makes each one a sign of an essence or power – as **man-enclosing earth** [B 148] for the body which contains the soul, **cloud-gathering** [B 149] for the air, and **blood-rich** [B 150] for the liver.

(Plutarch, *Table Talk* 683DE)

Concoction seems to be a sort of rotting, as Empedocles indicates when he says:

Wine is water from the bark which has rotted in the wood.
[B 81]

(Plutarch, *Scientific Explanations* 912C)

I am aware that Empedocles the natural scientist used the word *kamasênes* to cover all fish in general:

How the tall trees and the fish [*kamasênes*] of the sea . . .
[B 72]

(Athenaeus, *Deipnosophists* 334B)

As for animals themselves, you could not find any creature of land or air as prolific as all the creatures of the sea are. With that in mind, Empedocles wrote:

Leading the unmusical tribe of fertile fish . . . [B 74]

(Plutarch, *Table Talk* 685F)

Most of the irrational animals are better endowed by fortune and nature than we are. Some are armed with horns and teeth and stings,

and as for hedgehogs,

Empedocles says,

sharp-arrowed hairs bristle on their backs. [B 83]

Others are shod and clothed with scales and fur and claws and hard hoofs.

(Plutarch, *On Fortune* 98D)

(d) Biology

Empedocles and Democritus touched lightly on nature in the sense of form; for Empedocles, by placing Strife and Love among the principles as causes of form, and Democritus, by talking of shape and position and order, determine form, I suppose, by the ratio in which each item is made. He makes flesh and bone and the rest by a certain ratio – in the first book of the *Physics* he says:

Kindly earth in her well-made hollows
received of the eight parts two of bright Nestis
and four of Hephaestus. And white bones came into being,
wonderfully fitted together by the glue of Harmony [B 96]

– i.e. by divine causes, and in particular by Love or Harmony.

(Simplicius, *Commentary on the* Physics 300.16–26)

Vapour from woody bodies is smoke – I mean from bones and hair and everything else of that sort. They have not got a name in common, but none the less they are all the same by analogy, as Empedocles says:

The same are hair and leaves and the thick feathers of birds
and scales on strong members. [B 82]

(Aristotle, *Meteorology* 387b1–6)

When the sows live and feed together with the hogs it puts them in mind of sex and stimulates their desire. Empedocles says the same of humans:

And on him came desire †. . .† [B 64]

(Plutarch, *Scientific Explanations* 917C)

Empedocles the natural scientist allegorizes and speaks of the divided meadows of Aphrodite [B 66] wherein the generation of children takes place. (Scholia to Euripides, *Phoenician Women* 18)

Others of the older generation have also said that the male is conceived in the right-hand part of the womb. Parmenides put it like this:

In the right-hand parts boys, in the left girls [28 B 17];

and Empedocles says this:

For in the warmer limb was the male portion [B 67]

– and for that reason men are dark and more masculine and more hairy.

(Galen, *Commentary on Hippocrates'* Epidemics Book 6 XVIIA 1002)

Again, suppose that male and female are differentiated during gestation, as Empedocles says –

**they were poured into pure places: some flourish as women,
meeting with cold . . .** [B 65]

(Aristotle, *Generation of Animals* 723a23–25)

The body of the semen cannot be separated, part in the female and part in the male, as Empedocles says:

**But the nature of the members is separated, part in a
man's . . .** [B 63]

(Aristotle, *Generation of Animals* 764b15–18)

Empedocles knew of the double time of births: that is why he calls women **twice-bearing**. [B 69]

(Proclus, *Commentary on the* Republic II 34)

The embryo is enclosed in membranes, one of them fine and soft – Empedocles calls it the **lambkin**. [B 70]

(Rufus of Ephesus, *Names of the Parts of Man* 229)

Milk is blood concocted, not decomposed. Empedocles either misunderstood this or else used a poor metaphor when he said that milk **on the tenth day of the eighth month was white pus.** [B 68]

For rotting and concocting are opposites; and pus is a rotting whereas milk is something concocted.

(Aristotle, *Generation of Animals* 777a8–12)

Baubô: the nurse of Demeter; it also means belly, as in Empedocles. [B 153]   (Hesychius, s.v. *baubô*)

[Empedocles] says that inhalation and exhalation occur because there are certain vessels which contain blood (but are not full of blood) and which have channels leading into the external air, narrower than the parts of the body but broader than those of the air. Hence, since the blood naturally moves up and down, when it moves down the air flows in and inhalation occurs, and when it moves up the air goes outside and exhalation occurs. He compares the phenomenon to clepsydras:

> Everything inhales and exhales like this: all have bloodless
> tubes of flesh stretched over the surface of their bodies
> and at their mouths close-packed furrows are pierced
> all over the outer surface of the skin, so that the blood
> remains inside but routes are cut to give easy passage to the
>   ether.
> Whenever the soft blood rushes from them,
> the bubbling ether rushes down with a wild swell,
> and when it leaps back, it exhales again. As when a girl
> plays with a clepsydra of shining bronze –
> when she covers the neck of the tube with her pretty hand
> and dips it into the soft shape of shining water,
> no rain enters the vessel, but it is held back
> by the mass of air which presses from within on the
>   close-packed holes
> until she uncovers the dense stream. And then,
> as the breath leaves, water enters in proportion.
> Just so, when she holds the water in the depths of the
>   bronze,
> the neck and channel being blocked by human flesh,
> the ether outside valiantly holds the rain inside
> at the gates of the harsh-sounding strainer, controlling the
>   surface,
> until she releases it with her hand. Then again, the reverse
>   of before,
> as the air enters, water runs out in proportion.
> Just so with the soft blood pulsing through the limbs –
> whenever it rushes back into the recess,

**a stream of ether at once comes down swelling and surging,
and when it leaps back, it exhales again in equal quantity.**
[B 100]

(Aristotle, *On Respiration* 473b1–474a6)

(e) Perception and thought

Empedocles [says that the soul] is composed of all the elements and
that each of them actually is a soul. He says:

**For by earth we see earth, by water water,
by ether bright ether, and by fire destructive fire,
Love by Love and Strife by dismal Strife.** [B 109]

(Aristotle, *On the Soul* 404b11–15)

Empedocles seems to think that sometimes (as I said before) we see
when light leaves the eyes. At any rate, he says this:

**As when someone, intending a journey, prepares a lamp,
a flame of flashing fire through the winter night,
fastening the lantern-sides as protection against all the
      winds,
which divert the breeze when the winds blow,
but the light leaps through outside, inasmuch as it is
      finer-textured,
and illuminates the ground with its tireless rays:
so then the ancient fire, guarded in the membranes
and fine tissues, lies in ambush in the round pupil;
and they hold back the deep water which flows around,
but let the fire pass through inasmuch as it is finer-textured.**
[B 84]

Sometimes he says we see in this way, sometimes by effluences from
the objects seen.

(Aristotle, *On the Senses and their Objects* 437b23–438a5)

As Empedocles says,

from both [eyes] **comes a single vision.** [B 88]

(Strabo, *Geography* VIII v 3)

Do hounds, as Empedocles says,

> **tracking with their nostrils the fragments of animal
> members** [B 101.1],

pick up the effluences which the beasts leave on the matter?

(Plutarch, *Scientific Explanations* 917E)

Why do hounds not smell the tracks when the hare is dead? When it
is alive they perceive it because the smell is continuously given off by
the animal; but when it is dead the smell ceases to flow. For the smell
is not left behind in the way in which Empedocles says:

> **It leaves from its feet in the soft grass . . .** [B 101.2]

([Alexander], *Problems* 22.7)

Breathing is presumably a cause of smell not in itself but accidentally, as is clear from the case of animals and from the facts
just mentioned. But again at the end [of his account] Empedocles –
as if he were setting his seal on it – speaks as though this were the
cause:

> **Thus have all things been allotted breath and smells.** [B 102]

(Theophrastus, *On the Senses* 22)

Why does water look white on the surface but black in the depths? Is
it because depth is the mother of blackness inasmuch as it blunts and
weakens the rays of the sun before they descend, whereas the surface,
because it is immediately affected by the sun, can receive the whiteness
of the light? This is the view that Empedocles accepts:

> **In the bottom of the river the shadows make the colour
> black,**
> **and the same is seen in hollow caverns.** [B 94]

(Plutarch, *Scientific Explanations* 39)

(This last text survives only in Latin translation.)

Empedocles seems to treat the blood as the organ of understanding:

> **Nourished in seas of churning blood
> where what men call thought is especially found –**

for the blood about the heart is thought for men. [B 105]

(Porphyry, *On the Styx*, fragment 377 Smith, in
Stobaeus, *Anthology* I xlix 53)

In general, because they suppose that thought is perception and perception a sort of alteration, they say that what appears to perception is necessarily true. For these reasons Empedocles and Democritus and virtually all the others have been guilty of such opinions. Thus Empedocles says that our thoughts change as our condition changes:

For men's wit grows in relation to what is present. [B 106]

And elsewhere he says that

**Insofar as they become different, to that extent always
does their thought too present different objects.** [B 108]

(Aristotle, *Metaphysics* 1009b12–21)

Thinking, [Empedocles says,] depends on similars, ignorance on dissimilars, as though thought were the same as or similar to perception. For having enumerated the ways in which we recognize each thing by its like, at the end he adds that from these

**all things are harmonized and compacted,
and by these they think and feel pleasure and pain.** [B 107]

That is why we think especially with our blood; for in this the elements of the parts are best blended. (Theophrastus, *On the Senses* 10)

(8) REINCARNATION

The spirits whose crime is referred to in B 115 are condemned to a sequence of incarnations. These spirits are, or include, us; and thus Empedocles subscribes to the Pythagorean doctrine of metempsychosis or the transmigration of the soul.

The fate or nature of the change of shape itself is called by Empedocles a spirit which

wraps in an unrecognizable garment of flesh [B 126]

and gives the souls their new clothing.

(Porphyry, fragment 382, in Stobaeus, *Anthology* I xlix 60)

Empedocles says that the best change of dwelling for a man is to become a lion, if death changes him into an animal, and a laurel, if into a plant. This is what he says:

Among the beasts they become lions, mountain-laired,
sleeping on the ground,
and laurels among fair-tressed trees. [B 127]

(Aelian, *On Animals* XII 7)

Above all, [Empedocles] assents to the idea of reincarnation, saying:

For already have I become a boy and a girl
and a bush and a bird and a silent fish in the sea. [B 117]

He said that all souls change into every sort of animal.

(Hippolytus, *Refutation of All Heresies* I iii 2)

For some, the series of incarnations has a happy end:

Empedocles too says that the souls of the wise become gods. This is what he writes:

Finally, they are seers and hymnodists and doctors
and princes among earth-dwelling men;
and then they arise as gods, highest in honour. [B 146]

(Clement, *Miscellanies* IV xxiii 150.1)

If we live in a holy and just fashion, we shall be blessed here and more blessed after our departure hence, not possessing happiness for a period of time but being able to rest for eternity

at the same hearth and table as the other immortals,
relieved of mortal pains, tireless [B 147],

as Empedocles' philosophical poem puts it.

(Clement, *Miscellanies* V xiv 122.3)

(9) ETHICS

The doctrine of metempsychosis appeared to have implications for practical ethics.

As everyone somehow surmises, there is by nature a common justice and injustice, even if there is no shared community nor even a contract ... as Empedocles says about not killing living things: it is not the case that this is just for some and not just for others,

> **but this, a law for all, through the broad**
> **ether ever extends and through the boundless sunlight.**
>
> [B 135]

(Aristotle, *Rhetoric* 1373b6–9, 14–17)

Pythagoras and Empedocles and the rest of the Italians say that we have a community not only with one another and with the gods but also with the irrational animals. For there is a single spirit which pervades the whole world like a soul and which unites us with them. That is why, if we kill them and eat their flesh, we commit injustice and impiety, inasmuch as we are destroying our kin. Hence these philosophers urged us to abstain from meat ... Empedocles somewhere says:

> **Will you not cease from harsh-sounding slaughter? Do you**
> **not see**
> **that it is one another you devour in the carelessness of your**
> **thought?** [B 136]

And:

> **A father lifts up his own son, changed in form,**
> **and prays and slaughters him, the fool, †while he cries**
> **pitifully,†**
> **beseeching his sacrificer. But he, deaf to his cries,**
> **slaughters him in the halls and prepares an evil feast.**
> **Just so, a son takes his father, children their mother:**
> **they bereave them of life and eat the dear flesh.** [B 137]

(Sextus Empiricus, *Against the Mathematicians* IX 127–129)

When their leaves are torn off, plants as it were feel pain and are hurt, and they suffer a harmful wound and an unseemly nudity; and it seems that one should not only, with Empedocles,

keep altogether from the leaves of the laurel [B 140],
but also spare all other trees. (Plutarch, *Table Talk* 646D)

The mistake about not eating beans seems to have arisen because in a poem of Empedocles, who followed the teachings of Pythagoras, the following verse is found:

Wretches, utter wretches, keep your hands from beans. [B 141]
(Aulus Gellius, *Attic Nights* IV xi 9)

(Gellius' discussion of the prohibition on bean-eating is quoted in full in the next chapter.)

The teaching of Plato's doctrines requires, first, a sort of purification, i.e. training from childhood in the appropriate disciplines. For according to Empedocles, we should wash ourselves,

having cut with tireless bronze from five springs [B 143];
and Plato says that the purification must come from five disciplines.
(Theo of Smyrna, *Mathematics useful for reading Plato* 15.7–12)

Metaphor is applying to something a word which belongs to something else, the transference being from genus to species, from species to genus, from species to species ... From species to species, for example:

drawing off life with bronze [B 138]
or

having cut with tireless bronze [cf. B 143]
– here 'draw off' is used to mean 'cut' and 'cut' to mean 'draw off', both being forms of taking away.

(Aristotle, *Poetics* 1457b6–9, 13–16)

In all things I have thought Empedocles' phrase,

to abstain from evil [B 144],
important and divine. (Plutarch, *The Control of Anger* 464B)

(10) UTOPIA

*One of Empedocles' poems appears to have contained a description of a
Utopia or a Golden Age:*

In early times, sacrifices were in many places bloodless . . . Empedocles
is witness to this when, telling of the birth of the gods, he also indicates
his views on offerings:

> **Among them was no god Ares, nor Tumult,**
> **nor king Zeus, nor Cronus, nor Poseidon,**
> **but queen Cypris**

– she is Love –

> **whom they propitiated with pious statues**
> **and painted animals and subtly perfumed oils,**
> **with offerings of unmixed myrrh and of pungent**
> **frankincense,**
> **pouring libations of yellow honey onto the ground**
> [B 128.1–7]

– customs which even now are still preserved among some people,
being as it were traces of the truth.

> **But with the unspeakable slaughter of bulls their altar was**
> **not flooded.** [B 128.8]

(Porphyry, *On Abstinence* II 21)

By such [vegetarian] offerings nature and every sense of the human
soul was pleased:

> **But with the unspeakable slaughter of bulls their altar was**
> **not flooded;**
> **rather, this was the greatest defilement among men:**
> **to bereave of life and eat the gentle limbs.** [B 128.8–10]

(Porphyry, *On Abstinence* II 27)

The word *ktilos* is used of tame and domesticated animals, of the rams
who lead the flock, and of animals in good condition. Empedocles
uses it of tame and gentle animals:

> All were docile [*ktila*] and amenable to men,
> both beasts and birds; and friendliness glowed. [B 130]

So too Hesiod.   (Scholia on Nicander, *Theriaca* 453)

Empedocles refers to this when he says of [Pythagoras]:

> Among them was a man of immense knowledge,
> who had obtained the greatest wealth of mind,
> a master especially of every kind of wise deed.
> For when he reached out with all his mind
> he easily saw each and every thing
> in ten or twenty human generations. [B 129]

(Porphyry, *Life of Pythagoras* 30)

For reason, which leads to virtue by way of philosophy, always makes a man consistent with himself and unblamed by himself and full of peace and friendliness towards himself:

> There is no faction and no ill-proportioned discord in his
> members. [B 27a]

(Plutarch, *Philosophers and Princes* 777C)

(The ascription of this line to Empedocles is conjectural – and most scholars who do ascribe it to him suppose that it refers to the homogeneous Sphere.)

In the second book of Empedocles' *Purifications* one can find the alpha long, as is clear in the comparative form – for he uses *manoteros* like *tranoteros*:

> Of those which, with closer set roots beneath
> and looser set [*manoterois*] branches, thrive . . .

(Herodian, *On Accentuation in General* fragment)

13

Fifth-century Pythagoreanism

Pythagoras' followers in south Italy appear to have organized themselves into a sort of freemasonry; and they practised a communal way of life:

[Pythagoras], according to Timaeus, was the first to say that friends' possessions are held in common and that friendship is equality. And his pupils contributed their goods to a common store.

(Diogenes Laertius, Lives of the Philosophers VIII 10)

Pythagoras was revered, and all things were attributed to him: the phrase 'He said it himself' became a proverb. The Pythagoreans practised no ordinary silence and their views were not divulged to ordinary men.

The society is said to have had political ambitions and interests. In the middle of the fifth century, disaster struck.

At that time, in the regions of Italy which were then called Great Greece, the Pythagorean meeting places were burned down and general constitutional unrest ensued – a not unlikely event, given that the leading men in each state had been thus unexpectedly killed. The Greek cities in these regions were filled with bloodshed and revolution and turmoil of every kind. (Polybius, *Histories* II xxxix 1–3)

The Pythagoreans who survived dispersed, some of them eventually settling in mainland Greece.

At an early stage, Pythagoras' followers divided into two groups, the acusmatici *or Aphorists and the* mathematici *or Scientists.*

There were two forms of philosophy; for there were two kinds of people who practised it, the Aphorists and the Scientists. The Aphorists were allowed by the others to be Pythagorean, but they did not allow that the Scientists were Pythagoreans, saying that their work derived not from Pythagoras but from Hippasus. (Some say that Hippasus came from Croton, others from Metapontum.)

The philosophy of the Aphorists consists of unproven and unargued aphorisms about what should be done, and they attempt to preserve the other things [Pythagoras] said as though they were divine doctrines. They do not claim to say anything on their own behalf, nor do they think that they ought to say anything; rather, they hold that those of their number are best in wisdom who possess the most aphorisms.

All these aphorisms are divided into three kinds: some of them indicate what so and so is, others what is most such and such, others what one must do or must not do.

Those which indicate what so and so is are of the following sort. What are the Isles of the Blessed? – The sun and the moon. – What is the oracle at Delphi? – The *tetractys*, which is the harmony in which the Sirens sing.

What is most such and such: What is most just? – Sacrificing. – What is most wise? – Number (and secondly, the assigning of names to things). – What is most wise of the things among us? – Medicine. – What is most noble? – Harmony. – What is most powerful? – Knowledge. – What is most good? – Happiness. – What is most truly said? – That men are wretched. . .

The aphorisms indicating what should or should not be done are of the following sort. One must have children (for one must leave servants of God in one's place); one must put on one's right shoe first; one must not walk along the highways or dip one's hand in a font or wash in the bath-house (for in all these cases it is unclear whether one's fellows are pure). And others such as: Do not help anyone to put down a burden (for one must not become a cause of idleness); rather, help him to take it up. Do not have intercourse for the purpose of siring children with a woman who wears gold. Do not speak in the dark. Pour libations to the gods from near the handle of the cup – for the sake of the omen and so that no one will drink from the same place. Do not have an image of a god as a seal on your ring in case it is polluted; for it is a likeness †which one should set up in one's house†. Do not prosecute your own wife; for she is a suppliant (that is why a woman is married from her hearth and grasped by her right hand). Do not sacrifice a white cockerel; for it is a suppliant, sacred to the Month (which is why it signifies the hour). Give no advice which is not for the good of the receiver; for advice is sacred. Labour is good, pleasures of every sort are bad; for those who have come for punishment must be punished. One should sacrifice and approach the temples without shoes. One must not turn aside into a temple; for one must not treat God as a digression. It is good to stand fast, to receive wounds in the front, and so to die: the opposite is bad. Human souls enter all animals except those which it is right to sacrifice; that is why one must eat only sacrificial animals, which it is proper to eat, and no other animal.

Some of the aphorisms are of this sort. But the most extensive of them are concerned with sacrifices on various occasions and how they should be performed, with the other ways of honouring the gods, with our removal from this life, and with burials and how we must be buried. In some cases a reason is added – for example, that you must have children in order to leave behind another servant of the gods in your place. But others have no reason annexed to them. Of the additions, some will be thought to be naturally attached, others to be far-fetched – for example, not to break a loaf of bread because it is disadvantageous with regard to the judgement in Hades. The conjectural explanations added to such aphorisms are not Pythagorean but come from certain outsiders who make sophisticated attempts to attach conjectural reasons to them. For example, in the case just mentioned (why you must not break a loaf of bread), some say that you should not divide what brings people together (in the old days, after the foreign fashion, all friends came together over a single loaf), others ††that one must not make such an omen by breaking and crumbling it.†

Now all the aphorisms which deal with what to do and what not to do focus on the divine, and that is their source. The whole of their way of life is ordered with a view to following God. This is the very rationale of their philosophy. For they think it ridiculous for men to look for the good from anywhere except from the gods: it is as if you were living in a monarchy and paid service to some lieutenant among the citizens, ignoring the ruler of all – that, they think, is just what men actually do. For since God exists and is sovereign over everything, it is agreed that one must ask for the good from the sovereign; for everyone gives good things to those whom they love and in whom they delight, and the opposite to those to whom they are disposed in the opposite way.

(Iamblichus, *On the Pythagorean Way of Life* xviii 81–87)

There are numerous other accounts of the Pythagorean aphorisms, and of the modes of behaviour which they accompanied. One of the earliest notices is in Herodotus:

[The Egyptians] do not take woollen things into their temples or bury them with them: that is not holy. In this they are in agreement with those who are called Orphics and Pythagoreans. For it is not holy for one who partakes in these rites to be buried in woollen clothes. There is a sacred story told about this. (Herodotus, *Histories* II 81)

Dietary practice was important; but there was an ancient controversy over the true Pythagorean view of the matter:

A false opinion of long standing has gained ground and increased in strength – the opinion that Pythagoras the philosopher did not eat meat and also abstained from beans (for which the Greek is *kuamoi*). Following this opinion the poet Callimachus wrote:

Keep your hands from beans, a painful food:
as Pythagoras enjoined, so I too urge. [Callimachus, fragment 553 Pfeiffer]

Again, following the same opinion Cicero said this in the first book of his *On Divination*:

So Plato bids us go to bed with our bodies so composed that there is nothing which may bring distraction or disturbance to the mind. That, it is thought, is why the Pythagoreans are forbidden to eat beans which cause considerable flatulence and are thus inimical to those who seek peace of mind. [Cicero, *On Divination* I xxx 62]

Thus Cicero. But the musical scholar Aristoxenus, a man devoted to old texts and a pupil of Aristotle the philosopher, says in his book about Pythagoras that Pythagoras ate no vegetable more frequently than beans, because they soothe and gently relieve the bowels. I have written down Aristoxenus' very words:

Pythagoras esteemed the bean above all other vegetables; for he said that it was both soothing and laxative – that is why he made particular use of it. [Aristoxenus, *Pythagoras* fragment 25 Wehrli]

The same Aristoxenus also reports that [Pythagoras] used to eat small sucking-pigs and tender young goats. He seems to have acquired his information from the Pythagorean Xenophilus, who was his friend, and from certain other older men who were closer in time to Pythagoras. Alexis the poet, in his comedy *The Pythagorean Woman*, also makes the remark about animals.

The mistake about not eating beans seems to have arisen because in a poem of Empedocles, who followed the teachings of Pythagoras, the following verse is found:

Wretches, utter wretches, keep your hands from beans.

[31 B 141]

For most people have supposed that the word 'beans' is being used, as it normally is, to refer to the vegetable. But those who have considered Empedocles' poems more closely and in a more scholarly way assert that in this passage the word 'beans' signifies the testicles: they were called beans [*kuamoi*], obscurely and symbolically in the Pythagorean style, because they are the cause of being pregnant [*kuein*] and provide the impetus to human reproduction. Hence in this verse Empedocles wanted to deter men not from eating beans but from sexual indulgence.

Plutarch, too, who has considerable authority in scholarly matters, says in the first book of his *On Homer* that Aristotle the philosopher wrote the very same about the Pythagoreans – that they did not abstain from eating animals (except for a few sorts of meat). Since the point is surprising I have written down Plutarch's very words:

Aristotle says that the Pythagoreans abstain from womb, heart, sea-nettle and certain other things of that sort, but eat the rest. [Plutarch, *Homeric Studies* fragment 122 Sandbach, citing Aristotle, *On the Pythagoreans* fragment 194 Rose, 3rd edn]
(The sea-nettle is a sea creature which we call a sea-urchin.) But in his *Table Talk* Plutarch says that the Pythagoreans also abstain from mullet. (Aulus Gellius, *Attic Nights* IV xi 1–13)

Such practices were easily mocked. Several fourth-century BC comedies – like Alexis' Pythagorean Woman *– ridiculed the Pythagorean way of life. Here are some samples.*

If you love independence, my dear philosopher, why don't you imitate those Pythagoreans about whom Antiphanes says this in his *Memorials*:

> Some miserable Pythagorists were
> in the gully munching purslane
> and collecting the wretched stuff in sacks.

And in the play actually entitled *The Sack* he says:

> First, like a Pythagorizer, he eats
> no meat but takes and chews
> a blackened piece of cheap bread.

Alexis in *The Men from Tarentum*:

> – The Pythagorizers, as we hear,
> eat no fish nor anything else
> alive; and they're the only ones who don't drink wine.
> – But Epicharides eats dogs,
> and he's a Pythagorean. – Ah, but he kills them first
> and then they're no longer alive.

A little further on he says:

> – Pythagorisms and fine arguments
> and close-chopped thoughts
> nourish them. Their daily diet is this:
> one plain loaf each, and a cup
> of water. That's all. – A prison
> diet! Do all wise men

live like that and suffer such misery?
– These live in luxury compared to others. Don't you know
that Melanippides is one of them, and Phaon
and Phyromachus and Phanos: they
dine every four days on a single cup of bran.

(Athenaeus, *Deipnosophists* 160F–161C)

In *The Pythagorist* [Aristophon] says:
    As for going hungry and not eating anything,
    imagine you can see Tithymallus or Philippides.
    For drinking water they're frogs; for enjoying thyme
    and vegetables, caterpillars; for not being washed,
        chamber-pots;
    for staying out of doors all winter, blackbirds;
    for standing the heat and chattering at noon,
    cicadas; for never oiling themselves, dust-clouds;
    for walking about at dawn without any shoes,
    cranes; for not sleeping at all, bats.

(Athenaeus, *Deipnosophists* 238CD)

Among the Scientists or mathematici *are Hippasus and Philolaus,
who have chapters of their own. Here I cite a few texts of a more general
nature about the mathematical side of Pythagorean philosophy. The
most important passage comes from Aristotle.*

At the same time as [Leucippus and Democritus] and earlier, the
so-called Pythagoreans touched on the mathematical sciences: they
were the first to bring them forward and, having been brought up in
them, to think that their principles were the principles of everything
which exists. Since of mathematical principles numbers are by nature
the first, and since they thought they observed in numbers many
similarities to the things which exist and come into being (more so
than in fire and earth and water) – that justice is such and such a
property of numbers, soul and thought such and such, opportunity
something else, and so on for pretty well everything else – and they
also saw that the properties and ratios of harmonies depend on

numbers: since, then, other things appeared to have been modelled on numbers in their whole nature, while numbers appeared to be the first things in nature as a whole, they supposed that the elements of numbers were the elements of everything which exists, and that the whole heaven was harmony and number. Everything in numbers and harmonies which cohered with the properties and parts of the heavens and with the universe as a whole, they collected and fitted together; and if there was anything missing anywhere they eagerly made additions so that the whole of their theory should hang together. For example, since the number ten is thought to be perfect and to include the whole nature of numbers, they say that the bodies moving in the heavens are ten in number; and since only nine are apparent, for that reason they invent the counter-earth as the tenth.

I have given a more detailed account of these things elsewhere: I discuss them here in order to ascertain, in the case of the Pythagoreans too, what principles they posit and how they fit into the causes I have described. Now they, too, evidently believe that number is a principle both as matter for existing things and as their properties and states; they hold that the elements of number are the even and the odd, one of these being limited and the other limitless; that the number one derives from both elements (it is both even and odd) and numbers derive from the number one; and that the whole heaven, as I have said, is numbers.

Other members of the same school say that the principles are ten in number, and come in co-ordinate pairs: limit – limitless, odd – even, one – quantity, right – left, male – female, resting – moving, straight – crooked, light – darkness, good – bad, square – oblong . . . How [these ten principles] should be collected under the types of cause I have described they do not clearly articulate. But they seem to range the elements under the head of matter; for they say that they are inherent in substances, which are composed and fashioned from them. (Aristotle, *Metaphysics* 985b23–986a26, 986b4–8)

Aristotle says that the Pythagoreans 'touched on' mathematics. Later authors ascribe considerable mathematical achievements to them. For example:

Eudemus the Peripatetic ascribes to the Pythagoreans the discovery of the theorem that every triangle has internal angles equal to two right angles, and he says that they prove the proposition in this way: Let ABC be a triangle, and let DE be drawn through A parallel to BC. Then since BC and DE are parallel, the alternate angles are equal; so DAB is equal to ABC and EAC to ACB. Let BAC be added in common. Then angles DAB, BAC, CAE, i.e. angles DAB, BAE, i.e. two right angles, are equal to the three angles of the triangle ABC. Hence the three angles of the triangle are equal to two right angles.

(Proclus, *Commentary on Euclid* 379.2–16)

The most celebrated piece of Pythagorean mathematics is the theorem still known as Pythagoras' theorem:

'In right-angled triangles, the square on the side opposite to the right angle is equal to the squares on the sides next to the right angle': if we read those who like to record the ancient history of the subject we shall find them ascribing this theorem to Pythagoras and saying that he sacrificed an ox on its discovery.

(Proclus, *Commentary on Euclid* 426.1–9)

The story is not to be believed; and most scholars think that the Pythagoreans contributed little to mathematics.

According to Aristotle, they applied numbers to astronomy. In the chapter on Philolaus we shall rediscover the 'counter-earth'. Here is the Music of the Spheres:

It is clear from this that to say that [the heavenly bodies] produce a harmony as they move, their sounds being concordant, is an elegant and ingenious theory but is nevertheless untrue. Some think that when bodies of such a size move they must produce a sound, since this happens with bodies here below even though they are not of the same mass and do not move with such speed: when the sun and the moon, and the stars in such numbers and of such a magnitude, move in such a path at speed, it is impossible that they should not produce a sound of immense magnitude. Positing this, and supposing that their speeds, judging by their distances, have the ratios of the concords, they say that as the heavenly bodies move in a circle they produce a concordant sound. Since it seems unreasonable that we do not hear this sound, they say that the cause lies in the fact that the noise is with us from the moment of our birth so that it cannot be distinguished by reference to a contrary silence (for sound and silence are discriminated by reference to one another). Thus men are in the same case as blacksmiths whom habit makes insensible.

(Aristotle, *On the Heavens* 290b12–29)

The universe is infinite in extent, and it contains void or emptinesses:

All those who are thought to have touched significantly on natural philosophy have given some account of the limitless, and all posit it as a sort of principle of the things which exist. Some, like the Pythagoreans and Plato, make it a principle in its own right, supposing that the limitless exists in itself as a substance and not as an attribute of something else. The Pythagoreans locate it among perceptible objects (for they do not make numbers separate), and they say that the region outside the heavens is limitless. (Aristotle, *Physics* 203a1–8)

The Pythagoreans too said that the empty exists, and that it enters the heavens from the limitless breath, as though the heavens actually inhale the empty which distinguishes natural things and is a sort of separation and distinction of contiguous things. They hold that this occurs first among numbers; for the empty separates their natures.

(Aristotle, *Physics* 213b22–27)

Aristotle in the fourth book of the *Physics* writes:
    The Pythagoreans say that the empty exists, and that it enters the
    heavens from the limitless breath, as though the heavens inhale.
And in the first book of *On the Philosophy of Pythagoras* he writes that the heavens are one, and that from the limitless there enter time and breath and the empty which distinguishes the places of each thing for ever. [Aristotle, *On the Pythagoreans* fragment 201 Rose, 3rd edn]

(Stobaeus, *Anthology* I xviii 1c)

There were also theories about the nature of the soul. In the following extract, the speaker is Simmias, a Pythagorean:

And indeed, Socrates, I think that you yourself are aware that we suppose the soul to be something of this sort – our bodies being stretched and contracted by hot and cold and dry and wet and things of this sort, our souls are the blending and harmony of these things when they are well and appropriately blended with one another.

(Plato, *Phaedo* 86BC)

There is also another opinion handed down about the soul, an opinion which is no less plausible in the eyes of many people than any of the views we have mentioned but which has been found wanting even in public discussions: they say that the soul is a sort of harmony; for a harmony is a blending and composing of contraries, and bodies are composed of contraries. (Aristotle, *On the Soul* 407b27–32)

What the Pythagoreans say seems to have the same meaning. For some of them said that the motes in the air are soul, others that what moves them is soul. We have said how they can be seen to move continuously even if there is a complete calm.

(Aristotle, *On the Soul* 404a16–20)

The Aphorists and the Scientists seem to approach one another in the field of number mysticism. Some Pythagoreans played the numbers game in an extravagant fashion:

They did not determine in what way numbers are causes of substances and of their being. Are they boundaries (as points are of magnitudes)? – This is how Eurytus established what was the number of what (this the number of man, that the number of horse) – as people arrange numbers into squares and oblongs, so he modelled the shapes of plants with pebbles. (Aristotle, *Metaphysics* 1092b8–13)

Pythagoras himself had allegedly discovered the tetractys *or 'group of four': that is to say, the group of the first four integers, which together add up to the perfect number, ten.*

All these inventions and constructions, and many others like them, were devised by Pythagoras for the advantage and improvement of his followers. And the inventions were so admirable, and so divinized by those who understood them, that the sectaries used them as forms of oath:

> By him who handed to our generation the *tetractys*,
> source of the roots of ever-flowing nature.

(Iamblichus, *On the Pythagorean Way of Life* xxix 162)

14

Hippasus

Hippasus was a Pythagorean. His birthplace is variously reported, and our sources record no dates for him. It seems likely that he was active in the middle of the fifth century. He is said to have been the first of the Pythagorean mathematici *or* Scientists; *and he advanced opinions on natural science:*

Hippasus of Metapontum and Heraclitus of Ephesus also said that the principle is one, in motion, and limited; but they made it fire, and they produce existent things from fire by condensation and rarefaction, and resolve them into fire again, this being the one underlying nature.

(Simplicius, *Commentary on the* Physics 23.33–24.4)

We are ill-informed about the more distinctively Pythagorean aspects of Hippasus' thought. Two stories are worth setting down, though neither is beyond suspicion. First, Hippasus' name is associated with musical theory:

A certain Hippasus constructed four bronze discs in such a way that they all had equal diameters but the thickness of the first was one and a third times that of the second, one and a half times that of the third, and twice that of the fourth; and when they were struck they made a concord. (Scholia on Plato, *Phaedo* 108D)

The story means to ascribe to Hippasus the discovery of the fundamental musical ratios, 4:3, 3:2 and 2:1.

The second story concerns the mathematical achievements of the Pythagoreans:

About Hippasus they say that he was one of the Pythagoreans but that because he was the first to publish and construct a sphere based on twelve pentagons he died at sea for his impiety. He acquired the reputation for the discovery, although everything belongs to That Man (this is how they refer to Pythagoras, not calling him by his name).   (Iamblichus, *On the General Science of Mathematics* 25)

They say that the divinity punished those who made Pythagoras' views public. For the man who revealed the construction of the vigintiangle perished at sea for his impiety. (The vigintiangle is the dodecahedron, one of the so-called five solid figures, when it extends into a sphere.) Some said that it was the man who spoke about irrationality and incommensurability who suffered this fate.

(Iamblichus, *On the Pythagorean Way of Life* xxxiv 247)

15

Philolaus

Philolaus, a Pythagorean, was born in Croton in the 470s BC. When the Pythagorean school there was destroyed and its members dispersed, he retired to mainland Greece, where he spent some time at Thebes.

We possess several passages purporting to come from Philolaus' writings. Some scholars have regarded all of them as spurious; and some of them surely are – numerous Pythagorean forgeries were put together in antiquity. This chapter omits the texts which are uncontroversially inauthentic, translating those which the most recent scholarship is inclined to hold genuine.

One of Philolaus' works was later called On Nature. *The opening sentence is preserved:*

Demetrius in his *Homonyms* says that [Philolaus] was the first of the Pythagoreans to publish an *On Nature*. It begins as follows:
Nature in the world was harmonized from things limitless and things limiting, both the whole world and everything in it. [44 B 1]
(Diogenes Laertius, *Lives of the Philosophers* VIII 85)

Stobaeus transcribes a sequence of passages which, despite the different title, probably come from On Nature.

From Philolaus, *On the World*:
It is necessary that the things which exist should all be either limiting or limitless or both limiting and limitless. But they cannot be only limitless. Now since it is evident that they come neither from limiting things only nor from limitless things only, it is thus clear that the world and the things in it were harmonized from

both limiting and limitless things. The facts too make this clear: some, coming from limiting things, limit; some, coming from both limiting and limitless things, both limit and do not limit; some, coming from limitless things, are evidently limitless. [B 2]

And all things known have a number – for without this nothing could be thought of or known. [B 4]

Now number has two proper kinds, odd and even (and a third, even-odd, mixed from both); and of each of the two kinds there are many forms which each thing in itself signifies. [B 5]

On nature and harmony, matters stand thus: the being of things, which is eternal, and nature itself admit of divine and not of human knowledge – except that it was not possible that any of the things which exist and are known by us should have come into being had there not subsisted the being of the things from which the world was constituted, both the limiting things and the limitless things. And since the subsisting principles were neither similar nor of the same kind, it would thereby have been impossible for them to have been arranged had not a harmony supervened (in whatever way it may have done so). Now things similar and of the same kind had no need of a harmony; but things dissimilar and neither of the same kind nor equally matched must necessarily be locked together by a harmony if they are to be held together in a world. [B 6a]

The magnitude of a harmony is a fourth and a fifth. A fifth is greater than a fourth by nine to eight; for from the lowest to the middle is a fourth, from the middle to the top a fifth, from the top to the third a fourth, from the third to the lowest a fifth; and between middle and third there is nine to eight. A fourth is four to three, a fifth three to two, an octave two to one. Thus the harmony is five nine-to-eights and two semitones, a fifth is three nine-to-eights and a semitone, a fourth is two nine-to-eights and a semitone. [B 6b]

The first thing to have been harmonized, the One in the middle of the sphere, is called the hearth. [B 7]

(Stobaeus, *Anthology* I xxi 7–8)

A related fragment is preserved by Iamblichus:

In unified magnitudes, division is everywhere limitless, but extension is determined. For pluralities, it is the other way about: extension is limitless, division determined – though by nature, as far as their conception is concerned, both are limitless and therefore not capable of being scientifically circumscribed. For **nothing will have any knowledge at all if all things are limitless** [B 3], as Philolaus says.

(Iamblichus, *Commentary on Nicomachus'* Introduction
to Arithmetic vii [7.18–25])

The references to number find echoes in the following reports:

Plato teaches us many remarkable doctrines about the gods by means of mathematical forms, and the philosophy of the Pythagoreans uses these hangings to conceal the mysteries of its divine doctrines. For that is the case throughout the *Sacred Discourse*, in Philolaus' *Bacchae*, and in the whole of Pythagoras' teaching about the gods. [B 19]

(Proclus, *Commentary on Euclid* 22.9–16)

All the so-called mathematical sciences are like smooth flat mirrors in which traces and images of intelligible truth are reflected. But it is above all geometry which, according to Philolaus, being the principle and native city of the others, turns and elevates the mind which it purifies and gently releases from perception.

(Plutarch, *Table Talk* 718E)

The Pythagoreans say that reason [is the criterion of truth] – not reason in general, but mathematical reason, as Philolaus said, which, inasmuch as it considers the nature of the universe, has a certain affinity to it (for like is naturally apprehended by like).

(Sextus Empiricus, *Against the Mathematicians* VII 92)

Elsewhere there will be occasion to inquire further how, when numbers in a sequence are squared, no less plausible results follow –

by nature and not by convention, as Philolaus somewhere says. [B 9]
(Iamblichus, *Commentary on Nicomachus' Introduction
to Arithmetic* xxv [19.21–25])

*There is a text on cosmogony, and various reports about Philolaus'
astronomical theories:*

Philolaus' *Bacchae*:
**The world is one. It began to come into being at the middle, and
from the middle upwards and downwards in the same way; and
what is above the middle is the opposite way about from what is
below. For, to what is below the lowest part is like the highest, and
so on; for each has the same relation to the middle, except that
they are reversed.** [B 17]   (Stobaeus, *Anthology* I xv 7)

The others say that the earth is at rest. But Philolaus the Pythagorean
says that it is carried in a circle around the fire (in an oblique circle)
in the same way as the sun and the moon.

([Plutarch], *Opinions of the Philosophers on Nature* 896A)

Philolaus says that there is fire in the middle at the centre (he calls
this the hearth of the universe and the house of Zeus and the mother
of the gods, and the altar and bond and measure of nature), and again
more fire at the highest point and surrounding everything. By nature
the middle is first, and around it dance ten divine bodies – the sky,
the planets, then the sun, next the moon, next the earth, next the
counterearth, and after all of them the fire of the hearth which holds
position at the centre. The highest part of the surrounding, where the
elements are found in their purity, he calls Olympus; the regions
beneath the orbit of Olympus, where are the five planets with the sun
and the moon, he calls the world; the part under them, being beneath
the moon and around the earth, in which are found generation and
change, he calls the sky. Wisdom is concerned with the well-ordered
heavenly bodies, virtue with the products of disorderliness, the former
being perfect and the latter imperfect.

(Stobaeus, *Anthology* I xxii 1d)

Philolaus also had something to say on biological and psychological matters.

There are four principles of rational animals, as Philolaus says in his *On Nature* – brain, heart, navel, genitals:

Head of thought, heart of soul and perception, navel of rooting and first growth, genitals of depositing of seed and generation. Brain contains the principle of man, heart that of animal, navel that of plant, genitals that of all together (for all shoot and sprout from seed). [B 13]

([Iamblichus], *Theological Arithmetic* xx–xxi [25.17–26.3])

Philolaus of Croton says that our bodies are compounded from heat. For they have no share in coldness, as he argues from such considerations as these. Semen is hot, and it is semen which constitutes <animals>; the place into which semen is deposited, i.e. <the womb>, is hotter and similar to it; what is similar to something has the same power as what it is similar to. Now since what constitutes animals has no share in coldness and the place in which <it is deposited> has no share in coldness, clearly the animal that is being constituted will also be of the same sort. With regard to its constitution, he adds the following consideration: immediately after birth the animal draws in the external air, which is cold, and then discharges it like a debt. Now desire for the external air exists in order that, by drawing in breath from outside, our bodies, which are hotter, should be cooled by it. The composition of our bodies, he says, depends on these things.

He says that diseases occur because of bile and blood and phlegm, and that these are the principles of diseases. He says that blood is turned thick when the flesh is compressed internally, and that it becomes thin when the vessels in the flesh are divided. He says that phlegm is compounded from rain. He says that bile is the juice of the flesh. The same man makes a paradoxical remark on this subject: he says that bile is not found near the liver and yet that it is the juice of the flesh. Again, while most say that phlegm is cold, he supposes that it is by nature hot. For it is called phlegm from *phlegein* ['to burn'], and hence inflamed parts are inflamed by sharing in phlegm. These he supposes are the principles of diseases; contributory causes are excesses of heat or food or cooling and deficiencies <of these or> of things like them.

(anonymous *Medical Writings*, London Papyrus 137, cols. XVIII 8–XIX 1)

It is worth recording Philolaus' words; for the Pythagorean says this: **The old theologians and prophets also testify that the soul has been yoked to the body as a punishment and that it is buried in it as though in a tomb.** [B 14]   (Clement, *Miscellanies* III iii 17.1)

Cebes asked him: Socrates, why do you say that it is not right to do violence to oneself but that a philosopher will follow a dying man willingly?
– What, Cebes, didn't you and Simmias hear about these matters when you were in Philolaus' company?
– Nothing clear, Socrates . . . Why do they say that it is not right to kill oneself, Socrates? As for your question, I have heard from Philolaus when he was living among us, and from others too, that one should not do this. But I have never yet heard anything clear on the matter.

(Plato, *Phaedo* 61DE)

Certain thoughts and feelings – or else the actions based on such thoughts and reasonings – are not in our power; rather, as Philolaus said, some reasons are too strong for us. [B 16]

(Aristotle, *Eudemian Ethics* 1225a30–33)

16

Ion of Chios

Ion, who has already been cited in connection with Pythagoras, was born in about 485 BC on the island of Chios. He spent much of his life in Athens where he was a friend of many leading political and literary figures. He died in about 425.

The orator [Isocrates] here refers to Ion, the tragic poet, who was a Chian by birth, son of Orchomenus, known as Xuthus. He wrote many poems and tragedies and a philosophical treatise entitled *Triad*. Callimachus says that its authorship is disputed. In some copies it is entitled *Triads*, in the plural, according to Demetrius of Scepsis and Apollonides of Nicaea. They record this from it:

This is the beginning of my account: all things are three, and there is nothing more or fewer than these three things. Of each one the excellence is threefold: intelligence and power and fortune.

[36 B 1]   (Harpocration, *Lexicon*, s.v. Ion)

We have at most one other piece of information about Ion's philosophical thought. Plutarch may be referring to the Triad *when he reports that*

Ion the poet, in the work he wrote without metre and in prose, says that fortune, although a thing most dissimilar to wisdom, produces very similar results [B 3]: both will aggrandize States, adorn men and bring glory and power and dominion.

(Plutarch, *On the Fortune of the Romans* 316E)

17

Hippo

Hippo's dates are unknown; but he was lampooned by the comic poet Cratinus in the 420s and was therefore presumably active in the latter part of the fifth century BC. Cratinus attacked him for impiety, and at some point he won the epithet 'atheist'. Aristotle regarded him as a tawdry thinker:

One would not propose to place Hippo among these men because of the poverty of his thought.   (Aristotle, *Metaphysics* 984a3)

Simplicius gives a brief report of Hippo's view on the underlying nature of things:

Of those who say that the first principle is one and in motion ([Aristotle] calls them natural scientists in the narrow sense), some assert that it is limited. Thus Thales, son of Examyes, a Milesian, and Hippo, who is actually thought to have been an atheist, said that the principle is water. They were led to this view by the evidence of perception. For heat lives by moisture, dying things dry up, the seeds of all things are moist and all food is juicy. Now each thing is naturally nourished by that from which it is constituted; and water is the principle of natural moisture and conserves all moist things. That is why they supposed that water was the principle of everything and declared that the earth rests on water.   (Simplicius, *Commentary on the* Physics 23.21–29)

Hippo seems to have written at some length on biological matters, and his biological speculations had some connection with the doctrine that water is the principle of things. Here is one extract:

Hippo of Croton thinks that there is an appropriate moisture in us in virtue of which we perceive and by which we live. When this moisture is in an appropriate condition, the animal is healthy; when it dries up, the animal ceases to perceive and dies. That is why old men are dry and lack perception – they are without moisture. In the same way the soles of the feet lack perception because they have no share of moisture. That is as far as he goes on these points.

In another book the same man says that what he has named moisture changes through excess of heat and excess of cold and in this way brings on diseases. He says that it changes either to being more moist or to being drier or to being thicker textured or to being thinner textured or in other directions. This is how he explains diseases – but he does not name the diseases which come about.

(anonymous *Medical Writings*, London Papyrus 137, col. XI 22–42)

The one surviving fragment of Hippo's work is preserved in a note on the Iliad. *Homer refers to 'Ocean, from which flow all rivers and all seas and all springs and the deep wells'.*

In the third book [of his *Homeric Studies*, Crates] says that the later natural scientists also agreed that the water which surrounds the earth for most of its extent is Ocean, and that fresh water comes from it. Hippo:

All drinking waters come from the sea. For the wells from which we drink are surely not deeper than the sea is. If they were, the water would come not from the sea but from somewhere else. But in fact the sea is deeper than the waters. Now all waters that are higher than the sea come from the sea. [38 B 1]
Thus he said the same as Homer.

(Geneva scholia on Homer, *Iliad* XXI 195)

18

Anaxagoras

Anaxagoras was born at Clazomenae on the coast of Asia Minor in about 500 BC. He spent much of his life in Athens, where he was associated with Pericles, the leading statesman of the age, and with Euripides, the writer of tragedies. The dates of his stay in Athens are disputed: it is perhaps most probable that he came to the city in 480 and remained there until about 430. Tried for 'impiety' and condemned, he fled Athens and settled in Lampsacus in the Troad, where he died, an honoured guest, in 428.

Here, first, is the major portion of Diogenes' Life.

Anaxagoras, son of Hegesibulus (or of Eubulus), of Clazomenae. He was a follower of Anaximenes, and was the first to put thought in charge of matter – his treatise, which is written in a pleasant and lofty style, begins as follows:

All things were together. Then thought came and arranged them. [Cf. 59 B 1]

Hence he was nicknamed 'Thought', and Timon in his *Silli* says this about him:

> And they say, I suppose, that Anaxagoras is a stout hero,
> Thought; for he took thought, which suddenly rose up
> and pinched together everything, which before had been in
> disarray.

He was remarkable for his good birth and his wealth – and also for his generosity inasmuch as he ceded his inheritance to his relations. For when they accused him of neglecting it he said: 'Then why don't *you* look after it?' In the end he went into retirement and spent his time in scientific study, giving no thought to politics. When someone

185

asked him if he had no care for his country, he replied: 'Hush – I have the greatest care for my country,' pointing to the heavens.

He is said to have been twenty when Xerxes invaded Greece [480 BC], and to have lived for seventy-two years. Apollodorus in his *Chronicles* says that he was born in the seventieth Olympiad [500–497] and that he died in the first year of the eighty-eighth Olympiad [428]. He began to philosophize in Athens in the archonship of Callias when he was twenty, according to Demetrius of Phaleron in his *List of Archons*. They say that he stayed there for thirty years.

He said that the sun is a fiery mass, larger than the Peloponnese (but some ascribe this to Tantalus), and that the moon is inhabited and also contains hills and ravines. The uniform items are principles; for just as gold is compounded from what is called gold-dust, so the universe is put together from small uniform bodies. Thought is the principle of movement. Heavy bodies, like earth, occupy the lower regions, light bodies, like fire, the upper; water and air, the middle. For in this way the sea rests on the earth, which is flat, and its moisture is vaporized by the sun. At first the heavenly bodies moved as though in a rotunda so that the pole which is always visible was directly over the earth; later they acquired a tilt. The Milky Way is the sun's light, the stars being illuminated. Comets are conjunctions of planets which emit flames. Shooting stars are, as it were, sparks shaken from the ether. Winds occur when the air is rarefied by the sun. Thunder is a clash of clouds. Lightning is friction in the clouds. Earthquakes are a subsiding of air into the earth. Animals were generated from the moist, the hot and the earthy; and later from one another, males from the right-hand parts and females from the left.

They say that he predicted the fall of the stone which occurred at Aegospotami – he said that it would fall from the sun. That is why Euripides, who was his pupil, says in the *Phaethon* that the sun is a lump of gold. When he was going to Olympia he sat down under a waterproof as though it were going to rain – and it did. When someone asked him if the mountains at Lampsacus would ever become sea, they say he replied: 'Yes, if time doesn't give out.' Asked for what end he had been born, he said: 'To study the sun and the moon and the heavens.' When someone said, 'You have been parted from the Athenians,' he replied: 'No – they have been parted from me.' When he saw the tomb of Mausolus, he said: 'A rich tomb is the image of a substance turned to stone.' When someone complained that he was dying in a foreign country, he replied: 'Wherever you start from, the descent to Hades is the same.'

He is thought to have been the first – according to Favorinus in his *Encyclopaedia* – to have said that Homer's poetry is about virtue and justice. This theory was taken further by his acquaintance Metrodorus of Lampsacus, who was the first to occupy himself with the poet's ideas on natural science. Anaxagoras was also the first to publish a book in prose.

Silenus says in the first book of his *Histories* that the stone fell from the sky in the archonship of Demulus, and that Anaxagoras said that the whole heaven is constituted of stones – it is held together by its rapid rotation and will fall down if it slackens.

Different stories are told about his trial. Sotion, in his *Succession of Philosophers*, says that he was brought to trial for impiety by Cleon because he said that the sun was a fiery lump, and that when his pupil Pericles spoke in his defence he was fined five talents and exiled. Satyrus in his *Lives* says that the case was brought by Thucydides, Pericles' political opponent; that the charge was not only impiety but also collaboration with the Persians; and that he was condemned to death in his absence. When he was told both of the condemnation and of the death of his children, he said of the condemnation that 'Nature long ago condemned both them and me', and of his children that 'I knew they were mortal when I fathered them.' (Some ascribe this to Solon, others to Xenophon.) Demetrius of Phaleron, in his book *On Old Age*, says that he buried them with his own hands. Hermippus in his *Lives* says that he was held in prison to await his death. Pericles arrived and asked them if they had any charge to bring against *him* for his way of life. They said they had none. 'Yet I am his pupil,' he said. 'So do not yield to calumny and kill him, but listen to me and free him.' He was freed, but he could not bear the outrage and killed himself. Hieronymus, in the second book of his *Miscellaneous Notes*, says that Pericles led him to the court wasted and thin from disease, so that it was pity rather than judgement which freed him. So much for his trial.

He is thought somehow to have been hostile to Democritus, with whom he was not able to have any discussion. In the end he retired to Lampsacus and died there. When the magistrates of the city asked him what he would like to be done for him, he said: 'Let the children have a holiday each year in the month of my death.' The custom is still observed.   (Diogenes Laertius, *Lives of the Philosophers* II 6–14)

It is worth adding two anecdotes which Diogenes does not relate.

Pericles gained much from his association with Anaxagoras, and in particular he is thought to have risen above that superstition which amazement at the celestial phenomena produces in those who are ignorant of their causes and who, because of their inexperience, are fascinated and confused about things divine – a state of mind which is changed by a scientific account, which creates a sure piety based on good hopes in place of a fearful and feverish superstition.

It is said that the head of a one-horned ram was once brought to Pericles from the country, and that Lampon the seer, noting that the horn was strong and solid and grew from the middle of the forehead, said that, there being two powerful families in the city, that of Thucydides and that of Pericles, power would pass into the hands of one man – of him to whom the sign had appeared. But Anaxagoras had the skull cut open and showed that the brain had not filled out the cavity but rather, being sharp like an egg, had slipped from the whole vessel to the place where the root of the horn started. At the time it was Anaxagoras who was admired by those present; but a little later it was Lampon – for Thucydides was ousted and all public affairs came under Pericles.   (Plutarch, *Pericles* vi 155AB)

I once heard someone reading, as he said, from a book of Anaxagoras and saying that it is thought which arranges and is responsible for everything. This explanation delighted me and it seemed to me somehow to be a good thing that thought was responsible for everything – I believed that if that were so, then thought, in arranging all things, would arrange and place each in the best way possible. So if anyone wanted to discover the explanation of anything – how it comes into being or perishes or exists – he would have to discover how it is best for it to be or to be acted upon or to act in any way . . .

Now, my friend, this splendid hope was dashed. For as he continued reading I saw that the man didn't use thought at all, ascribing to it the explanation for the arranging of things; rather, he found explanations in air and ether and water and many other absurdities.

(Plato, *Phaedo* 97BC, 98BC)

It is clear from Diogenes' Life that Anaxagoras offered a complete account of the natural world on the old Milesian model. He was called a 'follower' of Anaximenes, and he was attempting to revive, in the post-Parmenidean period, the enterprise which the Milesians had carried out in the age of intellectual innocence.

Several later texts give details of his scientific views; but all the surviving fragments of his work deal with the most general and abstract part of his philosophy. Anaxagoras' universe began as an undifferentiated mass. Thought, or mind, worked on the mass, and the articulated world developed. The materials of Anaxagoras' world are uniform and continuous stuffs, not collections of particles or atoms. The cosmic development does not, and cannot, produce any 'pure' stuffs – every stuff always contains a 'portion' or 'share', however small, of every other stuff.

Most of what commonly pass as fragments of Anaxagoras are reconstructions built from different passages in Simplicius. Here the texts are presented in the form in which they are preserved. This makes for repetition; but it offers a better picture of the evidence.

In the first book of his *Physics* Anaxagoras says that
water is separated off from the clouds, earth from the water, and stones are compacted from the earth by the cold. [Cf. B 16]
Anaxagoras says that uniform things, limitless in quantity, separate off from a single mixture, all being present in all and each being characterized by what predominates. He makes this clear in the first book of his *Physics* at the beginning of which he says:
Together were all things, limitless both in quantity and in smallness

– for the small too was limitless. And when all were together, none was clear by reason of smallness; for air and ether covered all things, both being limitless – for in all things these are the greatest both in quantity and in size. [B 1]

And a little later:

For air and ether are separating off from the surrounding mass. And what surrounds is limitless in quantity. [B 2]

And a little later:

This being so, one should believe that in all things which are associating there are present many things of every sort and seeds of all things, having all kinds of shapes and colours and savours. And before they separated off, he says, when all were together, not even any colour was clear; for this was prevented by the mingling of all things – of the wet and the dry and the hot and the cold and the bright and the dark and much earth present in it and seeds, limitless in quantity and not at all like one another. For of the other things too, none is like any other. [Cf. B 4]

He makes it clear that none of the uniform items comes into being or is destroyed but that they are always the same:

These things being thus dissociated, one should recognize that all things are neither fewer nor more. For it is impossible for there to be more than all; rather, all are always equal. [B 5]

So much for the mixture and the uniform items. About thought he has written as follows:

Thought is something limitless and independent, and it has been mixed with no thing but is alone by itself. For if it were not by itself but had been mixed with some other thing, it would share in all things, if it had been mixed with any. For in everything there is present a portion of everything, as I have said earlier. And what was mingled with it would have prevented it from having power over anything in the way in which it does, being in fact alone by itself. For it is the finest of all things and the purest, and it possesses all knowledge about everything, and it has the greatest strength. And thought has power over all those things, both great and small, which possess soul. And thought had power over the whole revolution, so that it revolved in the first place. And first it began to revolve in a little region: it is revolving more widely, and it will revolve more widely. And thought knows everything which is mingling and separating off and dissociating. And what was to be and what was and what now is and what will be – all this thought arranged, and also this revolution in which now revolve the stars and the sun and the moon and the air and the ether which are separating off. The revolution itself made them separate them off. And the dense is separating off from the rare, and the hot from the cold, and the bright from the dark, and the dry from the wet. And there are many portions of many things, but nothing completely separates off or dissociates one from another except thought. All thought, both great and small, is alike. Nothing else is alike, but each single thing is and was most clearly those things of which it contains most. [B 12]

That he supposes a twofold world, one intelligible and the other (derivative from it) perceptible, is clear both from what we have already cited and from the following:

Thought †had power over whatever exists† and now is where all the other things also are – in the surrounding mass and in what has come together and in what has separated off. [B 14]

Now having said that

there are present in all things which are associating many things of every sort and seeds of all things, having all kinds of shapes and colours and savours, and men were compacted and also the other animals which possess souls,

he continues:

And the men possess inhabited cities and constructed goods, as with us, and there is a sun present among them and a moon and the rest, as with us, and the earth grows many things of every sort for them, the most serviceable of which they gather into their houses and use. [Cf. B 4]

The phrase 'as with us', which he uses more than once, shows that he is hinting at another world apart from ours. That he does not think that it is perceptible and earlier than ours in time is shown by the phrase 'the most serviceable of which they gather into their houses and use' – for he said 'use', not 'used'. Nor is he referring to a state of affairs similar to ours which now exists in another region of the world – for he did not say 'the sun and the moon are present to them as they are to us', but rather 'a sun and a moon, as with us', as though he meant a different sun and moon. But whether that is so or not demands further inquiry.

(Simplicius, *Commentary on the* Physics 155.21–157.24)

At the very beginning [of his book, Anaxagoras] says that things were limitless – **Together were all things, limitless both in quantity and in smallness** [cf. B 1] – and that among the principles there is neither a smallest nor a largest; for **of the small,** he says, **there is no smallest, but always a smaller. For what is cannot not be. And again of the large there is always a larger, and it is equal to the small in quantity. But in relation to itself each thing is both large and small.** [B 3]

For if everything is in everything and everything separates out of everything, then something smaller will be separated from what is supposed to be the smallest thing, and what is supposed to be the largest thing has been separated out of something larger than itself. He says clearly that **in everything there is present a portion of everything except thought – and in some things thought too is present.** [B 11]

And again:

Other things share a portion of everything, but thought is something limitless and independent, and it has been mixed with no thing. [Cf. B 12]

Elsewhere he puts it like this:

Now since there are equal portions of the great and of the small in quantity, for this reason too all things will be in everything; nor can they be separate, but all things share a portion of everything. Since there cannot be a smallest, things cannot be separated or come to be by themselves, but as they were in the beginning so too now are all things together. In all things many things are present, even what is separating off, equal in quantity in the larger and smaller. [B 6]

Anaxagoras also claims that each of the perceptible uniform items comes about and is characterized in virtue of the composition of similars. For he says:

But each single thing is and was most clearly those things of which it contains most. [Cf. B 12]

He seems, too, to say that thought attempts to dissociate them but cannot do so. (Simplicius, *Commentary on the* Physics 164.14–165.5)

Anaxagoras says at the beginning of his treatise:

Together were all things, limitless both in quantity and in smallness – for the small too was limitless. And when all were together, none was clear by reason of smallness. [Cf. B 1]

And:

One should believe that all things are present in the whole. [Cf. B 4]

Perhaps by 'limitless' he means what is for us ungraspable and unknowable – this is indicated by the phrase:

So that we do not know the quantity either in word or in deed of what is separating off. [B 7]

(That he thought them limited in form he makes clear by saying that thought knows them all.)

(Simplicius, *Commentary on* On the Heavens 608.21–28)

[Aristotle] did not mention Anaxagoras here, Alexander says, even though Anaxagoras placed thought among the principles – perhaps, he says, because he makes no use of it in generating things. But it is plain that he does make use of it, since he says that generation is nothing but separating out, that separating out comes about by motion, and that thought is responsible for the motion. This is what Anaxagoras says:

And when thought began to move things, things were separating off from everything which was being moved, and everything which thought moved was dissociated. And as they were moving and dissociating, the revolution made them dissociate far more. [B 13]

Rather, [Aristotle] did not mention Anaxagoras because Anaxagoras did not make thought an enmattered form (which is what he is investigating here) but a cause of dissociation and arrangement, separate from what is being arranged and belonging to a different order from what is being arranged. For **thought, he says, is something limitless and independent, and it has been mixed with no thing, but is alone by itself** [cf. B 12] – and he adds the reason for this. Perhaps this is another reason why [Aristotle] did not mention Anaxagoras – that his thought seems not to make the forms but to dissociate them when they already exist.

(Simplicius, *Commentary on the* Physics 300.27–301.10)

Anaxagoras of Clazomenae seems to have conceived of all the forms in three different ways. First, they are gathered together in an intelligible unity – as when he says:
Together were all things, limitless both in quantity and in smallness. [Cf. B 1]
And again he says:
But before these things separated off, when all were together, not even any colour was clear; for this was prevented by the mingling of all things – of the wet and the dry and the hot and the cold and the bright and the dark and much earth present in it and seeds, limitless in quantity and not at all like one another. This being so, one should believe that all things were present in the whole. [Cf. B 4]
(This totality will be the existent One of Parmenides.) Secondly, he conceived of them in an intellectual dissociation on which the dissociation in our world has been modelled. For in the first book of *On Nature*, shortly after the beginning, Anaxagoras says this:
This being so, one should believe that in all things which are associating there are present many things of every sort and seeds of all things, having all kinds of shapes and colours and savours, and men were compacted and also the other animals which possess souls. And the men possess inhabited cities and constructed goods, as with us, and there is a sun present among them and a moon and the rest, as with us, and the earth grows many things of every sort for them, the most serviceable of which they gather into their houses and use. This I have said about the separating off – that it will have occurred not only with us but also elsewhere. [Cf. B 4]

To some he will perhaps seem not to be contrasting a generative dissociation with an intellectual one but to be comparing our region to other places on the earth. But he would not have said of other places that there is a sun present among them and a moon and the rest, as with us; and it is the items in the intelligible world which he called seeds of all things and shapes. Read what he says a little later on when he compares the two:

As these things thus revolve and are separating off by force and speed (the speed produces the force), their speed is similar in speed to none of the things which now exist among men, but is certainly many times faster. [B 9]

And if this was his conception, he says that all things are in all things first in respect of intelligible unity, secondly in respect of intellectual consubstantiality, and thirdly in respect of perceptible conjunction or generation and dissolution from and into the same things.

(Simplicius, *Commentary on the* Physics 34.18–35.21)

When Anaxagoras says:

One thing neither dissociates nor separates off from another [cf. B 12] because everything is in everything, and elsewhere:

They have not been cut off by an axe, neither the hot from the cold nor the cold from the hot [B 8] (for there is nothing pure by itself) – this, [Aristotle] says, is not a matter of knowledge; for it is not because everything is in everything that the dissociation occurs.

(Simplicius, *Commentary on the* Physics 175.11–16)

In the first book of his *Physics*, Anaxagoras plainly says that generation and destruction are association and dissociation. This is what he writes:

The Greeks do not have a correct view of generation and destruction; for no thing is generated or destroyed; rather, they are mingled and dissociated from existing things. And for this reason they would be correct to call generation mingling and destruction dissociation. [B 17]

All this – that 'together were all things' and that generation takes place in virtue of alteration (or association and dissociation) – was assumed in order to show that nothing comes into being from what does not exist. (Simplicius, *Commentary on the* Physics 163.18–26)

Perhaps Anaxagoras posited compounds as elements, and not simple and original qualities, when he said:

The revolution itself made them separate off. And the dense is separating off from the rare, and the cold from the hot, and the bright from the dark, and the dry from the wet. [Cf. B 12]

And a little later he says:

The dense and the wet and the cold and the dark congregated here where now is the earth, and the rare and the hot and the dry moved out to the farther part of the ether. [B 15]

And he says that these original and very simple things are separating off, and he says that other things, more compound than these, sometimes become compacted like compounds and sometimes separate off like the earth. For he says:

In this way from these as they separate off earth is compacted; for water is separated off from the clouds, earth from the water, and stones are compacted from the earth by the cold. [Cf. B 16]

(Simplicius, *Commentary on the* Physics 178.33–179.10)

Perhaps all the opposites are actually in the elements, if the elements are principles, but not all of them directly (as they are in the case of the uniform items). For sweet and bitter, say, on the hypothesis of the elements do not inhere primarily in the elements but are there by way of heat and cold and dryness and moisture, whereas on the hypothesis of uniform items they inhere primarily and in their own right – as do the colour opposites. Or perhaps even in the case of the uniform items some opposites are prior to others, the secondary ones inhering because of the primary ones. At any rate, Anaxagoras says in the first book of his *Physics*:

For water is separated off from the clouds, earth from the water, and stones are compacted from the earth by the cold. And these move out further than the water. [Cf. B 16]

(Simplicius, *Commentary on the* Physics 155.13–23)

*The only other texts which preserve any of Anaxagoras' own words
are these:*

The distinguished natural scientist Anaxagoras, attacking the senses
for their weakness, says:
**We are not capable of discerning the truth by reason of their
feebleness** [B 21], and he offers as a proof of their untrustworthiness
the gradual change of colours. For if we take two colours, black and
white, and then pour from one to the other drop by drop, our eyes
will not be able to discriminate the gradual changes even though they
exist in nature.

(Sextus Empiricus, *Against the Mathematicians* VII 90)

Diotimus said that according to [Democritus] there are three criteria:
for the apprehension of what is unclear the criterion is the apparent
– for **what appears is the sight of what is unclear** [B 21a], as
Anaxagoras says (and Democritus praises him for this) . . .

(Sextus Empiricus, *Against the Mathematicians* VII 140)

Anaxagoras says:
A rainbow is the reflection of the sun in the clouds. [B 19]
Hence it is a sign of storms.

(Scholia b and T to Homer, *Iliad* XVII 547)

Some scholars have found further fragments in the following three texts:

Anaxagoras discovered the old doctrine that nothing comes into
being from what is not, and did away with generation, introducing
dissociation in its place. For he said that all things have been mixed
with one another and that as they grow they dissociate. For in the
same seed there are hairs and nails and veins and arteries and tendons
and bones. They are invisible because of the smallness of their parts;
but as they grow they gradually dissociate. For how, he says, could
hair come into being from what is not hair, or flesh from what is not
flesh? [B 10] And he says this not only of bodies but also of colours;
for black is present in white and white in black. And he posited the

same for weights, believing that the light was mingled with the heavy
and vice versa. All this is false – for how can opposites co-exist?
(Scholia on Gregory of Nazianzus [*Patrologia
Graeca* XXXVI 911BC])

In all these respects we are more unfortunate than the beasts. But by
experience and memory and wisdom and skill, according to Anaxagoras, †we exploit them,† taking their honey and their milk, and
plundering them and herding them together, so that here nothing
depends on fortune but everything on planning. [B 21b]
(Plutarch, *On Fortune* 98F)

Anaxagoras in his *Physics* says that what is called bird's milk is the
white of the egg. [B 22]   (Athenaeus, *Deipnosophists* 57D)

19

Archelaus

*Archelaus was the first Athenian philosopher. A pupil of Anaxagoras
and a teacher of Socrates, he was himself a minor figure in the history of
Greek thought, and no fragment of his works has survived. Yet he made
at least one striking remark (on the subject of ethics).*

Diogenes Laertius' brief Life *begins thus:*

Archelaus came from Athens or Miletus. His father was Apollodorus
or, according to some, Midon. He was a pupil of Anaxagoras and a
teacher of Socrates. He was the first to bring natural philosophy from
Ionia to Athens; and he was called a natural philosopher inasmuch as
natural philosophy actually ended with him, Socrates introducing
moral philosophy. But he too seems to have touched upon ethics; for
he philosophized about laws and about the noble and the just. Socrates
took this over from him and was supposed to have invented the
subject because he developed it to its height.

He said that there are two causes of generation, hot and cold, and
that animals were generated from the mud. And that things are just
or ignoble not by nature but by convention.

(Diogenes Laertius, *Lives of the Philosophers* II 16)

*Diogenes then gives a summary of Archelaus' natural philosophizing, a
fuller account of which is found in Hippolytus:*

Archelaus was Athenian by birth, son of Apollodorus. He spoke of
the mixing of matter in the same way as Anaxagoras, and similarly of
the principles of things. But he maintained that from the start there
is a mixture present in thought. The principle of motion is the

separating off from one another of the hot and the cold: the hot is in motion, the cold at rest.

As water liquefies it flows into the middle where it burns and becomes air and earth, the former of which is carried upwards while the latter settles below. The earth is at rest and comes into existence for these reasons, and it lies in the middle, being the merest fraction of the universe. <The air> given off by the conflagration <. . .>; from it as it is first burned off comes the nature of the heavenly bodies, of which the greatest is the sun and the second the moon (of the rest some are greater some smaller). He says that the heavens are tilted, and that in this way the sun sheds light on the earth and makes the air transparent and the earth dry. For at first the earth was a marsh, high at the circumference and hollow in the middle. He offers as evidence for its hollowness the fact that the sun does not rise and set at the same time for everyone – something which would be bound to occur were the earth level.

On the subject of animals, he says that, as the earth grew warm, it was first in the lower part, where the hot and the cold were mixing, that numerous other animals and also men appeared, all of them having the same way of life inasmuch as they were nourished by the mud. They were short-lived. Later they came to be generated from one another. Men were distinguished from the other animals and they established leaders and laws and skills and cities and the rest. He says that thought is naturally present in all animals alike; for each of the animals uses thought, some more slowly and others more quickly.   (Hippolytus, *Refutation of All Heresies* I ix 1–6)

20

Leucippus

Leucippus is a shadowy figure: his dates are not recorded, and even his birthplace is uncertain. He was the first to develop the theory of atomism, which was elaborated in far greater detail by his pupil and successor, Democritus of Abdera. Democritus overshadowed his master in the later tradition. The Greek historians of philosophy rarely distinguish between the views of the two men: they often refer, conjunctively, to 'Leucippus and Democritus'. We are rarely in a position to separate the contributions of the master from those of the pupil.

The atomist philosophy will be presented more fully in the next chapter. Here it is enough to cite one of the few passages which speak specifically of Leucippus, and to transcribe the solitary surviving fragment of Leucippus' writings.

Leucippus of Elea or of Miletus (both places are mentioned in connection with him) had something in common with Parmenides' philosophy but did not take the same path as Parmenides and Xenophanes about what exists – rather, as it seems, the contrary path. For whereas they made the universe one and motionless and ungenerated and limited, and did not allow anyone even to inquire into what does not exist, he posited limitless and eternally moving elements, the atoms, and a limitless quantity of shapes among them (since there is no more reason for them to have one shape than another), seeing that among what exists generation and change never cease. Again, he held that what exists no more is than what does not exist, and that both are similarly causes of what comes into being. For, supposing that the substance of the atoms is solid and full, he said that it exists and that it is carried about in what is empty, which he called non-existent and which he says exists no less than does what is existent.

(Simplicius, *Commentary on the* Physics 28.4–15)

Leucippus said that everything happens in accordance with necessity, and necessity is the same as fate. For he says in *On Thought*:

No thing happens in vain, but all things for a reason and by necessity. [67 B 2] (Stobaeus, *Anthology* I iv 7c)

21

Democritus

Democritus was born in Abdera in the north of Greece. He was the most prolific, and ultimately the most influential, of the Presocratic philosophers. Although Plato fails to mention his name, he was highly regarded by Aristotle, and his fundamental ideas were taken up and developed by Epicurus in the fourth century BC. None of Democritus' writings has survived intact, and there are, moreover, very few fragments bearing on his atomism, which we now think of as the central and most important part of his thought. It is indirectly, by way of Epicureanism, that Democritus has had a lasting effect on Western science and philosophy.

Little is known of his life. He is supposed to have learned from Leucippus and from Anaxagoras and from Philolaus. He is said to have travelled to Egypt, to Persia, to the Red Sea – and to Athens:

[Demetrius] says that he is thought to have visited Athens and not to have sought recognition, despising reputation. He knew Socrates but was not known by him. For he says:

I came to Athens and no one knew me. [68 B 116]

(Diogenes Laertius, *Lives of the Philosophers* IX 36)

He himself offered some chronological information:

As to his dates, he was, as he himself says in *The Little World-ordering*, a young man when Anaxagoras was old, being forty years younger than him. And he says that *The Little World-ordering* was composed 730 years after the capture of Troy [B 5]. So he will have been born, according to Apollodorus in his *Chronicles*, in the eightieth Olympiad

[460–457 BC] – or, according to Thrasyllus in his work entitled *Prolegomena to the Reading of the Books of Democritus*, in the third year of the seventy-seventh Olympiad [470/469 BC], being, he says, one year older than Socrates. So he will have been a contemporary of Archelaus, the pupil of Anaxagoras, and of Oenopides (men whom he mentions). He also mentions the opinion about the One held by Parmenides and Zeno as being particularly celebrated in his time – and also Protagoras of Abdera, who is agreed to have been a contemporary of Socrates.

(Diogenes Laertius, *Lives of the Philosophers* IX 41–42)

Some idea of Democritus' productivity, and of the breadth of his professional interests, may be gained from the list of his books which Diogenes Laertius preserves:

His books were catalogued and put in order by Thrasyllus in the same way as he arranged Plato's works – in tetralogies. His ethical works are these:

> *Pythagoras*; *On the Disposition of the Wise Man*; *On the Things in Hades*; *Tritogeneia* (so called because from her come three things which contain all human affairs).
>
> *On Manliness* or *On Virtue*; *The Horn of Amaltheia*; *On Contentment*; *Ethical Commentaries*. (*Well-being* is lost.)

Those are his ethical works; his works on natural science are:

> *The Great World-ordering* (which Theophrastus says was written by Leucippus); *The Little World-ordering*; *Description of the World*; *On the Planets*.
>
> *On Nature* (one book); *On the Nature of Man* or *On Flesh* (two books); *On Thought*; *On the Senses* (some put these together under the title *On the Soul*).
>
> *On Flavours*; *On Colours*; *On Different Shapes*; *On Changing Shape*.
>
> *Buttresses* (which supports the previous works); *On Images* or *On Providence*; *On Logic* or *The Rule* (three books); *Puzzles*.

Those are the works on nature. (Not so ordered are the following:

> *Heavenly Causes*; *Atmospheric Causes*; *Terrestrial Causes*; *Causes*

Concerned with Fire and Things in Fire; Causes Concerned with Sounds; Causes Concerned with Seeds and Plants and Fruits; Causes Concerned with Animals (three books); *Miscellaneous Causes; On the Stone.*

Those are the unordered works.) The mathematical works are these: *On Different Angles* or *On Contact with Circles and Spheres; On Geometry; Geometry; Numbers.*

On Irrational Lines and Solids (two books); *Planispheres; The Great Year* or *Astronomy* (a calendar); *Contest of the Waterclock. Description of the Heavens; Geography; Description of the Poles; Description of Rays of Light.*

Those are the mathematical works; the literary works are the following: *On Rhythms and Harmony; On Poetry; On the Beauty of Verses; On Euphonious and Cacophonous Letters.*

On Homer or *Correct Diction and Glosses; On Song; On Verbs; Vocabularies.*

Such are his literary works; his technical works are these: *Prognosis; On Diet* or *Dietetics; Medical Judgement; Causes Concerning Appropriate and Inappropriate Occasions.*

On Farming or *Farming Matters; On Painting; Tactics;* and *The Use of Arms.*

Such are these. Some order separately the following works from the *Commentaries:*

On the Sacred Writings in Babylon; On Those in Meroë; Circumnavigation of the Ocean; On History; Chaldaean Account; Phrygian Account; On Fever and Coughing Sicknesses; Legal Causes; Chamber-pots or *Problems.*

The other books which some ascribe to him are either compilations of his works or else agreed to be by others.

(Diogenes Laertius, *Lives of the Philosophers* IX 45–49)

The body of this chapter is divided into four sections. First, a selection of texts which describe the atomic theory. Then a section on Democritus' scientific and literary studies. Thirdly, passages which record Democritus' views on knowledge and scepticism. Finally, the longest section is given to the ethical fragments. The relative lengths of the four sections do not reflect the importance which Democritus – or we – might ascribe to the different aspects of his thought.

(1) ATOMISM

For Democritus' most celebrated doctrine, his atomism, we are obliged to rely on second-hand reports.

If the same atoms endure, being impassive, it is clear that [the Democriteans] too will say that the worlds are altered rather than destroyed just as Empedocles and Heraclitus seem to say. A short extract from Aristotle's work *On Democritus* will show what the view of these men was:

Democritus thinks that the nature of eternal things consists in small substances, limitless in quantity, and for them he posits a place, distinct from them and limitless in extent. He calls place by the names 'empty', 'nothing' and 'limitless'; and each of the substances he calls 'thing', 'solid' and 'existent'. He thinks that the substances are so small that they escape our senses, and that they possess all sorts of forms and all sorts of shapes and differences in size. From them, as from elements, he produces and compounds the visible and perceptible masses. The atoms struggle and are carried about in the empty because of their dissimilarities and the other differences mentioned, and as they are carried about they collide and intertwine in a way which makes them touch and be near one another but which does not produce any truly single nature whatever from them; for it is utterly foolish to think that two or more things might ever become one. He explains that the substances remain together for a certain time because the bodies entangle with and grasp hold of one another; for some of them are scalene, some hooked, some concave, some convex, and others have innumerable other differences. So he thinks that they hold on to one another and remain together up to the time when some stronger necessity reaches them from their surroundings and shakes them and scatters them apart. [Aristotle, *On Democritus* fragment 208 Rose, 3rd edn]

He speaks of generation and of its contrary, dissociation, not only of animals but also of plants and of worlds – and in general of all perceptible bodies. So if generation is an association of atoms, and destruction their dissociation, then according to Democritus too, generation will be an alteration.

(Simplicius, *Commentary on* On the Heavens 294.30–295.24)

The excerpt from Aristotle's lost essay on Democritus can be supplemented from his extant Metaphysics:

Leucippus and his colleague Democritus say that the full and the empty are elements, calling the one 'existent' and the other 'non-existent'; and of these the full and solid is existent, the empty non-existent (that is why they say that what exists no more exists than what does not exist – because body no more exists than what is empty), and these are the material causes of what exists. And just as those who take there to be a single underlying substance generate other things by its properties, taking the rare and the dense as principles of the properties, so these men say that the differences are causes of the other things. They say that the differences are three – shape, order and position. For they say that what exists differs only by rhythm, contact and turning – where rhythm is shape, contact is order and turning is position. Thus A differs from N in shape; AN from NA in order; and Z from N in position. As for motion (whence and how existing things acquire it), they too, like the others, blithely ignored the question. (Aristotle, *Metaphysics* 985b4–20)

Aristotle's final remark is echoed by Simplicius:

Democritus says that a whirl of every kind of forms was separated off from the whole [B 167]; but he does not say how or by what cause – so he seems to produce it spontaneously and by chance.

(Simplicius, *Commentary on the* Physics 327.23–26)

The same commentary contains a short section which adds a little to what we learn from Aristotle.

In the same way [Leucippus'] colleague Democritus of Abdera posited the full and the empty as principles, one of which he called existent and the other non-existent; for they posit the atoms as matter for what exists and produce everything else by their differences. These are three: rhythm, turning, contact – which is to say, shape and position and order. For by nature like is moved by like and things of the same kind are carried towards one another, and each of the shapes when arranged in a different compound produces a different condition. Hence, the principles being limitless, they reasonably undertook to account for all properties and substances and for how and by what cause they come into being. That is why they say that only for those who make the elements limitless does everything come out correctly. And they say that the quantity of shapes in the atoms is limitless because there is no more reason for them to be thus than thus. This is the explanation they themselves give for the limitlessness.

(Simplicius, *Commentary on the* Physics 28.15–27)

Atoms exist – they are 'the existent'. Empty space exists – even if it is paradoxically called 'the non-existent'. And nothing else exists:

Democritus sometimes does away with what appears to the senses and says that nothing of this sort appears in truth but only in opinion, truth about what exists lying in the fact that there are atoms and the empty. For he says:

By convention sweet and by convention bitter, by convention hot, by convention cold, by convention colour: in reality atoms and the empty. [Cf. B 125]

That is to say, objects of perception are thought and believed to exist but they do not exist in truth – only atoms and the empty do.

(Sextus Empiricus, *Against the Mathematicians* VII 135)

Several other texts refer to Democritus' celebrated claim that 'by convention colour' etc.

All these people suppose that the primary element is qualityless, having no natural whiteness or blackness or in general any colour whatever, and no sweetness or bitterness or heat or cold or in general any other quality whatever. For, Democritus says,

by convention colour, by convention sweet, by convention bitter: in reality atoms and the empty. [Cf. B 125]

And he thinks that it is from the congregation of atoms that all the perceptible qualities come to be – they are relative to us who perceive them, and in nature there is nothing white or black or yellow or red or bitter or sweet. For the term 'by convention' means 'as it were by custom and relatively to us, not in virtue of the nature of the things themselves'. This in turn he calls 'in reality', deriving the word from 'real' which means 'true'. So the sense of his remark, taken as a whole, will be this: Men think that there are white things and black things and sweet things and bitter things and so on; but in truth everything is things and nothing – this too he himself said, calling the atoms things and the empty nothing. Now all the atoms, being small bodies, lack qualities. The empty is a sort of space in which all these bodies are carried up and down for the whole of time, and either somehow intertwine with one another or else strike and rebound; and in these meetings they dissociate and again associate with one another and from this they make all compounds, including our own bodies and their properties and perceptions.

(Galen, *The Elements according to Hippocrates* I 417–418)

Everyone knows that the greatest charge against any argument is that it conflicts with what is evident. For since an argument cannot even start without self-evidence, how can it have any warranty if it attacks that from which it took its starting-points? Democritus was aware of this; for when he had brought charges against the apparent, saying:

By convention colour, by convention sweet, by convention bitter: in reality atoms and the empty,

he had the senses reply to the intellect as follows:

Poor thought, do you take your warrants from us and then overthrow us? Our overthrow is your fall. [B 125]

So one should condemn as unwarranted an argument which is so bad that its most persuasive part conflicts with the apparent items from which it took its start. (Galen, *On Medical Experience* XV 7–8)

According to [the Pyrrhonists], Xenophanes and Zeno of Elea and Democritus are sceptics . . . Democritus, who does away with qualities where he says:
By convention hot, by convention cold: in reality atoms and the empty. [Cf. B 125]
And again:
In reality we know nothing – for truth is in the depths. [B 117]
(Diogenes Laertius, *Lives of the Philosophers* IX 72)

The suggestion that the objects of everyday experience 'do not really exist' was rejected and ridiculed by the Epicureans:

[Colotes] fails to notice that he drives Epicurus out of life along with Democritus. For Democritus' remark that by convention is colour and by convention sweet and by convention compounds and the rest, in reality what is empty and the atoms [cf. B 125] was, he says, directed against the senses; and he holds that anyone who sticks by this argument and uses it cannot even think that he is himself a man and alive.

I cannot refute this argument; but I can say that these consequences are as inseparable from the doctrines of Epicurus as they say shape and weight are from the atoms. For what does Democritus say? – That substances limitless in quantity, atomic and indestructible, and also qualityless and impassive, are carried about scattered in what is empty. When they approach one another or collide or intertwine, the aggregates appear as water or fire or plants or men, but all things really are atomic forms, as he calls them, and nothing else. For there is no generation from what does not exist, while from what exists nothing can be generated since, because of their solidity, the atoms neither are affected nor change. Hence no colour can emerge from things which are colourless, and no nature or soul from things which are qualityless and impassive. (Plutarch, *Against Colotes* 1110F–1111A)

Democritus went wrong in a manner unworthy of himself when he said that in truth only the atoms are existent, all the rest being by custom. For according to your theory, Democritus, not only shall we not be able to discover the truth, we shall not even be able to live, taking no precaution against fire or death . . .

(Diogenes of Oenoanda, *Physics* fragment 7, col. II 4–14)

The texts so far cited do not explain why Democritus thought that the world consisted of atoms and empty space. The following passage does not claim to report Democritus' actual arguments, but it is presumably an adaptation of Democritean material.

Democritus seems to have been persuaded by appropriate and scientific arguments. What I mean will be clear as we proceed.

There is a difficulty if one supposes that there is a body or magnitude which is divisible everywhere and that this division is possible. For what will there be which escapes the division? If it is divisible everywhere, and the division is possible, then it might be so divided at one and the same time even if the divisions were not all made at the same time; and if this were to happen no impossibility would result. So if it is by nature everywhere divisible, whether at successive mid-points or in any other way at all, then if it is divided nothing impossible will have come about. (After all, if it were divided a thousand times into a thousand parts, nothing impossible would result, even though perhaps no one would actually so divide it.)

Now since the body is everywhere divisible, suppose it to have been divided. What will be left? A magnitude? That is not possible; for then there will be something which has not been divided, and yet we supposed it divisible everywhere. But if there is to be no body or magnitude left and yet the division is to take place, either it will consist of points and be composed of things with no magnitude, or else it will be nothing at all, so that even if it were to come to be from nothing and were composed from nothing, the whole body would be nothing but an appearance.

Similarly, if it consists of points it will not be a quantity. For when the points were in contact and were a single magnitude and were together, they did not make the whole any larger. For when it is divided into two or more, the whole is no smaller or larger than it was before, so that even if all the points are put together they will not make any magnitude.

If some sawdust, as it were, comes about when the body is being divided, and in this way a body escapes from the magnitude, the same argument applies: how is *that* body divisible?

But if it is not a body but a separable form or property which escapes, and the magnitude consists of points or contacts with such and such a property, it is absurd to think that a magnitude consists of what are not magnitudes.

Again, where will the points be, and are they motionless or moving? And a single contact always involves two things, so that there is something apart from the contact and the division and the point.

If one posits that any body of whatever size is everywhere divisible, these are the consequences.

Again, if I divide a log or anything else and then put it together, it is again a unit of the same size. This is so if I cut the log at any point whatever; for it was divided potentially everywhere. Then what is there apart from the division? Even if it has properties, how is a body resolved into these and how does it come into being from them? And how are they separated? So if it is impossible for magnitudes to consist of contacts or points, necessarily there are indivisible bodies and magnitudes.   (Aristotle, *On Generation and Corruption* 316a13–b16)

Atoms are ungenerated and indestructible. Democritus offered a curious argument to show that at least some things are ungenerated:

As for time, with one exception everyone seems to be in agreement: they say that it is ungenerated. That is how Democritus tries to show that it is impossible for everything to have come into being – for time is ungenerated.   (Aristotle, *Physics* 251b14–17)

(2) SCIENTIFIC AND LITERARY STUDIES

Like his predecessors, Democritus was concerned to understand and explain the varied phenomena of the world of nature:

Democritus, so they say, used to affirm that he would rather discover a single causal explanation than become king of the Persians [B 118] – although his causes were futile and causeless inasmuch as he started from an empty principle and an erroneous hypothesis.

(Dionysius of Alexandria, *On Nature* fragment 7 Routh, in
Eusebius, *Preparation for the Gospel* XIV xxvii 4)

Like his predecessors, Democritus had reflected on causation and on the nature and goal of scientific explanation. Aristotle, who had a high opinion of Democritus' scientific prowess, nevertheless found his ideas about causality somewhat primitive:

The earlier thinkers did not arrive at this method because essences and essential definition had not yet been discovered. Democritus was the first to touch on this – not as being necessary for scientific inquiry but because he was carried on by the facts themselves.

(Aristotle, *Parts of Animals* 642a24–27)

One important element in Democritean explanations (as a passage on psychology will further illustrate) was atomic shape or configuration:

For example, since fire moves readily and heats and burns, some made it a sphere and others a pyramid . . . If fire heats and burns because of its angles, then all the elements will heat (though some more than others); for they all have angles – for example an octahedron, a dodecahedron – and Democritus holds that a sphere too, being an angle, cuts because it moves easily. (Aristotle, *On the Heavens* 306b32–33, 307a13–17)

Another element is a principle according to which like is attracted to and acts upon like:

Democritus alone expressed a view of his own different from the others: he says that what acts and what is acted upon are the same and alike – it is not possible for items which are other and different to be acted upon by one another; rather, even if different items act upon one another, it is not insofar as they are different but insofar as they have something the same in common that this comes about.

(Aristotle, *On Generation and Corruption* 323b10–15)

There is an ancient opinion – which, as I have already said, has long been current among the natural scientists – to the effect that like recognizes like. Democritus is thought to have produced confirmation of this opinion and Plato to have touched on it in the *Timaeus*. Democritus bases his argument on both animate and inanimate things. For animals, he says, congregate with animals of the same kind – doves with doves, cranes with cranes, and so with the other irrational animals. Similarly in the case of inanimate things, as we can see from seeds which are being sieved and from pebbles where the waves break. For in the one case the whirling of the sieve separately arranges lentils with lentils, barley with barley, wheat with wheat; and in the other case, by the motion of the waves, oval pebbles are pushed into the same place as oval pebbles, and round pebbles as round pebbles, as though the likeness in things contained some sort of force for collecting things together [B 164]. That is Democritus' view.

(Sextus Empiricus, *Against the Mathematicians* VII 116–118)

[Democritus] says that in liquids like <associates> with like, just as in the universe as a whole, and that in this way the sea and all other <salty substances> were formed, as homogeneous items came together. That the sea is made of homogeneous items is also evident from other cases: frankincense, sulphur, silphium, nitre, alum, bitumen, and other great and remarkable things are not found in many parts of the earth.

(Theophrastus (?), *On Water*, Hibeh Papyrus 16 col. II 1–12)

These various notions, connected to a theory of 'effluences', collaborate in the following passage:

Democritus postulates that effluences are given off and that like is carried to like – but also that everything is carried to what is empty. Making these postulates, he assumes that the magnet and the iron are composed of similar atoms, and that the magnet is made of finer atoms and is more rarefied and contains more of the empty. For this reason, being more mobile, its atoms are carried towards the iron (for movement is toward likes) and entering the channels in the iron they set in motion the bodies which it contains, passing through them because of their fineness. The atoms thus set in motion are carried outside and flow towards the magnet because of the likeness and because it contains more of the empty; and the iron follows them because of their abundant discharge and movement, and is itself carried towards the magnet. The magnet is not carried towards the iron because the iron does not have as much of the empty as the magnet does.   (Alexander, *Problems and Solutions* ii 23 [72.28–73.7])

Alexander is no doubt drawing on Democritus' work 'On the Stone' (that is, 'On the Magnet'); and the catalogue of Democritus' writings gives an idea of the scientific topics which he addressed. But there are few fragments, and many of the numerous reports are of doubtful reliability, for

many fictions appear to have been ascribed to Democritus by unscrupulous authors who took refuge in his eminence and authority.   (Aulus Gellius, *Attic Nights* X xii 8)

The following passages, a small sample and roughly classified by topic, illustrate some of Democritus' scientific explorations.

(a) 'Meteorology'

I said that the fire associated with thunder is remarkably clear and fine: its very origin is in a pure and holy substance; and the swiftness of its motion shakes off and purifies it of anything moist or earthy which may have mingled with it; for **nothing struck by lightning,** as Democritus says, †**can withstand the brightness from the sky.**†
[B 152]   (Plutarch, *Table Talk* 665EF)

Later Democritus and Eudoxus and others wrote up journeys about
the earth and navigations round the earth. The old thinkers drew the
inhabited world as round, placing Greece in its centre and Delphi
in the centre of Greece (for Delphi holds the navel of the earth).
Democritus, a man of wide experience, was the first to appreciate that
the earth is elongated, its length being one and a half times its breadth.
[B 15]   (Agathemerus, *Geography* I i–ii)

(b) Mathematics

Consider the way in which [Chrysippus] answered the puzzle which
Democritus stated in such a vivid and scientific fashion. If a cone is
cut by a plane parallel to its base, what should we think of the surfaces
of the segments – are they equal or unequal? If unequal, they will
make the cone irregular, giving it a number of step-like notches or
roughnesses; if equal, the segments will be equal and the cone will
plainly have acquired the properties of a cylinder, since it will consist
of circles which are equal and not unequal – and that is utterly absurd
[B 155]. Here [Chrysippus] declares that Democritus is ignorant, and
says that the surfaces are neither equal nor unequal.

(Plutarch, *On Common Notions* 1079EF)

(c) Biology

The womb accepts the seed which has fallen into it and protects it as
it takes root – for first the navel grows in the womb, as Democritus
says [B 148], as an anchorage against rolling and drifting, as a rope
and a branch for the fruit which is being generated and coming to
be.   (Plutarch, *On Love for One's Offspring* 495E)

[The species of two forms of pulse] have in common what each form
got its name from – for wave-like pulses, the fact that waves, as it
were, form in the arteries one after another; for worm-like pulses,
the fact that they are like the movement of worms, animals which
themselves move in a wave-like manner, as Democritus I think says

where he discusses animals which wander wave-like in their movement. [B 126]   (Galen, *On the Difference of Pulses* VIII 551)

[Hippocrates] called veins not the vessels customarily so named but rather the arteries – and Democritus calls the movement in the arteries **vein-throbbing**. [B 120]

(Erotian, *On Expressions in Hippocrates* Φ 3 [90.18–20])

(d) Psychology

Some say that soul is especially and primarily a cause of movement; and, thinking that what is not itself moving cannot move anything else, they suppose that the soul is something moving. Thus Democritus says that it is a sort of fire, and hot; for, the shapes or atoms being limitless, he says that the spherical ones are fire and soul – like the so-called motes in the air which are seen in the sunbeams coming through windows.   (Aristotle, *On the Soul* 403b28–404a4)

In addition to such general theorizing, Democritus gave detailed attention to sense-perception. Theophrastus describes his views, of which the following two passages are representative.

Democritus does not determine whether perception takes place by opposites or by likes. For insofar as he makes perceiving come about by alteration, he will seem to have it take place by things which are different – for like is not altered by like. On the other hand, insofar as perceiving and alteration in general take place by being affected, and (as he says) it is impossible for things which are not the same to be affected (even if things which are different have an effect, they do so not insofar as they are different but insofar as they have something the same), then by likes. So on these matters you can take him in both ways.

He attempts to account for each [of the senses] in turn. He has sight occur by reflection, but he talks of reflection in a special way. The reflection does not take place immediately in the pupil; rather, the air between the eye and the seen object is imprinted when it is compressed by what is seen and what sees (for there are always effluences coming off everything). Then this air, which is solid and has a different colour, is reflected in the eyes, which are moist. What is dense does not receive it, but what is moist lets it pass through. That is why moist eyes are better at seeing than hard eyes – provided that the external membrane is extremely fine and dense, the internal parts are as spongy as possible and empty of any dense and tough flesh and also of any thick and oily liquid, and the vessels leading to the eyes are straight and dry so as to take the same shape as the objects imprinted – for each thing best recognizes what is akin to it.

(Theophrastus, *On the Senses* 49–50)

[A flavour] is sharp if in shape it is angular and crinkled and small and fine. For because of its pungency it quickly penetrates everywhere, and being rough and angular it gathers and holds things together. That is why it heats the body, by making empty spaces in it – for what is most empty is most heated.

Sweet flavour is constituted by round shapes which are not too small. That is why it relaxes the body completely and does not do everything violently or quickly. It disturbs the other flavours because as it passes through it makes the other shapes drift about and it moistens them; and when they are moistened and move out of order, they flow together into the stomach – that is the most accessible part since it is the emptiest.

Sour flavour is constituted by large shapes with many angles and as little roundness as possible. For when these enter the body they clog and stop the vessels and prevent things from flowing together. That is why they also settle the bowels.

Bitter flavour is constituted by small, smooth, rounded shapes, where the roundness also contains crinkles. That is why it is viscous and sticky.

Salty flavour is constituted by large shapes which are not rounded †nor yet scalene – and hence not crinkled.† (He calls scalene those which overlap and intertwine with one another.) They are large, because salt rises to the surface – if they were small and were hit by what surrounds them, they would mix with the whole. They are not round, because what is salty is rough while what is rounded is smooth. They are not scalene, because they are not entangled with one another – that is why [what is salty] is friable.

Pungent flavour is small, rounded and angular, but not scalene. For the pungent, being angular, heats by its roughness, and it relaxes because it is small and rounded and angular – that is what angular items are like.

He treats the other powers of each [flavour] in the same way, reducing them to the shapes. Of all the shapes none is pure and unmixed with the others; rather, there are many in each, the same flavour containing smooth and rough, rounded and sharp, and the rest. The shape which preponderates has a very great influence on perception and the power [of the flavour] – so too has the condition in which it finds us. For this too makes no little difference, since sometimes the same thing has opposite effects and opposites the same effect.

This is what he has said about flavours.

(Theophrastus, *On the Senses* 65–67)

There is also a theory of dreams:

[Favorinus] set down this standard thesis of Democritus, who says that images penetrate through the channels into the body and then surface to produce the visions we have during sleep. They come from everywhere, arising from furniture and clothing and plants – but especially from animals as a result of their motion and heat. They not only have impressed on them likenesses of the shapes of the bodies (as Epicurus thinks – he follows Democritus thus far but here departs from his account) but also take on reflections of the movements of the soul and of each man's plans and character and passions. They carry these along with them, and when they meet someone they speak like living things and announce to those who receive them the opinions and reasonings and impulses of those who sent them, whenever they arrive with the representations preserved in an articulated and distinct form.　　　　　(Plutarch, *Table Talk* 785AB)

(e) Theology

Democritus rightly says that

A few of the wise men, stretching up their hands to the place we Greeks now call the air, †spoke of Zeus; for† he knows all things and bestows all things and takes away, and he is king of all things.
[B 30]   (Clement, *Protreptic* VI 68.5)

Democritus says that certain images reach men, some of them beneficial and others harmful (which is why he prayed for propitious images); they are large and impressive, and difficult to destroy though not indestructible; and they indicate the future to men when they are seen and speak. So men of old, receiving the impression of these things, supposed that there were gods, there being no other god with an indestructible nature apart from these images. [B 166]
                    (Sextus Empiricus, *Against the Mathematicians* IX 19)

Some suppose that the strange things which happen in the world gave us the conception of gods. Democritus seems to be of this opinion; for he says that men in the distant past, remarking the events of the upper air – thunder and lightning, thunderbolts and conjunctions of stars, and eclipses of sun and moon – were frightened, thinking gods to be their cause.
                    (Sextus Empiricus, *Against the Mathematicians* IX 24)

It is absurd to pay careful attention to the cawing of rooks and the crowing of cocks and to pigs rooting among the rubbish, as Democritus puts it [B 147], and to treat these things as signs of wind and rain . . .   (Plutarch, *On Preserving Health* 129A)

(f) Anthropology

Democritus, like the voice of Zeus and 'saying this about all things', tried to explain the concept [of man] but could get no further than an amateur assertion, saying:

Man is what we all know. [B 165]

(Sextus Empiricus, *Against the Mathematicians* VII 265)

None the less, he had a certain amount to say on the subject. The following text is generally thought to reflect Democritean ideas (even though it does not explicitly mention Democritus).

They say that the first men lived an anarchic and bestial sort of life, going out to forage here and there and living off the most palatable herbs and the fruit which grew wild on the trees. Then, since they were attacked by wild animals, they helped one another (instructed by self-interest); and thus gathering together because of fear, they slowly came to recognize one another's shapes.

The sounds they made had no sense and were confused; but gradually they articulated their expressions, and by establishing symbols among themselves for every sort of object they came to express themselves on all matters in a way intelligible to one another. Such groups came into existence throughout the inhabited world, and not all men had the same language, since each group organized its expressions as chance had it. Hence there are languages of every type, and the groups who first came into existence are the founders of all the races.

Now the earliest men lived laboriously, none of the utilities of life having been discovered: they wore no clothes, they knew nothing of houses or of fire, they had not the slightest conception of cultivated foodstuffs. And not knowing how to harvest wild foodstuffs, they did not lay aside any fruits against need. Hence many of them died in winter from cold and from lack of food. Later, gradually instructed by experience, they took refuge in caves during the winter, and stored those fruits which could be preserved. Once fire and other utilities were recognized, the crafts were slowly discovered and with them whatever else can benefit communal life. For in general it was need itself which instructed men in everything, appropriately introducing knowledge of each thing to an animal which was naturally well endowed and had assistants for every purpose in its hands, its reason and its keenness of thought.

(Diodorus, *Universal History* I viii 1–9)

For the discovery of the crafts, primitive men had the example of the beasts to follow:

Perhaps we are foolish to admire animals for their learning, when Democritus asserts [B 154] that we are their pupils in all the most important things – of the spider in weaving and healing, of the swallow in building, of the song-birds (the swan and the nightingale) in singing.
(Plutarch, *On the Intelligence of Animals* 974A)

Democritus, a man who was not only the most scientific of the ancients but also the most industrious of all those of whom we have report, says that music is a young art, and he explains this by saying that it was not provoked by necessity but came into being from superfluity. [B 144]

(Philodemus, *On Music* IV, Herculaneum Papyrus 1497
col. XXXVI 29–39)

There are also some reflections on death:

Men seem to reject the very thought of death because of a love of life – which derives from a terror of death, not from an enjoyment of life; and then, when they have a clear view of death, it falls on them unexpectedly – and for that reason, not even bearing to make a will, they are caught and compelled to <. . .>, as Democritus says. [B 1a]

(Philodemus, *On Death* IV, Herculaneum Papyrus 1050
col. XXXIX 6–15)

Many of the old thinkers, among them the natural scientist Democritus in his writings about Hades, have collected stories of those who are thought to have died and then come to life again. [B 1]

(Proclus, *Commentary on the* Republic II 113)

(g) Literature and language

Democritus says:

What a poet writes with enthusiasm and holy inspiration is very fine. [B 18]

But we know what the poets say.

(Clement, *Miscellanies* VI xviii 168.2)

Democritus says this about Homer:

Homer, having a nature divinely inspired, fashioned a world of words of every sort [B 21],

implying that it is not possible to produce verses so fine and wise without a divine or superhuman nature.

(Dio Chrysostom, *On Homer* [*Discourse* liii] 1)

Again, as *chrusoöntai, chrusountai*, so *noöntai, nountai*. Democritus: **they think** [*nountai*] **divine thoughts in their minds.** [B 129]

(Herodian, *On Deformations* 240 [*Grammatici Graeci* III ii 253.8–10])

Democritus said that names are conventional, and he tried to establish this by four arguments. From homonymy: different things are called by the same name; therefore names are not natural. From polyonymy: if different names fit one and the same thing, then they also fit one another, which would be impossible. Thirdly, from the changes of names – why did we rename Aristocles Plato and Tyrtamus Theophrastus if names are natural? From the absence of similar forms – why do we say 'to think' from 'thought' when we do not derive anything from 'justice'? Therefore names are due to chance, not to nature. He calls the first argument **polysemy**, the second **equipollence**, <the third **metonymy**> and the fourth **anonymy**. [B 26]

(Proclus, *Commentary on the* Cratylus, preface 16)

Democritus, giving an etymology of the name [Tritogeneia], says that these three things come from wisdom: reasoning well, speaking well, and doing what you should. [B 2]

(Geneva scholia on Homer, *Iliad* VIII 39)

(3) KNOWLEDGE

Democritus' atomism was the framework within which he tried to understand the nature of the world. At the same time – as the celebrated remark 'By convention colour . . .' has already intimated – this atomism appeared to have sceptical implications.

According to [the Pyrrhonists], Xenophanes and Zeno of Elea and Democritus are sceptics . . . Democritus, who does away with qualities where he says:

By convention hot, by convention cold: in reality atoms and the empty. [Cf. B 125]

And again:

In reality we know nothing – for truth is in the depths. [B 117]

(Diogenes Laertius, *Lives of the Philosophers* IX 72)

The longest text on Democritean scepticism is the following:

Although in his *Buttresses* [Democritus] undertakes to ascribe power of warranty to the senses, he is none the less found condemning them. For he says:

We in reality know nothing firmly but only as it changes in accordance with the condition of the body and of the things which enter it and of the things which resist it. [B 9]

And again he says:

That in reality we do not understand how each thing is or is not has been shown in many ways. [B 10]

And in *On Forms* he says:

And a man must recognize by this rule that he is removed from reality [B 6];

and again:

This argument too shows that in reality we know nothing about anything, but our belief in each case is a changing of shape [B7];

and again:

Yet it will be clear that to know how each thing is in reality is baffling. [B 8]

Now in these passages he does away in effect with all apprehension, even if it is only the senses which he explicitly attacks. But in the *Rules* he says that there are two forms of knowledge, one by way of the senses and the other by way of the understanding. The one by way of the understanding he calls genuine, ascribing to it warranty with regard to the judgement of truth; the one by way of the senses he names dark, denying that it is unerring with regard to the discernment of what is true. These are his words:

There are two forms of knowledge, one genuine and the other dark. To the dark belong all these: sight, hearing, smell, taste, touch. The genuine, separated from this <. . .>. [B 11a]

Then, setting the genuine above the dark, he continues thus:

When the dark can no longer see more finely or hear or smell or taste or perceive by touch, but to a finer degree <. . .>. [B 11b]

So according to him too, reason, which he calls genuine knowledge, is a criterion.

But Diotimus said that according to him there are three criteria: for the apprehension of what is unclear the criterion is the apparent (for what appears is the sight of what is unclear, as Anaxagoras says [59 B 21a] – and Democritus praises him for this); for investigation, it is the concept ('for in every case, my son, there is one principle: to know what the investigation is about' [Plato, *Phaedrus* 273B]); of choice and avoidance, it is the passions (for what we find congenial is to be chosen and what we find alien to be avoided).

(Sextus Empiricus, *Against the Mathematicians* VII 136–140)

The remark on 'changing of shape' in B 7 is echoed in another text:

We know that what is hard to acquire is unnecessary and that what is necessary God has generously made easy to acquire. Hence Democritus well says that **Nature and teaching are similar**, and he briefly adds the reason:

for teaching changes a man's shape and nature acts by changing shape. [B 33]

There is no difference between being moulded in a certain way by nature and being shaped in that way by time and study.

(Clement, *Miscellanies* IV xxiii 149.3–4)

Aristotle offers a brief and puzzling analysis of what he took to be Democritus' error:

Many other animals receive impressions contrary to our own, and indeed things do not seem always the same to the perception of a single individual. So it is unclear which of them are true or false; for there is no more reason for this to be true than for that – they are on a par. That is why Democritus says that either nothing is true or to us at least it is unclear. In general, because they suppose that thought is perception and perception a sort of alteration, they say that what appears to perception is necessarily true. For these reasons, Empedocles and Democritus and virtually all of the others have been guilty of holding such opinions. (Aristotle, *Metaphysics* 1009b7–15)

And the Epicureans criticized Democritus for being unlivably sceptical:

[Colotes] first accuses [Democritus] of saying that each object is no more such-and-such than so-and-so, and thereby throwing life into confusion. But Democritus is so far from thinking that each object is no more such-and-such than so-and-so that he attacked Protagoras the sophist for saying just this and wrote many persuasive things against him. Colotes, having not the slightest acquaintance with these writings, has misunderstood Democritus' words: when he lays it down that things no more exist than does nothing, he means body by things and what is empty by nothing, indicating that the latter too has a sort of nature and subsistence of its own. [B 156]

(Plutarch, *Against Colotes* 1108F–1109A)

It may be noted, in passing, that the attack on Protagoras to which Plutarch here refers contained the first occurrence of an influential argument against relativism:

You cannot say that every impression is true, because of the reversal – as Democritus and Plato showed in their reply to Protagoras. For if every impression is true, then it will also be true that not every impression is true (since that is an impression), and thus it will be false that every impression is true.

(Sextus Empiricus, *Against the Mathematicians* VII 389–390)

(4) MORAL PHILOSOPHY

Numerous fragments of Democritus' moral and political philosophy are preserved. It is not clear whether they are the remains of a systematic theory, nor how that theory (if it existed) was connected to Democritus' other views. Most of the texts are found in the Anthology *of John Stobaeus; but before turning to Stobaeus a few passages from other sources may be set down.*

The overall goal of life, according to Democritus, is joy or contentment or tranquillity:

Democritus is said – whether truly or falsely we shall not ask – to have blinded himself; and certainly, so that his mind might be as little distracted from its thoughts as possible, he neglected his inheritance and left his land uncultivated – in search of what else if not of a happy life? And although he located such a life in the knowledge of things, nevertheless he wanted his inquiry into nature to put him into a good frame of mind – for the highest good he called contentment and, often, imperturbability (that is, a mind free from fear).

(Cicero, *On Ends* V xxix 87)

The Abderites too say that there is a goal of life. Democritus, in his work *On the Goal*, says that it is contentment, which he also calls well-being; and he often remarks:
For joy and absence of joy is the boundary <of advantage and disadvantage. [B 4; cf. B 188]
This, he says, is the goal of life for men both young> and old. Hecataeus holds that the goal is self-sufficiency, Apollodotus of Cyzicus that

it is amusement, Nausiphanes that it is unruffledness – and he says that this was called imperturbability by Democritus.

(Clement, *Miscellanies* II xxi 130.4–5)

If we miss contentment, then that is often our own fault – and the fault not of our bodies but of our souls:

Let us then say to ourselves that your body, my good man, produces diseases and afflictions by nature from within itself and receives many that strike it from without, and that if you open yourself up, you will find within a large and varied storehouse and treasury of evils, as Democritus says [B 149], which do not flow in from outside but have, as it were, internal and native springs.

(Plutarch, *On Afflictions of Mind and Body* 500DE)

The dispute between body and soul over the passions seems to be an old one. Democritus, ascribing our unhappiness to the soul, says that if the body were to take it to court for the pains and sufferings it had endured throughout its life, then if he were to be on the jury for the case he would gladly cast his vote against the soul inasmuch as it had destroyed some parts of the body by negligence or dissipated them by drunkenness, and had ruined and ravaged other parts by its pursuit of pleasures – just as he would blame the careless user if a tool or implement were in a bad condition. [B 159]

([Plutarch], *On Desire and Distress* 2)

To keep the instrument in good condition, we need wisdom and the use of reason:

Medicine, according to Democritus, **heals the diseases of the body, and wisdom takes away passions of the soul.** [B 31]

(Clement, *The Tutor* I ii 6.2)

When a man respects himself, not disparaging himself but rejoicing and being glad that he is a reliable witness and spectator of what is good, then he shows that reason is already nourished and rooted within him and, as Democritus says [B 146], is accustomed to take its pleasures from itself.   (Plutarch, *Progress in Virtue* 81AB)

Alongside such general musings, there are various particular reflections and counsels of a moral nature, among them the following:

Democritus:
Men enjoy scratching themselves – they get the same pleasure as those who are having sexual intercourse. [B 127]
(Herodian, *On Accentuation in General* XVI [*Grammatici Graeci* III i 445.9–11])

Light-hearted investigations move the souls [of symposiasts] in a harmonious and beneficial manner – but one should avoid speeches from wranglers and shysters, as Democritus styles them. [B 150]
(Plutarch, *Table Talk* 614E)

Lamprias said that it was hardly strange if Hagias was vexed when he got an equal share – after all, he carried a large paunch. And he confessed that he too was one of those who like their food – there are no bones in a shared fish, as Democritus says. [B 151]
(Plutarch, *Table Talk* 643E)

Hence it is well to interpose the night and sleep, to make an adequate interval and intermission, and to wake up fresh again, as at the beginning, and – as Democritus has it – thinking new thoughts each day. [B 158]   (Plutarch, *Table Talk* 655D)

Your sons should be kept away from bad language; for the word is shadow of the deed, according to Democritus. [B 145]
(Plutarch, *On Educating Children* 9F)

Democritus urges us to be instructed in the art of war, which is of the greatest importance, and to seek out labour, which is a source of great and glorious things for men. [B 157]

(Plutarch, *Against Colotes* 1126A)

Hence we shall not imitate those nations which eat flesh by necessity but rather those which are pious and closer to the gods. For to live badly and not wisely or temperately or piously, Democrates said, is not to live but to spend a long time dying. [B 160]

(Porphyry, *On Abstinence* IV 21)

In the preceding text, 'Democrates' is sometimes changed to 'Democritus'.

Now the fragments from Stobaeus, cited in the order in which they appear in the Anthology. *All the texts ascribed to Democritus (or to 'Democrates' or to 'Democ') are quoted; but some of the ascriptions are dubious.*

Democritus:

Do not be eager to know everything lest you become ignorant of everything. [B 169] (II i 12)

Democritus:

Reason is a powerful persuader. [Cf. B 51] (II iv 12)

Democritus and Plato both place happiness in the soul. Democritus writes thus:

Happiness and unhappiness belong to the soul. [B 170]

Happiness does not dwell in herds, nor yet in gold: the soul is the dwelling place of the spirit. [B 171]

He calls happiness contentment, well-being, harmony, orderliness, tranquillity. It is constituted by distinguishing and discriminating among pleasures, and this is the noblest and most advantageous thing for men. (II vii 3i)

Democritus:

Men fashioned an image of chance as an excuse for their own thoughtlessness; for chance rarely fights with wisdom, and a clear-sighted intelligence sets straight most things in life. [B 119]

(II viii 16)

Democritus:

From the same sources from which good things come to us we may also draw bad. But let us avoid the bad. For example, deep water is useful for many purposes, and then again it is bad – for there is danger of drowning. So a device has been discovered: teaching people to swim. [B 172]

idem:

For men, bad things spring from good when they do not know how to manage the good or to preserve them resourcefully. It is not just to judge such things bad; rather, they are good – †but anyone who wishes may use good things for bad ends.† [B 173]

A contented man who is led to deeds which are just and lawful rejoices night and day and is strengthened and free of care; but a man who pays no heed to justice, and does not do what he ought, finds all such things joyless; and when he remembers them, he is afraid and he reviles himself. [B 174]

The gods, both in the past and now, give men all things except those which are bad and harmful and useless. Neither in the past nor now do the gods bestow such things on men, but they come upon them by themselves because of blindness of thought and folly. [B 175]

Fortune offers many gifts, but is unstable: nature is self-sufficient. That is why, being smaller but stable, she conquers the greater force of hope. [B 176]   (II ix 1–5)

Democritus:

Many perform the foulest deeds and rehearse the fairest words. [B53a]   (II xv 33)

Democritus:

One should emulate the deeds and actions of virtue, not the words. [B 55]   (II xv 36)

Democritus:

Noble words do not obscure foul actions nor is a good action spoiled by slanderous words. [B 177]   (II xv 40)

Democrates:

Indulgence is the worst of all things with regard to the education of youth; for it is this which gives birth to the pleasures from which evil arises. [B 178]

idem:

Children who are given free rein <. . .> will learn neither letters nor music nor gymnastics nor yet – what most sustains virtue – a sense of shame; for it is precisely from this that shame usually arises. [B 179]

idem:

Education is an ornament for the fortunate, a refuge for the unfortunate. [B 180]

idem:

The use of exhortation and the persuasion of reason is clearly a stronger inducement to virtue than are law and necessity. For one who has been kept from injustice by law is likely to do wrong in secret, while one who has been led to duty by persuasion is unlikely to do anything improper either in secret or openly. That is why a man who acts uprightly from understanding and knowledge proves to be at the same time both courageous and right-thinking. [B 181]

(II xxxi 56–59)

Democ:

Nature and teaching are similar, for teaching changes a man's shape and nature acts by changing shape. [B 33]

idem:

Learning produces fine things by labour: foul things come to fruit spontaneously without labour. For even a man who is unwilling is often prevented <. . .> [B 182]   (II xxxi 65–66)

Democ:

Neither skill nor wisdom is attainable unless you learn. [B 59]

idem:

There is understanding among the young and lack of understanding among the old; for it is not time which teaches good sense but appropriate upbringing and nature. [B 183] idem:

Those who contradict and babble are ill-endowed for learning.
[Cf. B 85]   (II xxxi 71–73)

Democ:

Frequent association with the wicked increases a disposition to vice. [B 184]   (II xxxi 90)

Democ:

The hopes of the educated are stronger than the wealth of the ignorant. [B 185]   (II xxxi 94)

Democritus:

Like-mindedness makes for friendship. [B 186]   (II xxxiii 9)

Democritus:

It is fitting for men to take account of their souls rather than of their bodies; for a perfect soul corrects wickedness of body, but strength of body without reasoning makes the soul no better at all.
[B 187 = B 36]   (III i 27)

Democritus:

It is fitting to yield to the law, to the ruler, to the wiser. [B 47]

Democritus:

The boundary of advantage and disadvantage is joy and absence of joy. [B 188]

It is best for a man to live his life with as much contentment and as little grief as possible; this will come about if he does not take his pleasures in mortal things. [B 189]   (III i 45–47)

Democritus:

One should avoid even speaking of evil deeds. [B 190]   (III i 91)

Democrates:

One should refrain from wrong-doing not out of fear but out of duty. [B 41]   (III i 95)

Democritus:

For men gain contentment from moderation in joy and a measured life: deficiencies and excesses tend to change and to produce large movements in the soul, and souls which move across large intervals are neither stable nor content. Thus you must set your judgement on the possible and be satisfied with what you have, giving little thought to those who are envied and admired, and not dwelling on them in your thought; and you must observe the lives of those who are badly off, considering how much they undergo, so that what you have and what belongs to you may seem great and enviable, and so that you may no longer suffer in your soul by desiring more. For one who admires those who possess much and are deemed blessed by other men, and who dwells on them every hour in his memory, is compelled always to plan something new and, driven by desire, to set himself to do some desperate deed which the laws forbid. That is why you should not seek certain things and should be content with others, comparing your own life with that of those who act badly, and deeming yourself blessed when you reflect on what they undergo, acting and living so much better than they do. For if you hold fast to this judgement you will live in greater contentment and will drive away those not inconsiderable plagues of life, jealousy and envy and malice. [B 191]   (III i 210)

Democritus:

It is easy to praise and to blame what one should not; but each is the mark of a bad character. [B 192]   (III ii 36)

Democritus:

It is the task of good sense to guard against future injustice: it is a mark of insensibility not to defend yourself when it has occurred. [B 193]   (III iii 43)

Democritus:

Great joys come from contemplating noble deeds. [B 194]

(III iii 46)

Democritus:

Images are by their dress and adornment magnificent to observe; but they are empty of heart. [B 195]

Forgetting one's own ills produces boldness. [B 196]

Fools are shaped by the gifts of fortune, those who understand such things by the gifts of wisdom. [B 197]

That which is in need knows how much it needs: he who is in need does not recognize the fact. [B 198]

Fools, though they hate life, want to live – from fear of Hades. [B 199]

Fools live without enjoying life. [B 200]

Fools desire longevity but do not enjoy longevity. [B 201]

Fools desire what is absent: what is present, although it is more beneficial than what is past, they squander. [B 202]

In fleeing death men pursue it. [B 203]

Fools give no pleasure in the whole of their lives. [B 204]

Fools, fearing death, desire life. [B 205]

Fools, fearing death, want to grow old. [B 206]

Many have much learning and no thought. [B 64]

Reputation and wealth without understanding are not safe possessions. [B 77]   (III iv 69–82)

Democritus:

One should choose not every pleasure but those which aim at what is noble. [B 207]

Rightful love is a longing, without violence, for the noble. [B 73]

A father's good sense is the greatest precept for his children. [B 208]

With self-sufficiency in upbringing the night is never long. [B 209]

Fortune provides a rich table, good sense a self-sufficient one. [B 210]

Good sense increases joys and makes pleasure greater. [B 211]

                                                (III v 22–27)

Democritus:

Some men rule cities and are slaves to women. [Cf. B 214]

Sleeping during the day indicates a disturbed body or a troubled soul or idleness or lack of education. [B 212]

Coition is a mild madness; for a man rushes out of a man. [B 32]

(III vi 26–28)

Democritus:

Courage makes disasters small. [B 213]   (III vii 21)

Democritus:

A courageous man is not only one who conquers his enemies but also one who is superior to pleasures; some men rule cities and are slaves to women. [B 214]   (III vii 25)

Democritus:

The glory of justice is confidence of judgement and imperturbability: the end of injustice is fear of disaster. [B 215]   (III vii 31)

Democritus:

Imperturbable wisdom, being most honourable, is worth everything. [B 216]   (III vii 74)

Democritus:

It is not refraining from injustice which is good, but not even wanting it. [B 62]

Democritus:

Only those who hate injustice are loved by the gods. [B 217]

(III ix 29–30)

Democritus:

When wealth comes from wicked deeds it makes the disgrace more conspicuous. [B 218]   (III x 36)

Democritus:

One who offers advice to those who think they possess sense is wasting his time. [B 52]

idem:

Desire for money, if it is not limited by satiety, is far heavier than extreme poverty; for greater desires create greater needs. [B 219]

Democritus:

Evil gains bring loss of virtue. [B 220]   (III x 42–44)

Democritus:

Hope of evil gain is the beginning of loss. [B 221]   (III x 58)

Democritus:

The excessive accumulation of money for one's children is an excuse for avarice of a peculiar character. [B 222]

idem:

Whatever the body needs can readily be found by everyone, without trouble or distress; the things which need trouble and distress and make life painful are craved not by the body but by bad character of judgement. [B 223]   (III x 64–65)

Democritus:

The desire for more destroys what is present – like Aesop's dog. [B 224]   (III x 68)

Democritus:

One should tell the truth, not speak at length. [B 44 = B 225]
                                                       (III xii 13)

Democritus:

It is better to examine your own mistakes than those of others. [B 60]

Democritus:

Frankness is an aspect of liberty, but discerning the right occasion is hazardous. [B 226]   (III xiii 46–47)

Democritus:

Praise for noble deeds is noble; praise for bad deeds is the mark of a cheat and a deceiver. [B 63] (III xiv 8)

Democritus:

The thrifty behave like bees, working as though they are to live for ever. [B 227]

idem:

Ignorant children of thrifty fathers are like sword-dancers who are lost if they fail to land on the one place where they should set their feet (and it is difficult to land on the one place, for there is only room for a footprint). In the same way they too, if they fail to acquire their father's careful and thrifty character, are likely to be ruined. [B 228]

idem:

Thrift and hunger are good; so too on occasion is extravagance: it is the mark of a good man to recognize the occasion. [B 229] (III xvi 17–19)

Democritus:

A life without a feast is a long road without an inn. [B 230] (III xvi 22)

Democritus:

He is of sound judgement who is not grieved by what he does not possess but rejoices in what he does possess. [B 231] (III xvii 25)

Democritus:

Of pleasant things those which occur most rarely give most joy. [B 232]

idem:

If you exceed the measure, what is most enjoyable will become least enjoyable. [B 233]

idem:

A courageous man is not only one who conquers his enemies but also one who is superior to pleasures. [Cf. B 214] (III xvii 37–39)

Democritus:

Men ask for health from the gods in their prayers; they do not realize that the power to achieve it lies in themselves; lacking self-control, they act contrary to it and themselves betray health to their desires. [B 234]   (III xviii 30)

Democritus:

All those who get their pleasures from their bellies, exceeding the measure in food and drink and sex, find the pleasures slight and short-lived, lasting as long as they are eating or drinking. But the pains are many. For they always desire the same things; and when they obtain what they desire, the pleasure swiftly departs and they find nothing good but a brief joy – and a need for the same things again. [B 235]   (III xviii 35)

Democritus:

It is hard to fight against anger; to master it is the mark of a rational man. [B 236]   (III xx 56)

Democritus:

Ambition is always foolish: with its eye on what harms its enemy it does not see its own advantage. [B 237]   (III xx 62)

Democritus:

One who compares himself to his betters ends with a bad reputation. [B 238]

Democrates:

When he was an old man, Democrates climbed the acropolis and gasped for breath: he said that he was like the whole Athenian State – much hot air and little real puff.   (III xxii 42–43)

Democritus:

Oaths made from necessity are not kept by bad men once they have escaped. [B 239]   (III xxviii 13)

Democritus:
Voluntary labours make it easier to endure involuntary labours.
[B 240]
idem:
Continuous labour becomes lighter by custom. [B 241]
(III xxix 63–64)

Democritus:
More men are good by practice than by nature. [B 242]
idem:
Actions always planned are never completed. [B 81]
(III xxix 66–67)

Democritus:
All labours are more pleasant than rest when men achieve what they labour for or know that they will achieve it. †But if they fail, all† is equally painful and wretched. [B 243]   (III xxix 88)

Democ:
Even if you are alone, neither say nor do anything bad: learn to feel shame before yourself rather than before others. [B 244]
(III xxxi 7)

Democritus:
It is greedy to say everything and to want to listen to nothing.
[B 86]   (III xxxvi 24)

Democritus:
One should either be or imitate a good man. [B 39]
(III xxxvii 22)

Democritus:
If your character is orderly, your life too is well-ordered. [B 61]
(III xxxvii 25)

Democritus:

A good man takes no account of the censures of the bad. [B 48]
idem:
An envious man pains himself as though he were an enemy. [B 88]
(III xxxviii 46–47)

Democritus:

The laws would not forbid us to live each at his own pleasure if one man did not harm another; for envy makes the beginning of strife. [B 245] (III xxxviii 53)

Democritus:

Mercenary service teaches self-sufficiency in life; for bread and a straw mattress are the sweetest cures for hunger and exhaustion. [B 246]
idem:
To a wise man the whole earth is accessible; for the country of a good soul is the whole world. [B 247] (III xl 6–7)

Democritus:

The law wishes to benefit the life of men: it can do so when they themselves wish to be benefited – for to those who obey, it indicates their own virtue. [B 248]
idem:
Internecine strife is bad for both parties; for victor and vanquished suffer the same destruction. [B 249] (IV i 33–34)

Democritus:

From concord come great deeds, and for states the capacity to wage war – and in no other way. [B 250] (IV i 40)

Democritus:

Poverty in a democracy is preferable to what is called prosperity among tyrants – by as much as liberty is preferable to slavery. [B 251]
One should think it of greater moment than anything else that

the affairs of the State are well conducted, neither being contentious beyond what is proper nor gaining power for oneself beyond the common good. For a State which is well conducted is the best means to success: everything depends on it – if it is safeguarded everything is safeguarded and if it is destroyed everything is destroyed. [B 252]

It is not advantageous for good men to neglect themselves and look to other things; for their own affairs will go badly. But if anyone neglects public affairs he comes to have a bad reputation, even if he steals nothing and commits no injustice. For even if he is not negligent or unjust, there is a danger that he will get a bad reputation – and indeed fare badly: mistakes are inevitable and forgiveness is not easy for men. [B 253]

When bad men gain office, the more unworthy they are the more heedless they become and the more they are filled with folly and rashness. [B 254]

When those in power take it upon themselves to lend to the poor and to aid them and to favour them, then is there compassion and not isolation but companionship and mutual defence and concord among the citizens and other good things too many to catalogue. [B 255]   (IV i 42–46)

Democritus:
It is better for fools to be ruled than to rule. [B 75]

Justice is doing what should be done, injustice not doing what should be done but turning away from it. [B 256]

In the case of certain animals, it stands thus with killing and not killing: one who kills those which do or wish injustice is not punishable, and to do so conduces more to well-being than not to do so. [B 257]

One should kill at any cost all which offend against justice; and anyone who does this will in every society have a greater share of contentment and justice and boldness and property. [B 258]

Just as I have written about hostile beasts and brutes, so I think one should act in the case of men too: according to the traditional laws, you may kill an enemy in every society in which the law does not prohibit it – it is prohibited by the sacred customs of different countries, by treaties, by oaths. [B 259]

Anyone who kills any highwayman or pirate is not punishable, whether he does it by his own hand, by issuing an order or by casting a vote. [B 260]   (IV ii 13–18)

Democritus:
It is hard to be ruled by an inferior. [B 49]   (IV iv 27)

Democritus:
One should avenge to the best of one's ability those who are unjustly treated and not pass them by; for to do so is just and good, not to do so unjust and bad. [B 261]

Democritus:
Those who do deeds worthy of exile or imprisonment or who are worthy of punishment should be condemned and not acquitted; anyone who acquits them contrary to the law, judging by gain or by pleasure, acts unjustly – and this must lie heavy on his heart. [B 262]

idem:
He who †worthily administers the greatest offices† has the greatest share of justice and virtue. [B 263]

idem:
Feel shame before others no more than before yourself, and do wrong no more if no one is to know about it than if all men are; rather, feel shame above all before yourself and set this up as a law in your soul so that you may do nothing unsuitable. [B 264]

idem:
Men remember wrongs better than benefits. And that is just; for as those who repay their debts should not be praised, whereas those who do not should be blamed and suffer, so too is it with a ruler. For he was chosen not to do wrong but to do right. [B 265]

idem:
There is no device, in the present shape of things, whereby rulers may be protected from injustice, even if they are very good men.

<. . .> These things too should somehow be so arranged that one who commits no injustice, even if he severely examines doers of injustice, does not come under their power; rather, a statute, or something else, will protect those who do what is just. [B 266]

(IV v 43–48)

Democritus:
Ruling is by nature appropriate to the superior. [B 267]   (IV vi 19)

Democritus:
Fear produces flattery; it does not gain good-will. [B 268]

(IV vii 13)

Democritus:
Boldness is the beginning of action; chance determines the end. [B 269]   (IV x 28)

Democritus:
Use servants like parts of your body – one for one thing, one for another. [B 270]   (IV xix 45)

Democritus:
If a woman is loved, then no blame is attached to lust. [B 271]

(IV xx 33)

Democritus:
Democritus said that one who is lucky in his son-in-law gains a son, one who is unlucky loses a daughter. [B 272]   (IV xxii 108)

Democritus:
A woman is far sharper than a man when it comes to foolish counsels. [B 273]   (IV xxii 199)

Democritus:
To speak little is an adornment in a woman – and it is good to be sparing with adornments. [B 274]

Democritus:

To be ruled by a woman is the final insult for a man. [B 111]

(IV xxiii 38–39)

Democritus:

To bring up children is perilous; success is full of trouble and care, failure is unsurpassed by any other pain. [B 275]   (IV xxiv 29)

Democritus:

I think that one should not have children; for in the having of children I see many great dangers, many pains, few advantages – and those thin and weak. [B 276]

idem:

Anyone who has a need for children would do better, I think, to get them from his friends. He will then have the child he wishes – for he can choose the sort he wants, and one that seems suitable to him will by its nature best follow him. There is this great difference: here you may choose from many the child of your heart, of the sort you need; but if you produce a child yourself there are many dangers – for you must make do with the one you get. [B 277]

idem:

Men think that, by nature and some ancient constitution, it is a matter of necessity to get children. This is plain from the other animals too; for they all naturally get offspring, not with any benefit in view – rather, when they are born, they suffer and rear each as best they can, and fear for them as long as they are small, and grieve if they are hurt. Such is the nature of all things which have a soul; but for men it has come to be thought that some gain actually comes from offspring. [B 278]   (IV xxiv 31–33)

Democritus:

You should share your goods with your children so far as possible, and at the same time care for them lest they do any mischief with what they have in their hands. For they become at the same time far more thrifty with their money and keener to acquire it, and they compete with one another. For common expenditure does not

grieve us as much as private, nor common acquisition content us
– but far less. [B 279]

idem:

It is possible, without spending much money, to educate your
children and to build a wall and a protection about their goods and
their persons. [B 280]   (IV xxvi 25–26)

Democritus:

For beasts, good breeding is bodily strength; for men, grace of
character. [B 57]   (IV xxix 18)

Democritus:

Just as among wounds gangrene is the worst disease, so among
goods <. . .> [B 281]   (IV xxxi 49)

Democritus:

Money when used with thought promotes generosity and charity;
when used thoughtlessly it is a common expense. [B 282]

idem:

It is not useless to make money, but to do so unjustly is the worst
of all things. [B 78]   (IV xxxi 120–121)

Democritus:

Poverty and wealth are names for want and satisfaction; so one
who is in want is not wealthy and one who is not in want is not
poor. [B 283]

Democritus:

If you do not desire much, a little will seem much to you; for a
small appetite makes poverty as powerful as wealth. [B 284]

(IV xxxiii 23–25)

Democritus:

Those who seek good things find them with difficulty; bad things
come even to those who do not seek them. [B 108]   (IV xxxiv 58)

Democritus:

All men, conscious of their evil actions in life, suffer for their whole lifetime in trouble and fear, telling false stories about what comes after death. [Cf. B 297]   (IV xxxiv 62)

Democritus:

You must recognize that human life is frail and brief and confounded by many plagues and incapacities; then you will care for moderate possessions and your misery will be measured by necessity. [B 285]   (IV xxxiv 65)

Democritus:

Fortunate is he who is content with moderate goods, unfortunate he who is discontent with many. [B 286]   (IV xxxix 17)

Democritus:

If you are to be content you must not undertake many activities, whether as an individual or with others, nor choose activities beyond your own power and nature; rather, you must be on your guard so that even when fortune meets you and leads you further in your thoughts, you put it aside and do not attempt more than you can. It is safer to be well-built than fat. [B 3]   (IV xxxix 25)

Democritus:

Public poverty weighs heavier than private poverty; for no hope of relief remains. [B 287]

   Your house and your life, no less than your body, may fall ill. [B 288]   (IV xl 20–21)

Democritus:

It is irrational not to accommodate yourself to the necessities of life. [B 289]   (IV xliv 64)

Democritus:

Drive out by reasoning the unmastered pain of a numbed soul. [B 290] idem:

It is important to think as you should in times of misfortune. [B 42]

idem:

Magnanimity is bearing wrongs lightly. [B 46]

idem:

It is a mark of good sense to bear poverty well. [B 291]

(IV xliv 67–70)

Democritus:

The hopes of those who think aright are attainable; the hopes of the unintelligent are impossible. [B 58]

Democritus:

The hopes of the unintelligent are irrational. [B 292]

(IV xlvi 18–19)

Democritus:

Those who take pleasure in the disasters of their neighbours do not understand how the affairs of fortune are common to all, and they lack appropriate delight. [B 293] (IV xlviii 10)

Democritus:

Strength and shapeliness are the good things of youth; good sense is the flower of age. [B 294] (IV l 20)

Democritus:

Old men were young, but it is uncertain if the young will reach old age. Now a completed good is better than one which is still to come and is uncertain. [B 295] (IV l 22)

Democritus:

Old age is a general decrepitude: it has everything and lacks everything. [B 296] (IV l 76)

Democritus:

Some men who do not know how mortal nature dissolves but are conscious of their evil actions in life suffer for their whole lifetime

in trouble and fear, telling false stories about the time after death.
[B 297]   (IV lii 40)

The collection of sayings known as the 'Maxims of Democrates' con-
tains a number of items which have already made their appearance
under Democritus' name. Since many other of the sayings may well come
from the same source, I translate the collection as a whole and let it stand
as an Appendix to the ethical fragments of Democritus.

If anyone attends thoughtfully to these maxims of mine, he will do
many acts worthy of a good man and he will leave undone many
bad acts. [B 35]

It is fitting for men to take account of their souls rather than of
their bodies; for a perfect soul corrects wickedness of body, but
strength of body without reasoning makes the soul no better at all.
[B 187 = B 36]

He who chooses the goods of the soul chooses the more divine;
he who chooses the goods of the body, the human. [B 37]

It is noble to prevent injustice; or if not, not to collaborate in
injustice. [B 38]

One should either be or imitate a good man. [B 39]

Men flourish neither by their bodies nor by their wealth but by
uprightness and good sense. [B 40]

One should refrain from wrong-doing not out of fear but out of
duty. [B 41]

It is important to think as you should in times of misfortune.
[B 42]

Remorse for foul deeds is the salvation of life. [B 43]

One should tell the truth, not speak at length. [B 44]

A man who acts unjustly is more wretched than one who is
unjustly treated. [B 45]

Magnanimity is bearing wrongs lightly. [B 46]

It is fitting to yield to the law, to the ruler, to the wiser. [B 47]

A good man takes no account of the censures of the bad. [B 48]

It is hard to be ruled by an inferior. [B 49]

A man completely enslaved to money will never be just. [B 50]

Reason is often a more powerful persuader than gold. [B 51]

One who offers advice to those who think they possess sense is wasting his time. [B 52]

Many do not learn reason but live in accordance with reason. [B 53]

Many perform the foulest deeds and rehearse the fairest words. [B 53a]

The unintelligent gain good sense through misfortune. [B 54]

One should emulate the deeds and actions of virtue, not the words. [B 55]

It is those well-endowed for it who recognize and emulate the noble. [B 56]

For beasts, good breeding is bodily strength; for men, grace of character. [B 57]

The hopes of those who think aright are attainable; the hopes of the unintelligent are impossible. [B 58]

Neither skill nor wisdom is attainable unless you learn. [B 59]

It is better to examine your own mistakes than those of others. [B 60]

If your character is orderly, your life too is well-ordered. [B 61]

It is not refraining from injustice which is good but not even wanting it. [B 62]

Praise for noble deeds is noble; praise for bad deeds is the mark of a cheat and a deceiver. [B 63]

Many have much learning and no thought. [B 64]

One should cultivate much thought, not much learning. [B 65]

It is better to plan before acting than to repent. [B 66]

Do not trust everyone: trust the trustworthy – the former is foolish, the latter the mark of a man of good sense. [B 67]

A man is trustworthy or untrustworthy not only from what he does but also from what he wishes. [B 68]

Goodness and truth are the same for all men; pleasures differ for different men. [B 69]

Immoderate desire is the mark of a child, not of a man. [B 70]

Inopportune pleasures breed unpleasures. [B 71]

Violent appetite for one thing blinds the soul to everything else. [B 72]

Rightful love is a longing, without violence, for the noble. [B 73]

Accept nothing pleasant which is not advantageous. [B 74]

It is better for fools to be ruled than to rule. [B 75]

Silly people are taught not by reason but by misfortune. [B 76]

Reputation and wealth without understanding are not safe possessions. [B 77]

It is not useless to make money, but to do so unjustly is the worst of all things. [B 78]

It is wretched to imitate bad men and not even to wish to imitate good. [B 79]

It is disgraceful to busy yourself over the affairs of others and neglect your own. [B 80]

Actions always planned are never completed. [B 81]

Cheats and hypocrites are those who do everything in word and nothing in deed. [B 82]

Happy is the man who has property and sense; for he uses it nobly on what he should.

The cause of error is ignorance of what is better. [B 83]

One who does shameful deeds should first feel shame before himself. [B 84]

Those who contradict and babble on are ill-endowed for learning what they should. [B 85]

It is greedy to say everything and to want to listen to nothing. [B 86]

One should be on guard against bad men lest they take their opportunity. [B 87]

An envious man pains himself as though he were an enemy. [B 88]

An enemy is not he who acts unjustly but he who wishes to. [B 89]

Enmity among kin weighs far heavier than enmity among strangers. [B 90]

Do not suspect everyone – but be cautious and safe. [B 91]

You should accept favours only if you expect to give greater favours in return. [B 92]

When doing a favour keep watch on the receiver lest he prove a cheat and return evil for good. [B 93]

Small favours at the right time are very great for those who receive them. [B 94]

Honours count much with the intelligent who understand that they are being honoured. [B 95]

A generous man is not one who looks for a return but one who has chosen to do good. [B 96]

Many who seem to be friends are not; many who do not seem to be are. [B 97]

The friendship of one intelligent man is better than that of all the unintelligent. [B 98]

A man who has not a single good friend does not deserve to live. [B 99]

A man whose tried friends do not long stand by him has a bad character. [B 100]

Many avoid their friends when they fall from wealth to poverty. [B 101]

Equality is everywhere noble; excess and deficiency, I think, are not so. [B 102]

A man who loves no one, I think, is loved by no one. [B 103]

One who is wily and speaks seriously is an old man with charm. [B 104]

Beauty of body is an animal attribute if there is no thought beneath it. [B 105]

In good fortune it is easy to find a friend; in bad fortune nothing is harder. [B 106]

Not all our kindred are our friends – only those who agree with us over what is advantageous. [B 107]

Being men, it is fitting that we should not laugh at human misfortunes but mourn them. [B 107a]

Those who seek good things find them with difficulty; bad things come even to those who do not seek them. [B 108]

Those who like fault-finding are not well-endowed for friendship. [B 109]

Let not a woman argue: that is terrible. [B 110]

To be ruled by a woman is the final insult for a man. [B 111]

It is a mark of divine thought to consider always what is noble. [B 112]

If you believe that the gods observe everything, you will do wrong neither in secret nor openly.

Those who praise the unintelligent do them great harm. [B 113]

It is better to be praised by another than by yourself. [B 114]

If you do not understand the praise, suppose that you are being flattered. [B 115]

The world is a stage, life is our entrance: you came, you saw, you left.

The world is change; life is opinion.

A little wisdom is more honourable than a reputation for great folly. (Democrates, *Maxims* 1–86)

Diogenes of Apollonia

The Presocratic Diogenes, the first of several ancient philosophers to bear that name, came from a town called Apollonia – either Apollonia in Crete or Apollonia on the Black Sea. He is said to have been the last of the Presocratic natural philosophers, a remark which, together with certain parodies of his views found in the comic playwrights, suggests that he was active in the 430s and 420s.

Here is Diogenes Laertius' brief life of his namesake:

Diogenes, son of Apollothemis, of Apollonia, a natural scientist and extremely famous. He was a pupil, so Antisthenes says, of Anaximenes, but he lived in the time of Anaxagoras. Demetrius of Phaleron, in his *Defence of Socrates*, says that great jealousy nearly put his life in danger at Athens.

These were his views: Air is the element. There are limitless worlds and limitless empty space. The air when condensed and rarefied produces the worlds. Nothing comes into being from what does not exist, nor is anything destroyed into what does not exist. The earth is round and rests in the middle, having been formed by the rotation of the hot and the congealing of the cold.

This is how his book begins:

When beginning any account it seems to me that one should make the starting-point incontrovertible and the style simple and dignified. [64 B 1]

(Diogenes Laertius, *Lives of the Philosophers* IX 57)

Theophrastus wrote a monograph on him. His general line of interpretation emerges from the following passage:

Diogenes of Apollonia, perhaps the last of those who studied these subjects, wrote for the most part in a muddled fashion, sometimes following Anaxagoras and sometimes Leucippus.

He too says that the nature of the universe is air, limitless and eternal, from which, as it condenses and rarefies and changes its properties, the other forms come into being. This is what Theophrastus says about Diogenes, and the book of his entitled *On Nature*, which I have seen, clearly says that it is air from which everything else comes into being. But Nicolaus records that he posited as the element something between fire and air.

(Simplicius, *Commentary on the* Physics 25.1–9)

Most of our information about Diogenes derives from Simplicius, who records a disagreement among earlier interpreters.

Most say that Diogenes of Apollonia, like Anaximenes, posited air as the primary element. But Nicolaus in his treatise *On the Gods* records that he declared what is between fire and air to be the principle; and Porphyry, the most learned of philosophers, has followed Nicolaus. Now you should know that this Diogenes wrote several works, as he himself records in his book *On Nature*, where he says that he has written against the natural scientists (whom he himself calls sophists) and that he has composed a *Meteorology* (in which he says he has discussed the principle and also the nature of man). In *On Nature*, which is the only one of his works which I have seen, he proposes to show in many ways that there is much thinking in the principle which he posits. Immediately after the preface he writes as follows:

It seems to me, in a word, that all existing things are alterations of the same thing and are the same thing. This is quite clear. For if the things which now exist in this world – earth and water and air and fire and the other things which plainly exist in this world – if any one of them were different from any other, being different in its own peculiar nature, and were not the same thing changed in many ways and altered, then they could not mix with one another at all, nor could benefit or harm come to one from another, nor indeed could plants grow from the earth, or animals or anything

else come into being, unless they were so constituted as to be the same thing. But all these things, altering from some one thing, become different at different times and return to the same thing. [B 2]

I too, when I read those first remarks, thought that he had in mind as the common substrate something other than the four elements, since he says that these would not mingle with or change into one another if some one of them, having a peculiar nature of its own, were the principle, and if there were not some one thing underlying them all, of which all were alterations. But next, having shown that there is much thinking in this principle – for, he says,

Without thinking, things could not have been so distributed as to preserve measures of all things – of summer and winter and night and day and rain and wind and good weather; and all other things, if you will consider them, you will find to be disposed in the finest possible way [B 3] – he continues by urging that men and the other animals depend for their life and their soul and their thinking on this principle which is air. He says:

Again, in addition to these there are the following great signs. Men and the other animals, inasmuch as they breathe, live by the air. And this is for them both soul and thinking, as will have been shown clearly in this treatise; and if this departs, they die and their thinking stops. [B 4]

Then a little later he adds clearly:

And it seems to me that that which possesses thought is what men call air, and that by this everyone both is governed and has power over everything. For it is this which seems to me to be god and to have reached everything and to arrange everything and to be in everything. And there is not a single thing which does not share in it.

But no one thing shares in it in the same way as another; rather, there are many forms both of the air itself and of thinking. For it is multiform: hotter and colder, drier and wetter, more stable and with a swifter motion, and there are many – limitlessly many – other alterations in it both of flavour and of colour.

The souls of all animals are indeed the same – air hotter than

the external air in which we exist but much colder than the air by the sun. But this heat is not similar in different animals (for it is not similar even in different men); rather, it differs – not greatly, however, but to such an extent that they are still like one another. Yet none of the things which alter can become absolutely similar to another without becoming the same thing. Thus inasmuch as the alteration is multiform, so too are the animals multiform and many, and they resemble one another neither in shape nor in habit nor in thinking because of the multitude of the alterations. Nevertheless, it is by the same thing that they all live and see and hear, and they all get the rest of their thinking from the same source. [B 5]

Next he shows that the seed of animals is breath-like and that acts of thinking occur when the air together with the blood pervades the whole body through the vessels (and here he gives a precise anatomy of the vessels).

Here, then, he is found to say quite clearly that what men call air is the principle. It is noteworthy that, while he says that other things come into being by virtue of alterations in it, he nevertheless asserts that it is eternal:

And this itself is an eternal and immortal body; but by it some things come into being and others disappear. [B 7]

And elsewhere:

But this seems to me to be clear – that it is great and strong, eternal and immortal, and knows many things. [B 8]

So much for Diogenes.

(Simplicius, *Commentary on the* Physics 151.20–153.22)

Aristotle preserves Diogenes' 'precise anatomy of the vessels'.

Diogenes of Apollonia says this:

The vessels in men stand thus: There are two very large ones. They extend through the belly along the backbone, one to the right and the other to the left, into the legs, each on its own side, and upwards into the head past the collar-bones through the throat. From these, vessels extend throughout the whole of the body, from the right vessel to the right and from the left to the left, the largest two passing into the heart near the backbone itself, and others, a little higher up, passing through the chest under the armpits, each into the hand on its own side. One of these is called the splenetic vessel, the other the hepatic. Each of them divides at its extremity, one branch going into the thumb, one into the palm; and from them fine, many-branched vessels pass into the rest of the hand and the fingers. Other finer ones extend from the first vessels, from the right into the liver and from the left into the spleen and the kidneys. Those which extend into the legs divide at the junction and extend throughout the thighs. The largest of them extends down the back of the thigh and is seen to be thick; another passes inside the thigh, a little less thick than the former. Then they extend past the knee into the shin and the foot (like those which extend into the hands), descending to the sole of the foot and thence extending into the toes. Many fine vessels divide from them in the direction of the belly and the rib-cage.

Those which extend into the head through the throat show large in the neck. From each of them, where it ends, many vessels divide off into the head, those from the right towards the left and those from the left towards the right. Each ends at the ear. There is another vessel in the neck, next to the large vessel on each side and a little smaller than it, with which most of the vessels from the head itself connect. These extend through the throat on the inside. From each of them, vessels extend under the shoulder-blades and into the hands, and they are seen alongside the splenetic and the hepatic vessels, a little smaller in size. These are the vessels which are lanced when anything causes pain beneath the skin, whereas it is the hepatic and the splenetic vessels which are lanced when anything causes pain in the belly. Others extend from these under the breasts.

Other vessels extend from each of these through the spinal marrow into the testicles; these are fine. Others extend under the skin and through the flesh into the kidneys, and end in the case of men in the testicles and in the case of women in the womb. These are called spermatic. The vessels are broader as they first leave the belly, and then become finer until they change from the right to the left and vice versa.

The thickest part of the blood is drunk by the flesh; that which overflows into the regions just mentioned becomes fine and hot and frothy. [B 6]   (Aristotle, *History of Animals* 511b30–512b11)

The way in which air affects our mental lives may be illustrated by a passage from Theophrastus' account of Diogenes' psychological views:

Pleasure and pain come about in the following way. When a lot of air mixes with the blood and lightens it, being in a natural condition and pervading the whole body, there is pleasure; when the air is in an unnatural condition and does not mix, and the blood settles and becomes weaker and thicker, there is pain. Similarly with boldness and health and their opposites. The tongue is the best judge of pleasure, for it is very soft and rare and all the vessels lead into it. That is why the tongue provides a very large number of signs in the case of the sick, and in the case of the other animals it indicates their colours (for their varieties and characters are all reflected in it) . . .

We think, as has been said, by air which is pure and dry; for moisture inhibits thought. That is why when we are asleep or drunk or full we think less. There is a sign that dampness destroys thought in the fact that the other animals have weaker intellects; for they breathe air from the earth and the food they take is moister. Birds breathe pure air, but their nature is like that of fish; for their flesh is firm and the breath does not penetrate everywhere but comes to a stop in the belly. Hence they digest their food quickly but are themselves unthinking. In addition to their food, their mouths and tongues contribute to this; for they cannot understand one another. Plants, because they are not hollow and do not take in air, are completely incapable of thinking.

The same cause accounts for the fact that infants are unthinking. For they contain a great quantity of moisture with the result that [the air] cannot penetrate the whole body but is secreted in the chest. Hence they are dull and unthinking. They are prone to anger, and in general impetuous and volatile, because much air is moved from small bodies.

This is also the cause of forgetting. For because the air does not pass through the whole body we cannot understand things. A sign of this is the fact that when we try to remember something there is a constriction in the chest and when we find it, there is a relaxation and we are relieved of the pain.   (Theophrastus, *On the Senses* 43–45)

APPENDIX

The Sources

The following telegraphic notes convey a minimal idea of each of the authorities who are quoted in the course of this book. The list also includes the most important of the sources who are now read only at second hand, through quotation in later authors. The notes generally give, first, a date; then a place of birth (preceded by the letter 'b.') and a centre of activity (preceded by an arrow); thirdly, a hint of intellectual allegiances; fourthly, an indication – where apposite – of the works most pertinent to the study of the Presocratics.

The letter 'Q' in square brackets indicates that the source is known only indirectly; the letter 'L' in square brackets indicates that the source wrote in Latin (all sources not so stigmatized wrote in Greek).

The most important sources are marked by bold type. The length of a note is not proportional to the importance of its subject.

The sources are listed in alphabetical order, anonymous and pseudonymous works being placed at the end.

ACHILLES: third century AD (?); astronomer.

AELIAN: *c.* AD 170–230; b. Praeneste; → Rome; wrote *On Animals* and *Miscellaneous Inquiries*.

AGATHEMERUS: first century AD (?); geographer.

ALBERT THE GREAT: AD 1200–1280; theologian and scholar; teacher of Thomas Aquinas.

ALEXANDER OF APHRODISIAS: flourished *c.* AD 200; → Athens; Peripatetic philosopher; author of commentaries on Aristotle.

AMMONIUS: *c.* AD 440–*c.* 520; → Alexandria; pupil of Proclus; commentator on Aristotle.

APOLLODORUS [Q]: second century BC; b. Athens; → Alexandria; scholar and polymath, his lost *Chronicles* are a major source for Presocratic chronology.

APOLLONIUS: second century BC (?); compiler of *Marvellous Stories*.

ARISTOTLE: 384–322 BC; b. Stagira; → Athens (also worked at Assos, and at

Pella, where he tutored Alexander the Great). Pupil of Plato; founder of the Peripatetic school of philosophy. An unsurpassed polymath – scientist, philosopher, historian, scholar. He was interested in the history of philosophy and science; several of his surviving works (notably the *Physics* and the *Metaphysics*) contain invaluable information about the Presocratics.

ARISTOXENUS: fourth century BC; b. Tarentum; → Athens; associate of Aristotle; musical theorist, biographer, with interest in Pythagoreanism.

ARIUS DIDYMUS [Q]: first century AD (?); author of philosophical handbooks.

ATHENAEUS: flourished *c.* AD 200; b. Naucratis in Egypt; his *Deipnosophists* – *Professors at the Dining Table* – is an encyclopaedic farrago.

AULUS GELLIUS [L]: AD *c.* 125–*c.* 180; his *Attic Nights*, written in Athens, is a miscellany of essays on literary, historical and philosophical subjects.

CAELIUS AURELIANUS [L]: fifth century AD; b. Numidia; medical translator of Soranus (second century AD).

CALCIDIUS [L]: fourth century AD (?); Christian author of commentary on Plato's *Timaeus.*

CALLIMACHUS: *c.* 305–*c.* 240 BC; b. Cyrene; → Alexandria; poet and scholar.

CENSORINUS [L]: third century AD; → Rome; grammarian, his *On the Day of Birth* was written in 238.

CICERO [L]: 106–43 BC; b. Arpinum; → Rome; orator, politician, statesman; leading literary figure of his age; keen and learned philosopher.

CLEMENT OF ALEXANDRIA: *c.* AD 150–*c.* 215; b. Athens (?). The first Christian philosopher. His *Miscellanies* compares Greek and Christian thought, unsystematically but with a wealth of quotation.

COLUMELLA [L]: first century AD; b. Cadiz; writer on agriculture.

LUCIUS ANNAEUS CORNUTUS: first century AD; Stoic philosopher, scholar, friend of the poet Persius.

DAMASCIUS: *c.* AD 458–*c.* 540; b. Damascus; → Athens; Platonic philosopher.

DIO CHRYSOSTOM: *c.* AD 40–*c.* 120; b. Prusa in Bithynia; → Rome. Friend of the Emperor Trajan; orator, prolific author of belles lettres.

DIODORUS: first century BC; b. Agyrium in Sicily; → Alexandria and Rome; author of a *Universal History.*

DIOGENES LAERTIUS: third century AD (?). Nothing is known of his own life, but he survives in his *Lives of the Philosophers.* The work, in ten books, is derivative; despite its simplifications, confusions and occasional nonsense, it remains an invaluable source, both for the Presocratics and for later Greek philosophy.

DIOGENES OF OENOANDA: early second century AD; Epicurean philosopher who had his views carved on stone.

DIONYSIUS [Q]: *c.* AD 200–265; Bishop of Alexandria.

EROTIAN: first century AD; scholar and author of medical dictionary.

EUDEMUS [Q]: fourth century BC; b. Rhodes; → Athens; pupil of Aristotle; philosopher and historian of science.

EUSEBIUS: *c.* AD 260–*c.* 340; Bishop of Caesarea, voluminous author; his *Preparation for the Gospel* includes many quotations from otherwise lost works of pagan philosophy.

EUSTATHIUS: twelfth century AD; b. Constantinople; Archbishop of Thessalonica; wrote, among much else, a commentary on Homer.

GALEN: AD 129–*c.* 210; b. Pergamum; → Rome; eminent doctor and medical writer who was trained as a philosopher; his numerous writings make frequent reference to earlier philosophy.

HARPOCRATION: second century AD (?); → Alexandria; literary scholar.

HEPHAESTION: second century AD; → Alexandria; literary scholar.

HERACLIDES [Q]: *c.* 390–*c.* 310 BC; b. Heraclea on the Black Sea; → Athens; pupil of Plato; bellettrist and lightweight philosopher.

HERACLITUS: first century AD (?); author of allegorizing interpretations of Homer.

HERODIAN: second century AD; b. Alexandria; → Rome; works on grammar and literary theory.

HERODOTUS: *c.* 485–*c.* 420 BC; b. Halicarnassus, travelled widely; 'the father of history'.

HESYCHIUS: fifth century AD; → Alexandria; lexicographer.

HIEROCLES: fifth century AD; → Alexandria; Platonist philosopher; author of commentary on the so-called 'Golden Verses' of Pythagoras.

HIPPOLYTUS: *c.* AD 180–235; → Rome; bishop and controversialist, exiled to Sardinia. His *Refutation of All Heresies* contains much information about pagan philosophy.

HISDOSUS: flourished *c.* AD 1100; wrote commentary on Plato's *Timaeus*.

IAMBLICHUS: *c.* AD 250–*c.* 325; b. Chalcis; → Syria; Platonist philosopher; wrote at length on Pythagoreanism.

ISOCRATES: 436–338 BC; b. Athens; leading orator, political commentator, educational figure.

MACROBIUS [L]: early fifth century AD; his *Saturnalia* contains literary, scientific and philosophical discussions.

MARCUS AURELIUS: AD 121–180; b. Rome; Emperor and Stoic; his *Meditations* occasionally allude to the Presocratics.

MICHAEL OF EPHESUS: eleventh century AD; commentator on Aristotle.

NICOLAUS OF DAMASCUS: first century BC; scholar and author of commentaries on Aristotle.

NUMENIUS [Q]: end of second century AD; from Apamea in Syria; Platonico-Pythagorean philosopher.

ORIGEN: *c.* 185–*c.* 250 AD; b. Alexandria; → Caesarea; most influential of early Christian theologians; his *Against Celsus* contains frequent allusions to pagan philosophy.

PHILODEMUS: *c.* 110–*c.* 40 BC; b. Gadara; → Naples; Epicurean philosopher, many of whose works survive among the Herculaneum papyri.

JOHN PHILOPONUS: *c.* AD 490–*c.* 570; → Alexandria; Christian Platonist, author of commentaries on Aristotle.

PLATO: 428–348 BC; b. Athens; philosopher of all-pervasive influence; his works often allude to the Presocratics.

PLOTINUS: *c.* AD 205–270; b. Egypt; → Rome; Platonist and leading philosopher of his age; his *Enneads* contain occasional allusions to Presocratic thought.

PLUTARCH: *c.* AD 45–*c.* 120; b. Chaeronea; a man of learning and letters (history, biography, literary criticism, philosophy); several of his 'moral essays' contain quotations from and allusions to the Presocratics.

POLYBIUS: *c.* 200–*c.* 115 BC; b. Megalopolis; → Rome (as a prisoner of war); leading historian.

PORPHYRY: AD 233–*c.* 305; b. Tyre; → Rome; pupil of Plotinus, whose works he edited; Platonist philosopher and voluminous author.

PROCLUS: AD 412–485; b. Constantinople; → Athens; Platonist philosopher; his commentary on Euclid contains information about the early history of Greek mathematics.

RUFUS OF EPHESUS: early second century AD; medical writer.

SEXTUS EMPIRICUS: second century AD; major figure in sceptical philosophy; his *Outlines of Pyrrhonism* and *Against the Mathematicians* contain much information about earlier philosophers.

SIMPLICIUS: sixth century AD; trained in Alexandria, → Athens (529–534 in Persia); pagan, Platonist philosopher (an enemy of Philoponus). His commentaries on Aristotle, all written towards the end of his life, are remarkable for their learning; his commentary on the *Physics* is the single most important source for Presocratic philosophy.

JOHN STOBAEUS: fifth century AD; from Stobi in Macedonia; his *Anthology*, in four books, is a collection of excerpts from earlier Greek authors arranged by subject-matter.

STRABO: 64 BC–*c.* AD 25; b. Amasia in Asia Minor; → Rome; leading geographer.

THEMISTIUS: 317–388 AD; → Constantinople; renowned orator, commentator on Aristotle.

THEO OF SMYRNA: early second century AD; Platonist and mathematician.

THEOPHRASTUS: 371–287 BC; b. Lesbos; → Athens; Aristotle's leading pupil and successor, matching his master in the range of his interests. Had a profound influence on the historiography of Greek philosophy. Most of his works are lost; the essay *On the Senses*, discussing various pre-Aristotelian theories, survives.

THRASYLLUS [Q]: first century AD; b. Alexandria; → Rome; astrologer to the Emperor Tiberius; catalogued the works of Plato and Democritus.

TIMON [Q]: *c.* 320–*c.* 230 BC; b. Phlius; satirical poet of sceptical bent.

JOHN TZETZES: AD 1110–*c.* 1180; → Constantinople; scholar, polymath, prolific author.

Anonymous and Pseudonymous works

A few anonymous commentaries on classical texts have been cited, and also various scholia or marginal notes. Such items can rarely be dated with any certainty. Three other anonymous texts may be mentioned here: the *Medical Writings*, found on a papyrus, are the remains of an early history of medicine which had its origins in Aristotle's school; the *Theosophia*, dating from about AD 500, is a compilation of pagan texts which were taken to foretell the truths of Christianity; the *Etymologicum Magnum* is an encyclopaedic dictionary, compiled in about AD 1100.

The most important of the pseudonymous works, [Plutarch], *Opinions of the Philosophers on Nature*, is a superficial compilation, probably put together in the second century AD. Other works falsely ascribed to Plutarch are essays and fragments of uncertain date and provenance. Among the works falsely ascribed to Aristotle, all of which have a Peripatetic tinge to them, the most celebrated is [Aristotle], *On the World* – a brief summary of Peripatetic philosophy, dating perhaps from the first century BC, which was long used as an epitome of Aristotelianism. [Olympiodorus], *On the Divine and Sacred Art of the Philosopher's Stone* is a late essay on alchemy.

FURTHER READING

The literature on the Presocratics is extensive, and much of it is formidably technical. This list mentions a few of the more accessible items.

Most of the Greek texts are collected in
> H. Diels and W. Kranz, *Die Fragmente der Vorsokratiker* (Berlin, 1952 [10th edition]).

There is a useful anthology
> M. R. Wright, *The Presocratics* (Bristol, 1985).

A selection of Greek texts, together with translations and commentary, is printed in
> G. S. Kirk, J. E. Raven and M. Schofield, *The Presocratic Philosophers* (Cambridge, 1983 [2nd edition]).

There is an annotated selection of texts in English in
> R. Waterfield, *The First Philosophers* (Oxford, 2000).

The best brief and general introduction to the subject in English is
> E. Hussey, *The Presocratics* (London, 1972).

Longer and more philosophical treatments can be found in
> J. Barnes, *The Presocratic Philosophers* (London, 1982 [2nd edition]),
> A. A. Long (ed.), *The Cambridge Companion to Early Greek Philosophy* (Cambridge, 1999).

There is a detailed discussion of all aspects of Presocratic thought in the first three volumes of
> W. K. C. Guthrie, *A History of Greek Philosophy* (Cambridge, 1962, 1965, 1969).

See also:
> T. H. Irwin, *Classical Thought* (Oxford, 1989),
> C. C. W. Taylor (ed.), *Routledge History of Philosophy* – I: *From the beginning to Plato* (London, 1997).

Much of the best work on the subject has appeared in the form of articles. Samples can be found collected in

D. J. Furley and R. E. Allen (eds.), *Studies in Presocratic Philosophy* (London, 1970, 1975),

A. P. D. Mourelatos (ed.), *The Presocratics* (Garden City, NY, 1974),

G. Vlastos, *Studies in Ancient Greek Philosophy* – I: *The Presocratics* (Princeton, NJ, 1995).

On the general background to Presocratic philosophy, and on its predecessors

M. L. West, *Early Greek Philosophy and the Orient* (Oxford, 1971).

On the Milesian philosophers there is an outstanding study:

C. H. Kahn, *Anaximander and the Origins of Greek Cosmology* (New York, 1985 [2nd edition]).

For Xenophanes

J. H. Lesher, *Xenophanes: Fragments* (Toronto, 1992).

On Heraclitus

C. H. Kahn, *The Art and Thought of Heraclitus* (Cambridge, 1979).

For everything to do with Pythagoras and Pythagoreanism consult

W. Burkert, *Lore and Science in Ancient Pythagoreanism* (Cambridge, Mass., 1972).

Among innumerable studies of Parmenides, there is an edition, with translation and commentary,

A. H. Coxon, *The Fragments of Parmenides* (Assen, 1986).

For Zeno see the essays collected in

W. C. Salmon (ed.), *Zeno's Paradoxes* (Indianapolis, Ind., 1970).

There are notes on Empedocles in the edition by

M. R. Wright, *Empedocles – the Extant Fragments* (New Haven, Conn., 1981)

and the Strasbourg Papyrus is published and discussed in

A. Martin and O. Primavesi, *L'Empédocle de Strasbourg* (Berlin, 1999).

On Philolaus

C. Huffmann, *Philolaus of Croton: Pythagorean and Presocratic* (Cambridge, 1993).

For Anaxagoras

M. Schofield, *An Essay on Anaxagoras* (Cambridge, 1980).

On the Atomists

C. C. W. Taylor, *The Atomists: Leucippus and Democritus* (Toronto, 1999).

And for Diogenes of Apollonia

A. Laks, *Diogène d'Apollonie: la dernière cosmologie présocratique* (Lille, 1983).

Further bibliography can be found in Barnes, Guthrie, Long, Waterfield.

SUBJECT INDEX

INDEX OF QUOTED TEXTS

INDEX TO DIELS-KRANZ
B-TEXTS